WHAT YOUR COLLEAGUES

There are few individuals who can so deftly articulate a strong theory-into-practice orientation as does Lyn Sharratt. Why? Because she has done the work. Her credibility with the education community has been earned.

CLARITY weaves together theory, solid rationale, insights, reflective analysis, and guidance for teachers and leaders all underpinned with the "how" of practical, evidence-proven, and well-lived experiences. A topical book, CLARITY is available for practitioners who want to take their learning to new heights of understanding. A timely book, CLARITY is now, more than ever it seems, needed for the support it offers. In a noisy world, it provides an oasis of tranquility for those of us who want to reflect on proven ideas and gain keen insights as pathways to deep implementation. We need clarity on what matters most in learning, teaching, and leading.

—Avis Glaze
International Education Adviser;
Former Ontario Education Commissioner

CLARITY is practical, user-friendly, and grounded in current, evidence-based practices. Sharratt's focus remains on teachers using student data, working together to unpack the analysis, and collaborating on interventions and strategies to improve achievement. The book includes real case studies on lessons learned and successful examples from around the world. CLARITY empowers schools and systems to build on teachers' and leaders' expertise in shaping and informing improvement.

—Karen Grose
Vice President, TVOntario (TVO)

CLARITY is a must-read for all educators. Built on sound research and stories from the field, the book lays out a proven process for improving learning for all students. Lyn Sharratt does an outstanding job of showing the importance of clarity and precision in school leadership.

—Ruth Mattingley
Former Senior Executive Officer, Literacy
and Numeracy Secretariat,
Ontario Ministry of Education, and
Former Superintendent of Education, Lambton Kent District

CLARITY is a great resource for practicing school leaders, those working at division level, and those aspiring to such positions. The real-life examples clearly illustrate how schools can support all learners in their journey without suggesting a simplistic, cookie cutter approach to school improvement.

—Pamela Osmond-Johnson
Assistant Professor of Educational Leadership
University of Regina

In education today it is very easy to "muddy the waters" with what are perceived as competing initiatives or new ways forward. In CLARITY, Lyn Sharratt provides the precision, alignment, and direction that are needed to see what really matters in learning, teaching, and leading. It is sure to spark ideas as practitioners put learning into action. Readers will come away with a sense that CLARITY captures a learning journey that comes not just from theory but experience lived.

—Gale Harild
Author, Educational Pathway Consultant
Ontario, Canada

In an age of increasing measurement and accountability, it is heartening to see that Lyn Sharratt brings intentional CLARITY to the real work of what matters MOST in learning, teaching, and leading – our students! At the same time, Sharratt demonstrates the impact that collaboration has on all levels of learning - teachers, leaders, students and community. Authentic examples from the field provide the reader with what it looks like, sounds like, and feels like to use precision as a tool for improvement. The vignettes, case studies, quotes and examples of practice provide us with a "mental picture" of what is possible in our own contexts when we stay the course and commit to the 14 Parameters. However, this book is more than that, it is a way to challenge and shape our individual and collective dispositions and actions in what matters most in learning, teaching and leading.

—Joanne Casey
Educational Consultant, Literary Coach, and Instructional Mentor
Queensland, Australia

Educational leaders improve learning experiences for all students when they believe and trust that day-to-day quality teaching promotes high expectations of all students; teachers' working collaboratively; coherence between the vision of the future and daily practice; and being across all classrooms, inquiring and sharing about the learning done. These concrete actions fill schools with life, energy and successful achievement of high expectations.

—Isidora Recart
Chief Executive Officer, and

—Simón Rodriguez Espinoza
Director of Professional Development
Arauco Foundation, Chile

In her latest book, CLARITY, Lyn Sharratt continues to bring invaluable insights to education practitioners to make a positive difference for all learners. The invitation at the close of each chapter to take a deliberate pause to create clarity provides a powerful structure for practitioners to reflect upon ways to progress educational achievement in their own context.

—Maggie Ogram
Educational Leadership Coach
Osprey Consulting Ltd.

At the heart of what has instigated amazing change in Brisbane Catholic Education (BCE) is Lyn Sharratt's work around the 14 Parameters. Sharratt's extraordinary contribution to our work in BCE, her resilience and demand for excellence, has been so critical to our growth. What I admire most is her commitment to all students—regardless of their circumstances—be they in Chile, the Cape, Sunnybank, or Saskatoon.

—David Greig
Senior Executive Officer
Brisbane Catholic Education

Education systems and schools operate in complex environments. CLARITY provides an explicit, practical model that can be utilized by each layer within a system – system leaders, principals, teachers, and students – to ensure that there is an unrelenting focus on what matters most: student learning. This carefully constructed text breaks through educational jargon to purposefully illustrate how clarity can be realized and evidenced in student improvement through the use of real case studies.

—Tania Leach
Education Consultant, Lecturer
Toowoomba, Queensland, Australia

Lyn Sharratt is the ultimate teacher – guiding, supporting, and challenging us to be the high-quality educators who keep every FACE at the center. The fruits of her labor are powerfully demonstrated in every school across our diocese. With this book, Sharratt brings CLARITY to us in such an inspiring way.

—Anthony Gordon
Executive Director of Education, and

—Mary-Ellen Demsey
Director of Teaching and Learning
Diocese of Wilcannia-Forbes, Australia

Educational change happens when the vision and purpose of diverse stakeholders converge around students' learning. Lyn Sharratt demonstrates not only why educational improvement is important, but also how to achieve it. The narrative style and powerful content of CLARITY *will engage academics, practitioners, and everyone who cares about improving the learning opportunities of all children.*

—Sergio Galdames
Chilean Educational Researcher and
PhD Candidate at the Institute of Education UCL

For over a decade now, Dr. Sharratt has been bringing clarity to educational audiences around the globe. She has now put her profound messages into print in CLARITY. *Drawing on research, case studies, and front-line experience, this book draws the reader in and clearly paves the path for us, as leaders in the profession, to implement, monitor, and assess very effective and clearly described practices.* CLARITY *calls upon us to be reflective practitioners who are willing to learn alongside one another while ensuring the needs of each and every one of our students are met.*

—Kim Newlove
Former Superintendent of Education
Saskatoon Public Schools

CLARITY

What Matters MOST in Learning, Teaching, and Leading

Lyn Sharratt

Foreword by John Hattie

Introduction by Alma Harris

A Joint Publication

CORWIN
A SAGE Publishing Company

FOR INFORMATION:

Corwin
A SAGE Company
2455 Teller Road
Thousand Oaks, California 91320
(800) 233-9936
www.corwin.com

SAGE Publications Ltd.
1 Oliver's Yard
55 City Road
London EC1Y 1SP
United Kingdom

SAGE Publications India Pvt. Ltd.
B 1/I 1 Mohan Cooperative Industrial Area
Mathura Road, New Delhi 110 044
India

SAGE Publications Asia-Pacific Pte. Ltd.
3 Church Street
#10-04 Samsung Hub
Singapore 049483

Publisher: Arnis Burvikovs
Development Editor: Desirée A. Bartlett
Editorial Assistant: Eliza B. Erickson
Production Editor: Amy Schroller
Copy Editor: Diana Breti
Typesetter: C&M Digitals (P) Ltd.
Proofreader: Dennis W. Webb
Indexer: Maria Sosnowski
Cover and Interior Designer: Anupama Krishnan
Marketing Manager: Sharon Pendergast

Printed in the United States of America

ISBN 978-1-5063-5872-7

This book is printed on acid-free paper.

FSC
www.fsc.org
MIX
Paper from
responsible sources
FSC® C005010

19 20 21 22 10 9 8 7 6 5 4 3

DISCLAIMER: This book may direct you to access third-party content via Web links, QR codes, or other scannable technologies, which are provided for your reference by the author(s). Corwin makes no guarantee that such third-party content will be available for your use and encourages you to review the terms and conditions of such third-party content. Corwin takes no responsibility and assumes no liability for your use of any third-party content, nor does Corwin approve, sponsor, endorse, verify, or certify such third-party content.

CONTENTS

Visit the companion website at
resources.corwin.com/CLARITY
for videos and downloadable resources

LIST OF ONLINE RESOURCES

Note From the Publisher: The author has provided web content throughout the book that is available to you through QR (quick response) codes. To read a QR code, you must have a smartphone or tablet with a camera. We recommend that you download a QR code reader app that is made specifically for your phone or tablet brand.

Web Resources

Content may also be accessed at **resources.corwin.com/CLARITY**

Web Resource 1: Using the 14 Parameters as a System and School Self-Assessment Tool for Improvement

Web Resource 2: Darling Downs Template to Track the 14 Parameter Work

Web Resource 3: Organizing and Mobilizing a Learning Event—The Learning Fair

Web Resource 4: One Principal's Thoughts on Building Capacity in a Secondary School

Web Resource 5: A Professional Learning Protocol for Collaborative Assessment of Student Work

Web Resource 6: School Case Management Meeting Teacher and Participant Template

Web Resource 7: Follow-Up Case Management Meeting Template

Web Resource 8: System Case Management Meeting Facilitator's/ Chair's Script

Web Resource 9: Creating QR Codes for Your Data Wall

Web Resource 10: Self-Assessing Against the Six Leadership Dimension Skills

Web Resource 11: Knowledge Building From a Principal's Perspective

LIST OF ACRONYMS

CMA: Case Management Approach

CMM: Case Management Meeting

CI: Collaborative Inquiry

DC: Demonstration Classrooms

FIL: Fellowship of Instructional Leaders

GRR: Gradual Release and Acceptance of Responsibility

IT: Integrative Thinking

KO: Knowledgeable Other

KB: Knowledge Building

KBC: Knowledge-Building Circle

LI: Learning Intention

PD: Professional Development

PL: Professional Learning

PLC: Professional Learning Community

SIP: School Improvement Plan

SC: Success Criteria

FOREWORD

In 1990, Frank Fendick began his PhD dissertation with a quote from William Cowper (1731–1800):

A tale should be judicious, clear, succinct;

The language plain, the incidents well link'd;

Tell not as new what ev'ry body knows;

And, new or old, still hasten to a close.

His thesis was a meta-analysis of *teacher clarity*, which he referred to as **clarity of speech** (so all can hear, does not use few vague terms), **organization** (starts with Success Criteria, covers all topics on post-test, reviews student work), **explanation** (explains simply and interestingly, at the right pace), **providing examples** and **guiding practice** (gives examples of how to do the work, answers student questions, gives enough time, gives feedback), and **assessing student learning** (asks questions, encourages discussions, checks work).

Fendick located 39 studies reporting 100 correlations between one of these dimensions and class achievement gain. When transposed, the correlations become approximate effects of .46 to .70 across verbal and numerical subjects, larger and smaller class sizes, for less and greater experienced teachers. These effects increased across grade levels (from .52 in elementary, .60 in secondary, to .82 in college) and were higher when rated by the students than by independent observers. They are large effects relative to other influences on student learning. Fendick provides clear evidence that *teacher clarity* is critically important and matters greatly in the learning process.

Lyn Sharratt provides the detail, the theory, and the practical applications of these important dimensions of *teacher clarity*. It seems a hands-down misère or simply common sense that if students do not understand the teacher's instructions or lessons, then there is unlikely to be much comprehension and engagement. But Sharratt's *CLARITY* is more than comprehension; it is about "being explicit about precision in practice," and she outlines the 14 Parameters of system and school improvement. The major headings are shared beliefs and understanding, the centrality of the student, the learning of the adults working together about their impact on their students, shared responsibility and accountability, and smelling the roses where there is this enhanced impact on the learning lives of students. Sharratt articulates the 14 Parameters in detail in the book, but her watermark on each page is "precision."

The model depends very much on "data"—but data shared with students and teachers to understand the effects of their instruction. There is an emphasis on the fidelity of planning, the implementation of assessment and instruction, and continuing to develop and refine action plans to improve the impact. Most important, collaborative work is across all teachers and leaders.

There are few schools that are excellent without an excellent leader—and a common trait in *CLARITY* is that this leader is the first among equals—leading the narrative in the school about the impact of the adults on the students, gaining—and, more important, interpreting—the data and the information from the classroom observations, and challenging the expectations of all in the school. This requires skills, and here is where Sharratt's Professional Learning focus can enhance the leader's role to ensure optimal CLARITY of impact—what it means, who gains this impact, and to what magnitude.

Throughout, Sharratt puts FACES to the message of precision in this book, from students sharing in the construction of Success Criteria, collaborative planning before teaching, assessment and instruction waterfall charts, to walking with Lyn as she works in schools throughout the world.

One of my concerns is that Professional Learning Communities (PLCs) are plentiful, but too often they fail to have much effect as the focus of many PLCs is wrong. Too often, PLCs are about the "nice" stuff—curricula, difficult students (never difficult teachers), resources—and not about the "right" stuff—what does impact mean in this school, how would we know we are attaining this impact, and how can we work together to help each other understand how we think about what we do, appreciate, and mean by impact on the learning lives of students? All these require the precision of CLARITY that weaves its message on every page of this book.

This book is judicious, clear, succinct, the language plain, the incidents linked. Yes, everybody knows about teacher clarity, but too often students do not experience clarity. Thus, this book is for all, new or old, and there is no necessity to "hasten to a close."

—**John Hattie**, Creator of Visible Learning
Laureate Professor at the University of Melbourne, Australia

PREFACE

CLARITY is being explicit about precision in practice through research done, experiences lived, and knowledge gained from collaboratively working side by side to improve the outcomes for all students. CLARITY of expectations is reflected by equity and excellence in every system, in every school, and in every classroom.

I began the work on explicitly bringing CLARITY to my improvement research as a practitioner, first by modeling a belief that *literacy is everyone's business*, and second by demonstrating in practical ways that distinctive moral imperative. This book is about *the what and the how*—the practical, tangible ways of bringing CLARITY to increasing all students' achievement. Bringing CLARITY to expected, effective practice *is everyone's business!*

My leadership journey to realizing CLARITY in delivering effective practice began by stating the obvious: **illiteracy is unacceptable**. The percentage of illiterate citizens currently around the world is too high. Astonishing as it may seem in the 21st century, 12% of the world's population is considered functionally illiterate, with only basic or below-basic literacy levels in their native languages. Seven hundred eighty-one million people across the globe still cannot read or write. One hundred twenty-six million youth, worldwide, are illiterate (International Literacy Association, 2018).

The absolute need to achieve "every graduate a literate graduate" compels me to think not simply about the right of all students to read, write, do mathematics, and to think critically, but about "the how" of how to achieve this worthy goal. We have a moral imperative to increase levels of literacy around the world, starting in our classrooms. Hence the beginnings of CLARITY. I define literacy as the development of a continuum of skills, knowledge, and dispositions that prepare all learners for a changing world community. It **begins** with the fundamental acquisition of skills in reading, writing, listening, speaking, viewing, representing, responding, and in mathematics. It **becomes** the ability to understand, think critically, apply new knowledge and skills, and communicate effectively and creatively in all subject areas in a variety of multimodal, multimedia ways and for a variety of purposes (adapted from York Region District School Board, 2007).

As John Hattie said in his Jack Keating Memorial Lecture in June 2016,

> Literacy and numeracy remain the critical bases of any educated person, and while many would (correctly) argue that these are attributes of narrow excellence; they are the building blocks of the wider excellence many aspire toward. Literacy and numeracy are capabilities which facilitate higher learning, not necessarily ends in themselves. (2016c)

Canada considers both equity and excellence in determining a clear path forward in learning, teaching, and leading. Ontario, Canada's largest and most diverse province, supports that focus. It should be no secret why Canada's 15-year-olds ranked #2 in reading, #4 in science, and #5 in collaborative problem solving in the worldwide 2015 PISA survey. Our nation is resolute in its determination to reduce the percentage of the population who are illiterate.

To that end, this book is about the CLARITY needed—that teaching is informed by learning about learning, underpinned by CLARITY of foundational literacy skills and being supported by consistent, persistent, insistent leadership. We remember:

- Hope is not a strategy!

- Don't blame the kids or the parents.

- Our work is all about learning: having relevant assessment data that improves instruction for all—every student, every day.

- It is critical to have a laser-like focus on every FACE in order to increase achievement.

- Prepackaged, purchased solutions don't work. What works? Teacher and leader capacity building for assessment that informs instruction.

- It's not random acts of self-improvement or "Choose Your Own Adventure" that improve schools or systems. What works is relentless, focused direction. Leadership commitment to "the work" matters. Leadership commitment to equity and excellence matters. "The standard you walk past is the standard you accept" (Chief of Army, Lieutenant General David Morrison AO, Australia, 2013).

- Leaders must be present and "in the moment" continuously.

Ontario educators focus on precision in classroom practice and building collaborative cultures, where co-learning is valued as the format for collective capacity building. As that requires both technical (first-order) and cultural, embedded (second-order) change, this means that collaboration is about purposeful work focused on what can influence students' growth and achievement.

We know first-order changes (structural frameworks and organizational structures) are foundational but do not represent silver bullets for change in themselves, unless second-order changes (adaptive changes to implement a pervasive culture of learning) focused on impact are embedded (Planche, Sharratt, & Belchetz, 2008; Sharratt & Planche, 2016). Educators everywhere need to move to making second-order changes that promote precision in practice and measure increased student achievement. You will find guidance for **how to do this** throughout this book.

A precondition for improving schools is the existence of a culture focused on learning in which professionals

- talk about practice

- share their "craft knowledge" as co-learners and as Knowledgeable Others

- conduct Learning Walks and Talks in classrooms daily

- support and celebrate each other's successes unconditionally

Without purposeful culture, no meaningful improvement—no Professional Learning, no curriculum development, no teacher leadership, no student self-assessment, no co-teaching, no parent involvement, and no sustainable change—is possible (Barth, 2006).

Empowerment, recognition, satisfaction, and success in our work—all in scarce supply within our schools globally—will never stem from "going it alone" as a masterful teacher, principal, or student, no matter how accomplished one is. The culture must lead to engagement; engagement must move those involved to empowerment. Success comes only from being an active participant within a masterful group of colleagues. Leaders and teachers teaching with and learning from each other is the only answer (Barth, 2006).

The contents of this book are divided into the three "big ideas" that reflect the flow of my thinking: Part I: Learning (Chapters 1, 2, 3); Part II: Teaching (Chapters 4, 5, 6, 7); and Part III: Leading (Chapters 8, 9, 10), a progression that provides CLARITY for me and hopefully for you.

During 2016, 2017, and 2018, thousands of teachers and leaders participated in Professional Learning sessions with me on system and school improvement, during which I had opportunities to ask the classic knowledge-building and Collaborative Inquiry questions:

1. Given what you know now, what are you still wondering about?

2. What are you thinking you can do with the knowledge you have gained?

3. To what can you commit tomorrow to make a difference for each student?

Each chapter begins with a sample of these Wonderings that identify the *what* and introduce the *how*. All chapters conclude with a Deliberate Pause to Create CLARITY and participant Commitments that are meant to establish CLARITY of first- and second-order changes necessary to achieve our collective goal of all students progressing toward at least one year's growth for each year of school (Hattie, 2012). Further resources for the text can be found online at **resources.corwin.com/CLARITY**.

Throughout the book, I have co-written vignettes and case studies and captured quotes from my colleagues. My narrative co-authors are gifted and talented teachers and leaders who make the theory of the 14 Parameters for improvement come to life in their detailed descriptions of what constitutes successful practice. They are practitioners who do this work and reflect on it every day, providing CLARITY for all of us.

ACKNOWLEDGMENTS

Practitioners highlighted in this book through their honest and reflective quotes, vignettes, and case studies exemplify the FACES of CLARITY. They are the model teachers and leaders, too many to mention here, who strive to ensure all learners are improving beyond what was ever thought possible. I wish to thank them, my many colleagues from across the globe, who have become such good friends over the years of our work together. Your gifts of knowledge about teaching and learning have had a huge impact on my thinking and have contributed to this writing. Your skills, professionalism, wisdom, warmth, and generosity of spirit are reflected in every chapter. You inspire me to write about your accomplishments.

Thank you to Professor John Hattie, whose continuing work and writing is a constant source of reflection, energy, and confirmation of my own thinking. It causes me to ponder and wonder, "What if?" His formidable research affirms the text in this book and the work of so many in making learning visible for students, teachers, and leaders.

Thank you to Professor Alma Harris who, to me and for me, is an authentic researcher, author, and advocate for all students, teachers, and leaders. Not only is Alma a strong leader of learning, she is a role model to me and so many women and men working in the field of educational reform.

Thank you, sincerely, to my editor, Arnis Burvikovs, Publisher, Corwin Press. Thank you, Arnis, for believing in my work across the globe putting FACES on the data and for supporting my efforts in putting that work on paper in order to energize others. Arnis, thank you for being with me through the production of five beautiful books. Thank you, Desirée Bartlett, content development editor, for "being there" and for your invaluable editing expertise. This book couldn't have been published without the dedication and attention to detail of Eliza Erickson, who has worked tirelessly to make it perfect—I owe my sincere thanks to you, Eliza, for "going the extra mile" for me. Thank you, too, to Amy Schroller, Laureen Gleason, Melanie Birdsall, Diana Breti, and the whole Corwin design and production team who made this book an incredible educational resource.

Finally, "thank you" is not ever enough to thank Jim, my constant cheerleader, colleague, and best friend who is truly encouraging and supportive of my work. Thank you to our very special children, Robert, Michelle, Stephanie, and Taylor and their spouses for the joy our eight grandchildren—Robbie, Madeleine, Jackson, Ryan, Aeson, Clarke, Audrey, and Penelope—bring us! Our family members give both Jim and me such pleasure as they are individually and collectively highly accomplished, creative, considerate, and lovingly supportive. We are blessed.

PUBLISHER'S ACKNOWLEDGMENTS

Joanne Casey
Literacy Coach and Mentor
Bokarina, QLD, Australia

Beverley Freedman
Education Consultant, Author
Maple, ON, Canada

Gale Harild
Educational Pathway Consultant, Author
Thornhill, ON, Canada

Tania Leach
Academic Specialist—Teacher Education
University of Southern Queensland, Australia

Ruth Mattingley
Senior Executive Officer (Retired), Literacy and Numeracy Secretariat,
Ontario Ministry of Education, Author, ON, Canada

Pamela Osmond-Johnson
Assistant Professor of Educational Leadership
Regina, SK, Canada

ABOUT THE AUTHOR

Dr. Lyn Sharratt is a highly accomplished practitioner, researcher, author, and presenter. She graduated with a BA in social work from the University of Waterloo, a BEd from the University of Western Ontario, an MEd from the Ontario Institute for Studies in Education, and a doctorate from the University of Toronto. Lyn coordinates the doctoral internship program in the Leadership, Higher and Adult Education department at the Ontario Institute for Studies in Education, University of Toronto. She has worked in four school districts across Ontario as a school superintendent, superintendent of curriculum and instruction, administrator, curriculum leader, and K–10 and Special Education teacher. Lyn has taught all elementary grades and secondary-aged students in inner-city and rural settings. She has analyzed and commented on public policy for a provincial trustee organization, the Ontario Public School Boards' Association; has taught preservice education at York University and master's and doctoral students at University of Toronto and Nipissing University; and has led inservice professional development in a provincial teachers' union head office. Lyn is a widely published researcher and author. She is lead author, with Michael Fullan, of *Realization: The Change Imperative for Increasing District-Wide Reform* (Corwin, 2009) and *Putting FACES on the Data: What Great Leaders Do!* (Corwin, 2012, published in English, Spanish, and Arabic). Lyn is lead author of *Good to Great to Innovate: Recalculating the Route K–12* (Corwin, 2015) with Gale Harild and of *Leading Collaborative Learning: Empowering Excellence* (Corwin, 2016) with Beate Planche. *CLARITY: What Matters*

MOST in Learning, Teaching, and Leading (Corwin, 2019) is her fifth book that reflects all of her work across the globe from 2009–2019. As well as an author and practitioner working in remote and urban settings worldwide, Lyn is an advisor for International School Leadership with the Ontario Principals' Council; is an author consultant for Corwin Press; and consults internationally, working with system, school, and teacher leaders at all levels in Australia, Canada, Chile, the Netherlands, the United Kingdom, and the United States. She works tirelessly, focusing her time and efforts on increasing each student's achievement by working alongside leaders and teachers to put FACES on their data, taking intentional action to make equity and excellence a reality for *all* students. Visit her at www.lynsharratt.com; Twitter @LynSharratt; and on LinkedIn where Lyn owns the "Educational Leadership" LinkedIn group made up of 69,000+ members. Search for Lyn's "Good to Great to Innovate" video on www.thelearningexchange.ca. There you will see her speaking in Ontario about the leadership it takes to achieve system and school improvement.

IN MEMORIAM

Melanie Greenan was an outstanding doctoral student in my cohort of EdD students at the Ontario Institute for Studies in Education, University of Toronto, Canada. Mel became a treasured friend. She was an insightful school leader and a critical thinker as a system consultant who worked at the elbow of teachers and leaders, as a vice-principal in the Dufferin-Peel Catholic District School Board, and as a student achievement officer across Ontario at the Ministry of Education. Mel was a Knowledgeable Other to whom so many of us turned for her wisdom, wit, faith, and inspiring spirit. She gave me extremely helpful feedback on the work in this book. Totally unforgettable. Mel passed away in August 2017. She was a tenacious fighter in battling cancer and never gave up the fight—and that is how she lived every part of her life. Mel was and remains a true role model for us in Ontario. We all miss her.

To Jim

Who is always beside me as a guide, mentor, and best friend.

Your tenacity and positive spirit inspire me.

With Love,

Lyn

INTRODUCTION

Occasionally, a book comes along that stops you in your tracks. This is such a book. Written with passion and purpose, the expertise and experience of the author simply shines through every page. This is a timely book, particularly as the educational discourse in recent years has tended to be preoccupied with big data and international comparisons, largely overshadowing the micro-world of the classroom. It is an important book because it reminds us that teachers have the biggest impact on students' learning (Hattie, 2009) and the work that they undertake, collaboratively, can have a profound influence on the way teachers and students interact.

The mantra of this book is CLARITY, defined as "being coherent and intelligible." Around the world we see far too many examples of education policy that does not meet these two core principles. For teachers, the policy making process can be remote, obscure, and sometimes highly contestable. The imperatives for educational change are often very far removed from the realities of the classroom (Fullan, Quinn, & McEachen, 2017) and factors such as poverty, inequality, and inequity are often discounted in the policy rush for better performance (Harris & Jones, 2010; Harris, Jones, & Huffman, 2017). The educational landscape is littered with failed initiatives and failed promises of better schools and better outcomes. The key reason for this resides in a significant disconnect between policy makers and the profession. This broken link means that professional expertise and professional leverage are often sidelined in policy making and implementation.

There is a growing evidential base that posits an alternative of thinking about educational change and reform (Evers & Kneyber, 2015). This approach puts teachers in the driving seat of improvement, innovation, and change and calls upon their collective expertise to shape and inform policy decisions (Zhao, 2018). This shift in responsibility and accountability positions teachers at the center rather than the periphery of educational reform. It gives teachers voice, authority, and agency to create and innovate in ways that they know will make a positive difference to learners.

In many ways, this book is a clarion call to action asking us to appraise how teachers work together, to be most effective, and to have the greatest impact on learners. This is not an overly abstract or theoretical book, but it is a grounded and evidence-based treatise on leading successful classroom change. As Kurt Lewin famously said, "there is nothing so practical as a good theory," and this book is replete with practitioner-based theorizing and embedded practical knowledge.

COLLABORATION MATTERS

At the heart of this book is a focus on professional collaboration and the engagement of teachers in focused, purposeful collaborative activities with the core aim of improving student outcomes. Recently, other writers have referred to the importance of "collaborative professionalism" in the pursuit of school and system improvement (Hargreaves & O'Connor, 2017). It could be argued that these two phrases mean the same thing, but in fact, there are important differences. The first emphasizes "professional," placing importance on the norms of professional engagement, trust, and interdependency that are necessary for professional collaboration. The second emphasizes "collaborative," which implies that the nature of collaboration, the form it takes, its intentions are significant contributory factors in generating shared professional practice or *professional capital* (Hargreaves & Fullan, 2012). The differences may be subtle, but they are important as they imply alternative starting points in initiating, supporting, and sustaining teachers' collaborative practice.

In *CLARITY*, the existence of a collaborative culture of learning is described as the Third Teacher. Not only is this insightful, but it absolutely encapsulates the power and potential of shared professional engagement and its impact on the classroom environment. The classroom is, and should be, a second home for students, particularly those at risk. It should offer a safety net, a sanctuary, and a safe place to learn. The emphasis in this book on the learning environment as the Third Teacher and the way it describes the construction of such a learning environment is the book's core strength. It is a timely reminder that what happens in the classroom is critically important to the young people who learn there; it is their second home and it is their Third Teacher. The evidence also clearly shows a positive classroom environment is no accidental matter but the net result of the care, attention, and purposeful scaffolding by teachers.

14 PARAMETERS

The key to a positive classroom environment is encapsulated in the 14 Parameters that are at the heart of this book. As the author notes, the 14 Parameters "were present to high levels within systems and schools and where leaders focused on them, system and school leaders and teachers increased students' growth and achievement. Where they were not found, or only some were found, or where system and school leaders did not focus on them, there was no or very low improvement in student outcomes." The book shows that incorporating all 14 Parameters is one of the ways of building the capacity for Professional Learning and system learning.

The Parameters are also value based and driven. At the core of this book is a deep conviction that all students can learn and an authentic moral stance founded on principles of equity and equality. Each Parameter is explained and explored in this book, based on evidence and substantiated knowledge. These Parameters are not just some loosely coupled whims but are based on the author's lifetime of experience in supporting school and system improvement. These are grounded, verified, and proven approaches to school-level change and improvement.

LEADERSHIP MATTERS

There is a great deal of international literature that reinforces the importance of leadership in securing school and system improvement (Leithwood, Harris, & Hopkins, 2008). The educational leadership field is replete with study after study emphasizing how school leadership can make or break productive organizational change. In this book, leadership is also center stage in the amalgam of strategies and approaches that contribute to positive learning outcomes for students. Parameter #4 is principals as "lead learners" with a key responsibility "to work alongside teachers at Professional Learning sessions, modeling and monitoring effective and expected practices as learning leaders, always looking to find the evidence of those practices that most benefit student learning. Principals use data, collaboratively with all staff, to inform school planning, to select resources, and to co-lead assessment practices that inform instruction for all students in their care. In other words, instructional leaders."

Generally, within the research literature, there is considerable agreement on the broad nature of instructional leadership as well as a clear understanding about its impact on key school and student learning conditions (Robinson, Lloyd, & Rowe, 2008). In general, instructional leadership is defined as strategies and actions carried out by the principal and other school leaders to support and strengthen teaching and learning quality. Instructional leaders have been described as "strong, directive leaders" who accept responsibility for results and are able to improve teaching and learning processes in the school (Hallinger & Murphy, 1985). Thus, attention to instructional leadership practices would seem appropriate and helpful in steering a path toward classroom improvement.

In short, the emphasis on instructional leadership in this book is, again, timely and prescient. There are two important points that are reinforced: first, that the leadership focus should be explicitly on improving learning and teaching and second, that this can only be achieved through shared or *distributed* leadership practices (Harris, 2014). CLARITY, in the way this book describes it, will only be achieved through the coherent selection and implementation of certain practices and the collective intelligibility to focus on the right things. Without the support of the formal leadership, this is unlikely to happen and any efforts in this direction will be derailed. We already know more than we need to about the centrality of school leadership in the pursuit of better outcomes for learners and equality for all students in all settings. The real challenge now is to make this happen, not just in some schools but all schools.

CODA

CLARITY is not just a practical guide; it is an uplifting account of what can be achieved when professionals work together in a supportive, focused, and meaningful way. It demonstrates that change may appear technically simple, but it is fraught and culturally complex. The core message in this book is the importance of "learning, teaching, and leading with persistence, insistence, and consistency that results in CLARITY of purpose and practice." It reminds us that improvement is a shared responsibility and that collective and sustained professional effort is much more likely to bring successful improvement than individual and isolated endeavor.

There is no simple recipe for school and system improvement, but there are some key principles or Parameters. In this book, Lyn Sharratt, in her inimitable way, presents the practical tools to realize the goal of lasting classroom change and transformation. She provides CLARITY in a cluttered educational world overflowing with quick fixes, gimmicks, promises, and dubious evidence.

Ultimately, Lyn is clear about *who* matters most of all and ensures that students are at the epicenter in her model of change. A long time ago, I met Lyn in Ontario. The years may have passed but her passion remains fixed, her moral purpose is unquestionable, and her practical wisdom is irrefutable.

—**Alma Harris**, Author of *Distributed Leadership Matters*
Professor of Educational Leadership and Policy, University of Bath

PART I
Learning

CLARITY
The 14 Parameters:
A Learning Framework

CHAPTER I

Wonderings...

1. How can we break down assumptions and perceptions to ensure we target the right things?

2. How can we work collaboratively in an evidence-based way to improve student outcomes?

3. How can we differentiate professional development on pedagogy to meet individual teachers' needs?

4. How can we implement the 14 Parameters strategically, so staff won't feel overwhelmed?

5. How can we build, maintain, and sustain momentum for continuous improvement?

What are you, the reader, wondering?

Figure 1.1

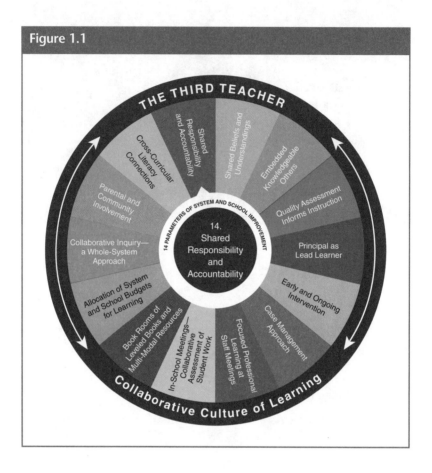

This graphic, displayed throughout the book, depicts the 14 Parameters. The graphic is a visual representation of how the parameters—when all are applied together—can exponentially increase the achievement of all students. You will see examples of this in the many case studies and vignettes in this book. The parameters are discussed and defined, not in order, but when a "big idea" is related to a particular parameter. The dial in the middle of the circle points to a specific parameter as it is being discussed. Encompassing the parameters is the wrap-around concept of establishing a culture of learning at every level of a system: classroom, school, district, state. I call that culture of learning the Third Teacher.

THE THIRD TEACHER: CREATING A COLLABORATIVE CULTURE OF LEARNING

After parents and teachers, the classroom environment is **the Third Teacher**. Paying attention to the teaching and learning environment is a critical first step. The learning space becomes a strategic tool in promoting creativity, originality, perseverance, risk taking, learning from mistakes, problem solving, resolving conflict, collaboration, and critical thinking.

Thus, careful consideration and **co-construction** of the Third Teacher with students is extraordinarily important.

What is created to put on the walls, who creates it, and where it is placed tells a lot about the teacher's understanding of the iterative process of leading and learning in the classroom. Learning to critically observe this aspect of instruction is best accomplished by "walking the walls" in many classrooms, looking for evidence of students' thinking.

Intentionally co-constructed learning spaces and walls are quite different from cluttered ones in which scaffolds for students may be irrelevant, overwhelming, disorganized, and distracting rather than supportive. From observing literally thousands of classrooms, asking students questions about their learning, and watching them refer to the walls, I have a strong belief that a heightened sense of ownership results when teachers and students co-construct the learning environment, agreeing on displays of visual prompts to track learning. Displayed student work must be central so it can be quickly referenced as a targeted, focused response to students' needs at "just the right time." No prepackaged, purchased, or laminated materials can do that.

Classroom walls that become interactive learning spaces and show evidence of use move from being "pretty" to being "pretty useful." Materials on classroom walls that have not been used by students in two weeks (my rule of thumb) need to be revised or culled as they become stagnant wallpaper instead of students' and teachers' pedagogical documentation. Before they approach the teacher when they are stuck, students learn to refer to the Third Teacher prompts or scaffolds that are available to them in the learning space, such as,

- co-created **anchor charts**

- deconstructed **Learning Intentions**

- co-constructed **Success Criteria**

- co-developed Learning Walls with "big idea thinking" signposts along the way

- co-designed **Bump-It-Up Walls**

- collaboratively annotated student work using strong and weak examples

- co-defined acceptable behaviors and collective learner community responsibilities

These scaffolds in classrooms are the Success Criteria that indicate to leaders, principals, and colleagues who do Learning Walks and Talks (see Chapter 9) that students in the classrooms are living in meaningful, supportive learning spaces and that teachers have a fundamental understanding of both the learning that should be happening and how the Third Teacher can be a supportive colleague.

Every learning space in schools and in systems must be scrutinized for risk-free environments that promote curiosity, wondering, thinking, questioning, inclusivity, and risk taking. These same criteria apply to the culture of learning established in system and school meetings: welcoming environments that invite people to take risks, **fail fast**, and feel safe to think out loud without being thwarted and/or dismissed. Crafting the cultural aspect of the Third Teacher is everyone's responsibility. It underpins every parameter in our research. In the absence of a safe learning culture, very few will be brave enough to speak up and speak out without fear of retribution. Consideration of the Third Teacher is necessary at every level—the system, the school, and the classroom—and is reinforced in the bookends: Parameters #1 and #14.

INTRODUCTION TO THE 14 PARAMETERS

In *Realization: The Change Imperative for Deepening District-Wide Reform* (Sharratt & Fullan, 2009) and *Putting FACES on the Data: What Great Leaders Do* (Sharratt & Fullan, 2012), we unwrapped our research neatly summarized as the 14 Parameters of system and school improvement, displayed in Figure 1.2.

Figure 1.2 The 14 Parameters of System and School Improvement

1. Shared beliefs and understandings

    a. All students can achieve high standards given the right time and the right support.

    b. All teachers can teach to high standards given time and the right assistance.

    c. High expectations and early and ongoing intervention are essential.

    d. All leaders, teachers, and students can articulate what they do and why they lead, teach, and learn the way they do. (Adapted from Hill & Crévola, 1999)

2. Embedded Knowledgeable Others

3. Quality assessment informs instruction

4. Principal as lead learner

5. Early and ongoing intervention

6. Case management approach

7. Focused Professional Learning at staff meetings

8. In-school meetings—collaborative assessment of student work

9. Book rooms of leveled books and multi-modal resources

10. Allocation of system and school budgets for learning

11. Collaborative Inquiry—a whole-system approach

12. Parental and community involvement

13. Cross-curricular literacy connections

14. Shared responsibility and accountability

    a. We all own all the FACES!

Our research established that when these 14 Parameters were present at high levels, in systems and schools where leaders focused on them, the system, school leaders, and teachers increased students' growth and achievement. If they were not found, or only some were found, or system and school leaders did not focus on them, there was no or very little improvement in student outcomes (Sharratt & Fullan, 2012). We learned that incorporating all 14 Parameters at high levels was achievable in every school that focused and committed to understanding how all interweave to support each other (see Figure 1.2). We also reported that hundreds of leaders helped us to coin three words—Knowledge-ability, Mobilize-ability, and Sustain-ability (see Chapter 9)—as the initial three of six leadership dimensions that school leaders must demonstrate in order to bring about needed, sharply focused changes to the system and school performance (Fullan & Sharratt, 2007; Sharratt & Fullan, 2012).

Our research continues to be well-received as highly impactful descriptions of not only *what* must happen in systems and schools but *how* to make it happen. I have introduced the 14 Parameters and established their ongoing use in many large, small, urban, and rural districts in several countries across the globe with measurable success. I challenge and encourage system and school leaders to be continually vigilant by implementing and continuously reviewing the 14 Parameters to ensure they and their teams of leaders and teachers are doing the best they can for *all* students—and to never default to what is comfortable, easiest, or status quo. The tools enabling teachers and leaders to become more precise in the work to improve student achievement are embedded throughout this book. To begin, explore **Web Resource 1: Using the 14 Parameters as a System and School Self-Assessment Tool for Improvement** with your teams of leaders and teachers, to determine how well you are doing against the proven 14 and to identify next steps.

Web Resource 1: Using the 14 Parameters as a System and School Self-Assessment Tool for Improvement.

ACHIEVE CLARITY USING THE 14 PARAMETERS

In my work with system and school leaders developing high-impact improvement approaches, the 14 Parameters have consistently proven to work—across contexts—in countries, states, districts, and schools, each with differing variables. In our early work together, leaders in Metro Region Queensland implemented the 14 Parameters and simplified their System Improvement Plan to include a one-page document with the imprinted **watermark** "Precision" (see Figure 1.3). I emphasize a

Figure 1.3 Precision Watermark Underpinning System Improvement Plan

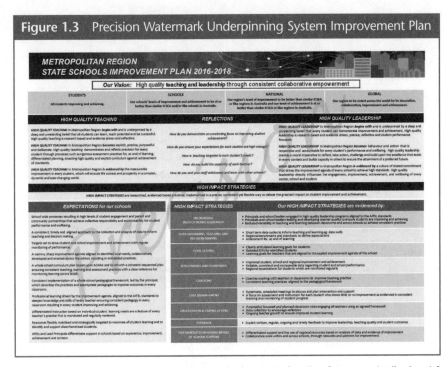

Source: © State of Queensland (Department of Education) Creative Commons Attribution 4.0 International (CC BY 4.0)

one-word watermark that is subtly visible beneath the text on the page as an ever-present descriptor that defines the system and what it stands for. The watermark is the reminder of their collective passion and determination to increase all students' growth and achievement by teaching with "precision" in every classroom.

FUNDAMENTAL CHALLENGE

Can you define your vision on one page? What is your one-word watermark? Take a minute and jot a note to yourself. List the characteristics that will help you define your watermark. What one word describes the measurable and observable high expectations you have for your classroom, school, or system?

Dr. Liam Smith, executive director of the School Improvement Unit, Department of Education and Training in Queensland, writes,

A pre-condition to improving student learning outcomes is whether the leadership team and staff members have a clear understanding of the school's improvement plan—the what and how—and have developed clear Success Criteria for measuring their collective and individual successes. Individual members of the leadership team must be able to articulate their roles and responsibilities in relation to the improvement agenda and they must have collectively developed accountability mechanisms to ensure each team member is able to regularly reflect on and report back their progress to the other team members. Teachers in highly successful schools, then, are able to articulate and demonstrate through their teaching practice the intent of the improvement plan and are able to monitor how they are working toward the fulfilment of the plan. (personal communication, 2017)

Successful, high-focus systems and schools understand the "simplexity" (Sharratt & Fullan, 2012) of the 14 Parameters; however, the less successful see only the complexity. Mark Campling (personal communication, 2017), regional director, Metro Region, points out that he and his high-performance, results-oriented team are focused on the following:

- using research-informed practice as found in the 14 Parameters (Chapter 1)

- scrutinizing data to take precise action that is differentiated to the needs of each school and student (Chapter 2)

- setting precise performance targets for each student using Data Walls and case management meetings (CMMs) across the system (Chapter 7)

- providing unrelenting, differentiated support for leaders, teachers, and students (Chapters 4 and 5)

- empowering leaders in collaborative networks at every level (Chapter 3)

- establishing clear governance structures and transparent decision-making processes (Chapter 9)

Given these precisely targeted strategies, it is not surprising that this high-performance leadership team has outperformed most public schools in Australia.

We developed the 14 Parameters, or integrated performance characteristics, from our research into why similarly supported schools showed different trajectories—dramatic, sustained improvement in achievement; slow to no improvement; or widely variable year after year. The most successful were assessed as "highly focused" against the 14 Parameters; the less successful were "low focused" (Sharratt & Fullan, 2009, 2012). The process of using the 14 Parameters as a reflective tool for improvement is ongoing and responsive to feedback and new information to move a system and its schools forward together.

UNPACKING THE 14 PARAMETERS

The following is a brief synopsis of each parameter, with a discussion of the impact of collaborative formal and informal leadership roles at every level.

Parameter #1: Shared Beliefs and Understandings

This parameter is number 1 for a reason: it is *the vision*. We must believe the following:

a. All students can achieve high standards given the right time and the right support.

b. All teachers can teach to high standards given time and the right assistance.

c. High expectations and early and ongoing intervention are essential.

d. All leaders, teachers, and students can articulate what they do and why they lead, teach, and learn the way they do. (Adapted from Hill & Crévola, 1999)

It is impossible to lead a team without establishing a shared vision of common beliefs and understandings as these are foundational to systems and schools as learning organizations (Sharratt, 1996). They must be revisited at every opportunity as the evidence of student achievement is gathered and reviewed. Whenever there is a conflict, team members need to revisit these beliefs because the four dimensions of Parameter #1 are the glue or first principles that must be present within every system and school. System and school leaders together with teachers must be driven by a deep belief that all students can achieve high standards given the right time and the right support. Similarly, leaders must believe and expect that all teachers can learn to teach to high standards when given the right assistance. It is expected that leaders, teachers, and students can articulate why they do what they do and why they lead, teach, and learn the way they do. To me, this is the equity issue, that, when embraced, leads to equity and excellence. With staff turnover a reality everywhere, at least annual renewal of the shared beliefs among returning staff becomes an ongoing culture-building opportunity that provides a solid platform of consistency in welcoming new team members. Continuously refreshing Parameter #1 as the vision establishes shared beliefs and understandings, which is a must before the improvement work can have an impact.

Parameter #2: Embedded Knowledgeable Others

An expert teaching team is necessary. Leaders and teachers must "attach" themselves to a Knowledgeable Other; every school must have at least one respected and respectful master teacher who has time during the day to *co-teach* with classroom teachers. These Knowledgeable Others are instructional coaches who have time purposefully scheduled during the school day to work alongside classroom teachers, supporting focused work on assessment that informs instruction. Knowledgeable Others must have strong interpersonal skills to build relational trust while co-laboring with teachers (Sharratt & Planche, 2016). Selection on the basis of this proven and reference-evidenced characteristic is key to successful deployment of the role. *Only after being certain* the person has strong interpersonal skills do selectors consider the candidate's other evidence-proven skills in leading instruction, assessment, and managing change. It is crucial to be deliberate about possessing relational skills because Knowledgeable Others plan, scaffold, and facilitate Professional Learning through group processes such as lesson study, co-teaching cycles, and the collaborative assessment of student work (see Chapter 8). They must be seen as critical members of the school leadership team. Having a Knowledgeable Other, part time in every school, is key to moving a system forward as consistent messages can be delivered when all Knowledgeable Others and their principals participate in learning sessions together and are then expected to deliver the same Professional Learning in their schools. This creates the coherence in improvement messages needed across a system and in a school.

Parameter #3: Quality Assessment Informs Instruction

This parameter is about the need for pervasive high-impact classroom practice. Evidence-proven, high-impact practices, like using ongoing assessment data that differentiate instruction, are embedded in the planning for daily, uninterrupted literacy and numeracy blocks of instructional time or in specific subject classes where every lesson features a literacy skill and teachers embed assessment *for* and *as* learning practices (see Chapter 4), to inform their next steps for instruction. Thus, data today is instruction tomorrow. The Knowledgeable Other's timetable aligns with the literacy block at the elementary level and with that of teachers most in need of instructional support at the secondary level. Knowledgeable Others use the **Gradual Release and Acceptance of Responsibility** (GRR) model to ensure precision in practice. The GRR is a pedagogical framework designed to teach all students how to make meaning, gain conceptual understanding, and communicate effectively, as discussed in Chapter 5.

Parameter #4: Principal as Lead Learner

System and school leaders attend, participate, and are "present"—learning together. They *work alongside* teachers at Professional Learning sessions, modeling and monitoring effective and expected practices as learning leaders, always looking to find evidence of those practices that most benefit student learning. Principals use data, collaboratively with all staff, to inform school planning, to select resources, and to co-lead assessment practices that inform instruction for all students in their care. In other words, instructional leaders

- put FACES on the data and take action to make a difference for each and every student;

- acquire a deep understanding of effective classroom practices by participating in ongoing Professional Learning Community (PLC) work focused on data and driven by professional Collaborative Inquiry about high-impact practices;

- take part, with their leadership teams, in system learning sessions and plan how they will replicate the learning back in their schools, always focused on the FACES of students; and

- conduct Learning Walks and Talks daily in classrooms, collecting evidence of students' thinking and teachers' use of cutting-edge practices to increase their students' achievement because they know that learning happens in the classroom, not in their offices (see Chapter 9).

Parameter #5: Early and Ongoing Intervention

Intervention is critical in the early years, but it is not limited to them and it must be ongoing throughout the grade levels. Individual student need is determined by the ongoing scrutiny of a variety of assessment data. Intervention is not a purchased program; there is no one intervention program that will "fix" students. Intervention is most effective when it is sharply focused on individual learning needs; money for human and material resources is best spent in the early years, when the foundations for learning are developed and shaped. However, intervention practices must be seen by the system and schools as an ongoing, central resource with which teachers can collaboratively engage and from which they can learn. A structured, collaboratively planned approach by all teachers (e.g., classroom, special education, Reading Recovery, English language learner, and support teachers) is necessary to design and deliver units and lessons with an integrated co-teaching approach to supporting *all* students. All teachers must strive to become intervention teachers capable of teaching all students (see Chapter 7).

Parameter #6: Case Management Approach

Putting FACES on the data using the case management approach is a two-pronged process: (1) prevention: the co-construction of **Data Walls** allows staff members to stand back and discuss students' areas of need, to set targets, and to decide what is possible for each FACE, and (2) intervention: **case management meetings** (CMMs) in which a teacher presents one student at a time, through a work sample, to a *problem-solving forum* focused on supporting the classroom teacher with a recommended instructional strategy to try. It requires school leaders and teachers to come together as co-learners. Data Walls and CMMs precisely determine next steps to meet the differentiated learning needs of teachers and students in each school. At the system level, Data Walls and CMMs mirror those at the school level, precisely determining next steps in providing differentiated resourcing and Professional Learning in each school across a system (see Chapter 7).

Parameter #7: Focused Professional Learning at Staff and Professional Learning Community Meetings

Using meeting times for Professional Learning builds teacher and leader **collective capacity** and develops a common language across all learning areas. Starting with data, teachers who are Knowledgeable Others and leaders *together* provide the Professional Learning needed at staff meetings, at division meetings, and during Professional Learning Community (PLC) time (see Chapter 3), modeling a culture of learning—the Third Teacher—that reflects clear expectations about precision in practice. Rather than spending precious meeting time on operational issues, leaders relegate them to emails or shared sites so that *learning* is the focus of all meetings. During meetings it is the capacity of the group that is built, as well as a collective understanding of the vision for the improvement work. Meeting times are spent talking about and sharing impactful teaching strategies. It is key that classroom teachers share leadership in planning and designing their Professional Learning, to ensure they are learning what they think they need to learn and to create commitment to and ownership of their learning. As Campbell et al. (2016) stated, "Teachers value Professional Learning that is relevant and practical for their work; 'job-embedded' should not mean school-based exclusively as opportunities to engage in and with external expertise as these sources of professional development matter also" (p. 8). Across their Canadian case study interviews, a key finding they reported was the importance of Professional Learning that is teacher- and leader-driven. Their findings support the critical importance of Parameter #7.

Parameter #8: In-School Meetings— Collaborative Assessment of Student Work

It is often noted that the greatest variation in teaching in a system is not between schools; it is between classrooms in the same school. To reduce that variation, evidence of learning through student work samples is used in regular, ongoing **co-teaching conversations** in which teachers collaboratively determine how to

- sharpen their use of assessment data, every minute, to drive precise instruction;

- broaden their individual and collective instructional repertoire;

- challenge assumptions in a respectful way;

- improve immediate Descriptive Feedback strategies;

- move students from one level of work to the next and beyond expectations.

This powerful collaborative assessment of student work process begins when teachers and leaders gather at their Data Wall and begin to "wonder why" they are seeing a worrying trend, spike, or individual student with an issue. At regularly planned meetings to discuss the literacy and numeracy achievement of individual students, staff, facilitated by Knowledgeable Others and leaders,

- co-develop common assessment tools,

- collaboratively assess student work,

- give one another evidence-based feedback,

- co-create curriculum-based exemplars in order to reduce variation in practice among classrooms.

Collaborative processes such as the case management approach, lesson study, the Co-Teaching Cycle, and Collaborative Inquiry are used by leaders, Knowledgeable Others, and teachers to promote ongoing rich discussion about changed classroom practices and their evidence-informed impact on student learning.

Parameter #9: Book Rooms of Leveled Books and Multi-Modal Resources

Resources that support differentiated instruction are compiled and organized in a multimedia room or resource center for teachers' access to just-right, just-in-time resources. These high-quality, multi-modal resources reflect the diversity of the community, meet a range of abilities and needs, and address a range of student interests. They are easily accessible and support teachers' implementation of the curriculum at students' point of need. Processes are established for regular auditing of system and school resources by leaders and teachers to sustain quality assurance of resources and refresh understanding of what is available to teams of like-grade teachers. For example, in-school and cross-school dialogue leads to a deeper understanding of what constitutes a high-quality literacy resource that promotes critical literacy skills and results in "teachable moments" that empower critical thinking by all students.

Parameter #10: Allocation of System and School Budgets for Learning

Principals and leadership teams intentionally allocate budget items for resources that address instructional needs revealed by school and classroom assessment data. Leaders can articulate why they are doing what they are choosing to do. Equity of outcomes for all learners is assured through budget resourcing (human and material) to support learning and learners. Some centrally retained funds are available to flexibly and responsively apply resources to meet emerging learning needs. Frequently, system needs are *collaboratively triaged*; that is, needs are prioritized so that support is allocated (to schools and teachers) using data, not by applying resources equally. Firsthand situational knowledge is based on the ever-present vision of increasing all students' achievement.

Parameter #11: Collaborative Inquiry— A Whole-System, School, and Classroom Approach

Every system or school meeting begins with a review of data, searching for the impact of actions taken on previously identified issues. Questions about the data are the basis of SMART goals. Collaborative Inquiry (CI) questions follow and are developed by system leaders, principals, and groups of teachers to test pedagogical approaches they feel will enable instruction to elevate student achievement to meet their collective SMART goals. Development of CI questions is deliberate using a structured, collaboratively planned approach; it is not left to system teams or schools to independently create their own processes because "being systematic" counts. The CI learning cycle (Sharratt & Fullan, 2009, 2012;

Sharratt & Harild, 2015) in Chapter 3 is a model for collaboratively interrogating the data in a knowledge-building process. The model results in coherent, reportable pedagogical documentation that must be shared across the system and schools to ensure knowledge utilization and mobilization by all (Sharratt, 1996). Professional CI allows teachers and leaders to investigate the cause and effect relationship between their practices and the evidence of student learning. CI is one example of job-embedded Professional Learning that involves a structured process of turning continuous teacher inquiry into high-impact classroom practice. Teachers and leaders work collaboratively to design specifically focused questions arising from issues identified in their system, school, and classroom assessment data. The system supports the work of school teams by providing funds and offering Professional Learning sessions focused on how time is spent on collaborating and on developing the necessary research skills to do the CI work. At the end of the research cycle, inquiry teams make available reports documenting their learning journeys and findings. Systems find ways, such as the Learning Fair, discussed later in this chapter, to celebrate the learning and mobilize the knowledge gained across schools. Being involved and comfortable with professional inquiry leads to teachers replicating that process for students in classrooms (see Chapter 6). Engaging students in processes to uncover their wonderings and excite their inquisitiveness results in empowered student learning of the curriculum content.

Parameter #12: Parental and Community Involvement

System and school leadership teams work toward establishing strong community-home-school relationships (see Chapter 2). Research indicates that parent and community involvement increase all students' achievement. Schools build strong relationships with parents by keeping them informed about their children's progress and by involving them in the why and how the school is teaching literacy skills, for example, in every subject area. Parents, caregivers, and the broader community are helped to understand how they can support their children and are continuously invited to provide input into annual system and school plans for improvement. Then, when these plans are drafted, they are shared once again. Parents and the broader community are seen as *partners in decision-making processes* focused on growth and achievement for all students (Sharratt & Harild, 2015).

Parameter #13: Cross-Curricular Literacy Connections

System and school improvement requires a definitive focus on literacy and critical thinking skills across all subject areas, woven into rigorous, cognitively demanding performance tasks. The components of balanced literacy instruction allow teachers to support students to develop meaning-making skills in all subject areas. Assessment data determine what literacy skills each student will need to develop in order to access a subject's curriculum content; however, teachers in all content areas can further students' achievement by modeling the skills, sharing in the making of meaning, guiding students toward independence, and monitoring their independent work using the Gradual Release and Acceptance of Responsibility model in all subject areas (see Chapter 5). Adopting that model, schoolwide, enables literacy development, for example, in every subject area, affording the opportunity for differentiated instruction.

Parameter #14: Shared Responsibility and Accountability

Parameter #14 is the "bookend" parameter to Parameter #1. Leaders care about the schools down the road as much as they do their own. Thus, *everyone is responsible* and *accountable* for every learner within and across schools in a district and a state. That is, everyone knows and can clearly articulate the system, school, and classroom priority because SMART Goals and CI questions are aligned, clear, precise, intentional, and published. Everyone sees himself or herself as responsible for achieving the goals and accountable for the learning that results from their implementation. Intentional procedures and processes encourage system- and schoolwide shared responsibility and ownership for student learning (see Chapter 9 and Conclusion).

POWER LIVES IN THE INTERSECTION OF THE 14 PARAMETERS

Acknowledging shared responsibility develops a culture that encourages continuous professional improvement. Triangulation of data informs the Professional Learning needed in districts and schools and impacts the allocation and selection of resources. Districts disaggregate standards-based assessments, delivering them to leaders' and teachers' desktops to put individual FACES on the data to assist in the development of improvement plans

Source: Lyn Sharratt, Brisbane Catholic Education, 2017.

and collaborative actions. Through the co-construction of Data Walls, principals, leadership teams, and teachers can name at-risk students individually, and through CMMs they can clearly articulate what they are doing for each one.

School staff members work on finding and sharing the results of CI questions. Principals and teachers conduct Learning Walks and Talks daily to look for evidence-proven, agreed-upon assessment and instructional strategies discovered through their CIs. Systems host evidence-based Learning Fairs for all school teams to share their CI journeys that highlight student improvement data. System and school leaders and teachers learn from each other by having this forum to mobilize knowledge of "What works?" "What doesn't?" and "What did we do differently?" This information is documented, curated, and shared on internal system websites. Schools also host their own Learning Fairs for parents and the community to keep them well-informed of progress.

None of the improvement work progresses smoothly unless the bookends—Parameter 1: Shared Beliefs and Understandings and Parameter 14: Shared Responsibility and Accountability—are in place for each and every student. The process of using the 14 Parameters is ongoing, reflective, and responsive to feedback and new information to move systems and their schools forward together; the intersection of all 14 Parameters, as illustrated in Figure 1.4, ensures that system and school improvement will occur.

HOW TO BEGIN IMPLEMENTING THE 14 PARAMETERS

Although the 14 Parameters may seem complicated, systems and schools begin simply as follows:

- using their data to consider their areas of immediate need

- selecting two or three of the Parameters as immediate goals to be actioned, in addition to Parameters 1, 6, and 14, which are always the nonnegotiables

- developing an action plan with benchmarks and timelines to progress the work of implementing the selected Parameters in addition to the three nonnegotiable Parameters, as depicted in Figure 1.5

Using data to select areas of immediate need enables professionals in educational systems to collaboratively focus their work to further develop their collective capacity. Once these areas of need are transparent, teams select the parameters that are likely to be most impactful in addressing student need. With success in the two or three selected first, teams can move toward their next collaboratively selected priority within the 14, and the next, until they are self-assessing as "high" against all 14 Parameters. We can demonstrate that student achievement has increased under this collective professional enterprise more than it has in systems we have examined where schools have worked individually, "choosing their own adventure" (adapted from Sharratt & Fullan, 2009, 2012). The 14 Parameters represent a "system-ness approach" to improvement for every FACE. System-ness demands that everyone is responsible and accountable (Parameter #14). System-level educators are not just part of the background noise in system and school improvement. Rather, they exercise essential leadership, with school leaders, to build collective capacity throughout systems for teaching and learning improvements (Honig et al., 2010, in Watterston & Kimber, 2017).

The case study schools and systems highlighted throughout this text show that astonishing progress is possible when focused on the 14 Parameters for improvement. Systems and schools that align their work with these 14 areas make a difference to increasing all students' achievement. How can leaders not afford to reallocate the time when many large

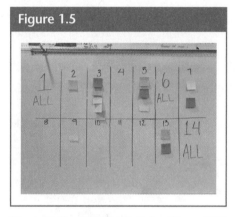

Figure 1.5

Source: Lyn Sharratt, Wilcannia-Forbes Diocese, 2017.

Web Resource 1:
Using the 14
Parameters as a
System and School
Self-Assessment Tool
for Improvement

and small diverse systems and schools that have done so are successfully raising student achievement levels?

SELF-ASSESS YOUR SYSTEM AND SCHOOL PROGRESS USING THE 14 PARAMETERS

Instructional coach Tracey Petersen and I developed a matrix of expected outcomes when using the 14 Parameters as the lens to self-reflect, measure, and ensure that all students' achievement is progressed and sustained.

The first page of the matrix is displayed in Figure 1.6; the entire System and Self-Assessment Tool using the 14 Parameters as the lens to determine improvement is available online as **Web Resource 1: Using the 14 Parameters as a System and School Self-Assessment Tool for Improvement.**

FUNDAMENTAL CHALLENGE

As you view the complete matrix online (Web Resource 1), note how you might use it to establish the vision or set an improvement goal that focuses on taking action at every level of your system and schools. How will you know that leaders, teachers, and students can express what has improved and *why* it has improved, using evidence?

CREATE AN ACTION PLAN FOR SYSTEM AND SCHOOL IMPROVEMENT

Effective leaders at every level have a clearly articulated vision; a short, sharply focused plan; and a clear line of sight to every classroom. They relentlessly follow up on codetermined, widely known system, school, and classroom nonnegotiables, using the 14 Parameter Framework to assess ongoing improvement. This takes leaders who are consistent, insistent, and persistent, as discussed in Chapter 9. Figure 1.7 illustrates the precision in practice developed and implemented with integrity by system leaders in the Diocese of Wilcannia-Forbes. The action plan in Figure 1.8 (see p. 34) provides CLARITY and incorporates scheduled timely follow up. These leaders hold each other accountable for increasing all students' achievement.

The 14 Parameters	Assessment literate learners	Teaching with a literacy focus K–12	Early leveled literacy K–2	Instructional coaching cycle	Collaborative Inquiry	Leadership skills and behaviors
1. **Shared Beliefs and Understandings** • **All students** can achieve high standards given the right time and the right support. • **All teachers** can teach to high standards given time and the right assistance. • **High expectations and early and ongoing intervention** are essential.	• Believe that assessment literacy is foundation of quality teaching & right of every student • Demonstrate belief that students are partners in learning • Empower students to own their learning • Articulate how the assessment literacy of teachers and students is	• Create the right Learning Intentions and Success Criteria (SC) to ensure that every student can achieve • Open up critical thinking to be "A"-level thinking to all students • Articulate the processes in every subject area used to	• Know that what happens in Kindergarten predicts secondary school graduation • Witness literacy explicitly taught in a joyful learning environment • Embrace that early literacy includes oral language, reading, writing, viewing, representing, mathematics, and critical thinking	• Co-plan how to deconstruct Learning Intentions from curriculum and co-construct Success Criteria with students that opens critical thinking ("A"-level thinking) to all learners • Articulate and demonstrate how teachers' capacity	• Reflect continuously on data to inform Collaborative Inquiry (CI) that is grounded in evidence of student learning to progress the teaching • Examine and co-assess student work as evidence of learning • Stay true to the CI cycle with operating norms, protocols, and	• Build consensus with all staff about shared beliefs and understandings • Model the consistent belief that all teachers can learn to teach and all students can learn, given the right time and assistance • Articulate the above vision; provide rationale why teachers, students do what they do every day

(Continued)

Figure 1.6 (Continued)

The 14 Parameters	Assessment literate learners	Teaching with a literacy focus K–12	Early leveled literacy K–2	Instructional coaching cycle	Collaborative Inquiry	Leadership skills and behaviors
• **All leaders, teachers, and students** can articulate what they do and why they lead, teach, learn the way they do every day (adapted from Hill & Crévola, 1999).	built through collaborative learning processes	move from curriculum expectations addressed in Learning Intentions, through SC and Descriptive Feedback, to rich assessment tasks	• Use an effective balanced literacy approach to ensure all students are reading with fluency and comprehension by the end of Grade 1 • Expect that students will progress in literacy learning in alignment with the expectations for their grade level • Articulate how the three cueing systems are used as a tool to target book introductions and instruction within early leveled reading	is built by assessing individual needs through the 4 C's Cycle: Co-Planning, Co-Teaching, Co-Debriefing and Co-Reflecting	a structured, collaboratively planned approach to inquiry	• Model and monitor high expectations for all learners • Ask, continuously, if the expectations are set high enough • Ask, "Is the teaching aligned to the curriculum expectations?" and "How has the teaching caused learning?" • Participate in CI alongside teachers

Figure 1.7 Wilcannia-Forbes Education Services Action Plan

2017 Education Services Team ACTION PLAN

Rationale:

This Action Plan is intended to prioritize and track the work of the Wilcannia-Forbes (WF) Education Services team following the ongoing Professional Learning during 2017–2019.

List of Priority Actions

1. All stakeholders clearly articulate system priorities with a laser-like focus on the priority of literacy, including numeracy.

2. Go deeper into 2nd order change to ensure precision in assessment to inform literacy instruction.

3. Central Education Office (CEO) staff model alongside teachers using Lesson Study and the 4 Cs model.

4. Build all teacher and leader capacity in teaching reading/writing and numeracy by identifying strong practitioners who deeply understand their impact in classrooms and using them to demonstrate best practice.

5. Data will drive differentiation in human and material resourcing in schools, resulting in agile ways in providing support where it is needed.

6. Regular and ongoing communication between CEO teams to ensure alignment and laser-like focus on the priority of literacy.

7. Model what we expect of schools.

Focus Area	Timeframe	Details of Tasks to Be Completed	Key Person/s	ACTIONED
CEO Data Wall—where are the pockets of excellence? Who are our most vulnerable students? Schools?	Term 2, 2017	• Chris and Prue to gather examples of potential Data Walls to share with the team • Simone will have Kindergarten Data reading levels to present at next meeting.	Simone Prue Chris	Completed as of 29/5/17 Physical Data Wall Updated for Term 2. 24/7/2017

(Continued)

Figure 1.7 (Continued)

Focus Area	Timeframe	Details of Tasks to Be Completed	Key Person/s	ACTIONED
		• Prue to purchase bi-fold display board for use. • Follow up discussions at planning day on Monday 15th May • Oversee/review the process ONGOING ITEMS: • Collection of Kindergarten (K) reading levels at the end of each term • Data Wall: Adjust co-constructed Data Wall to reflect reading levels	Suz/Chris Simone Chris Simmy/Prue Natalie/Deb	Nat to put update in Principals' Bulletin Board about our Data Wall
Professional Learning (PL) on administering Running Records accurately for all teachers	Term 2 Week 4/5	• PL opportunity for all Ed Services team and Focus Teachers • Reading expectations updated Shared beliefs among team are consistent; Reading expectations reflect both Accuracy/Comprehension across all schools. • Compare and contrast various Reading Assessment Benchmark Kits and present back to team in Term 4	Natalie Suz/Mary-Ellen Natalie Ange & Prue	WF Expectations—to be finalized Nat to update schools via Principal Bulletin Board and email Focus Teachers
Develop School Action Plans to focus work being actioned in schools	Term 2 Week 4	• Stimulus Paper completed for sharing at Principals' Meeting 16/5/17 ONGOING ITEM: • Regular follow-up and check-ins with Ed Services team—review school discussions from Principals' Meeting Record of the author's work to date in schools	Deb Natalie/Deb	Completed at Principals Workshop 16/5/17 Ongoing check-ins

Focus Area	Timeframe	Details of Tasks to Be Completed	Key Person/s	ACTIONED
Review Sharratt's Instructional Coach role compared with our Focus Teacher Role	Term 2 Week 3	• Karen O'Malley to email author for copy of her Role Description • Updated Role Description completed after Focus Teacher Workshop	Natalie Ange	Ange and Nat to confer and finalize what is not included in Role Description
Establish networking groups for Stage 1, Stage 2, Stage 3	25 October	• Planning meeting for 2018 • Education Officers to each take responsibility for a key learning stage	Education Services Team	Discussion 25th October, 2017
Ed Services writing a Literacy Strategy	Working on it from present time Initial Draft September 4	• Shared Beliefs & Understandings (Parameter#1) document to be developed • A subcommittee of Literacy Strategy Group to work on a Literacy Strategy paper to discuss with author as our Critical Friend • Literacy Strategy group to meet outside of Ed Services meeting—develop a Literacy Strategy e-FOLDER ◦ 1st meeting 22 June (9–12) • Initial draft paper to be brought to Ed Services Team meeting September 4 (Term 3—Week 8)	Education Services Team	*Good to Great to Innovate,* Sharratt & Harild, 2015—team encouraged to refer to text in developing Literacy Strategy; Literacy Strategy Group reconvene 29th August 2017, 9–10 am Simmy to scan and upload to folder
Develop PL to deliver to Focus Teachers reflecting author's work	Term 2 Week 5 Term 2 21st June	• Explore the possibility of systemwide Professional Learning day in 2018 with author • 14 Parameters Professional Learning - for Focus teachers	Natalie Ed Officers	Nat has flagged with Mary-Ellen. Ongoing Suz has uploaded.
Regular Principal's Bulletin Board Updates	Ongoing	• Regular check-ins and updates via Principals' Bulletin Board and standing item at Principals' Meeting to inform schools of Ed Services actions	Natalie	Ongoing

Source: Mary-Ellen Dempsey, 2017.

An additional monitoring framework for following up this improvement work, used in Darling Downs South West Region, can be found in **Web Resource 2: Darling Downs Template to Track the 14 Parameter Work.**

The following case study demonstrates how a leader in a large urban and rural district used the 14 Parameter Framework to co-create an action-oriented improvement plan that led to impressive school improvement results. As you read, note the cluster work does not follow Parameters 1 to 14 in sequential order, but the leader aligns them with the ongoing work and the language of improvement developed internally.

CASE STUDY: USING THE 14 PARAMETERS AS A TAKE-ACTION TOOL

The Queensland government's Department of Education and Training (DET) is made up of seven education regions with the metropolitan region, covering the area of capital city Brisbane and the Brisbane Western Corridor to the west, including the city of Ipswich, located about 40 kilometers from Brisbane Central Business District.

Many of the families in the Ipswich area cluster of primary schools are low-income earners and at high levels of social disadvantage. Not only do school staff teams provide education, they offer social and emotional support to students and intervention programs to counter serious student behavior issues at all grade levels. Student performance data sources have consistently presented as very low and have been flagged "red" for "below national minimum standard" in national testing programs. Attracting high-quality beginning and experienced teachers has been challenging due to the poor reputation of schools in this area.

The Ipswich cluster, supported by Assistant Regional Director Helen Kenworthy, consists of 25 primary schools, 798 teachers, and 12,065 students. Kenworthy's role is to support principals and schools to improve performance and outcomes for all students. Coming from her deep belief in Parameter #1, that every student can learn given the right time and right support, her vision from the start was "to make a difference in the lives of the students in Ipswich." Together with school leaders, Kenworthy focused on the Region's goal: "to ensure all students reach National

Minimum Standard in Grade 3 with a specific focus on indigenous student achievement being monitored and known personally by each ARD."

Focus for Kenworthy and her colleagues is driven by their *Metropolitan Region State Schools Improvement Plan (SIP) 2016–2019*. The initial one-pager of their comprehensive plan is displayed in Figure 1.3. The SIP plan identifies nine high-impact strategies that positively impact student improvement and achievement:

- intentional instructional leadership (Parameter #4)

- data-informed teaching and decision making (Parameter #3)

- goal setting (Parameter #1)

- benchmarks and standards (Parameter #14)

- coaching (Parameter #2)

- case management (Parameter #6)

- classroom observation and taking action (Parameters #3, #4, and #14)

- ongoing feedback (Parameter #3)

- differentiated model of school support (Parameters #5 and #6)

Nineteen of the 25 schools in Kenworthy's cluster agreed to focus intensely on the following:

- using data to drive instruction (Parameter #6)

- early and ongoing intervention (Parameter #5)

- Professional Learning at staff meetings (Parameter #7)

- building leader and teacher capacity for focused literacy assessment and instruction (Parameters #3, #4, and #14)

School cluster meetings were led the same way a principal would lead Professional Learning at staff meetings, ensuring there was a sustained focus on literacy assessment and instruction (Parameter #3). The agenda for every cluster meeting was an unwavering focus on (1) analyzing data

(Continued)

(Continued)

and (2) reading *Putting FACES on the Data* (Sharratt & Fullan, 2012). Two cluster meetings were held in each of the four school terms, a total of eight per year, and an additional series of fortnightly workshops was also provided with a focus on developing a school reading framework and reading program.

The focus of Kenworthy's work in schools was centered on putting FACES on the data. Every school was supported to develop a Data Wall that put FACES on reading data and raised awareness that student achievement was not as high as it should be. The region's expected reading benchmarks were included on every Data Wall and provided a standard of achievement that was the goal for each grade level. Their mantra became, "a year's worth of learning in one year" (Hattie, 2012). School Data Walls, as shown in Figures 1.8A and 1.8B, were used by schools to monitor and track individual student progress to ensure every student was making predicted and expected progress.

Figure 1.8 Examples of School Data Walls in the Ipswich Cluster

Source: Helen Kenworthy, assistant regional director, Metro Region.

Kenworthy participated in CMMs beside principals and teachers and provided advice and guidance about protocols, questioning techniques, teaching strategies, and follow-up support. Each CMM was held in front of the school Data Wall, and the progress of individual students and groups of students was closely monitored. One of the biggest shifts in thinking was identified in discussions about instruction. A key question was, "What do students need to learn and to be able to do to move to the next reading level?" From this understanding, the focus of the case management approach became

- What needs to be planned and taught to move this student forward?

- How will we monitor this so that this student continues to make progress?

- How will we make sure what is learned in the CMM is sustained and shared with other teachers?

(Continued)

(Continued)

In reflecting on the number of students still on the lowest reading level (0–4) at the end of Term 3, a four-term school year, a group of Kindergarten teachers from one of the larger schools in the cluster stated,

> If we had known what we know now about data and understanding individual students, looking at what the data is telling us about what students know and what our students need to know, we could have made a difference sooner. Our teaching practice has changed; every student has different needs and we really need to teach them differently. We will start earlier next year and make a bigger difference.

School leadership teams accompanied Kenworthy on Learning Walks and Talks (see Chapter 9) at other schools to observe Data Walls and CMMs in action. Schools shared their practices about how they provided intervention and monitored the effectiveness of the intervention. Collaborative learning groups were established across schools and driven by school leaders, with Kenworthy participating. Participants reflected on the progress of work in each school, shared practice, and discussed professional reading.

Supporting school leaders to develop a deep understanding of how to analyze and use student data was also a significant focus of the initial work. Data analysis experts were used to teach school leaders about national data sets, and curriculum advisors provided training and insight into how to use and interpret diagnostic reading assessment tools. A deep understanding of how to assess reading provided the catalyst for ensuring that all school leaders understood how to teach reading, and Professional Learning was ongoing to build leadership capacity in this area. The result of the above focused work is a group of highly capable, competent instructional leaders in the cluster schools who work with teachers to ensure every student is learning and achieving.

Source: Helen Kenworthy, assistant regional director, Metropolitan Region, personal communication, 2017.

IMPACT!

The outcomes of this focused work are tangible and inspiring for Kenworthy and the school leaders. After only 16 months, results for Grade 3 and 5 reading and writing improved dramatically in 18 of the 25 schools in this cluster. Their ongoing data collection indicates where their next focus and differentiated Professional Learning must be.

School leaders and teachers are proud of their work; their teaching practice has changed, and students have celebrated the improvements they have made. Kenworthy's knowledge of teaching and learning combined with her strategic and focused leadership has resulted in the following:

- dramatic changes in pedagogical practice across all the schools

- an unwavering focus on literacy

- a moral imperative to improve the lives of all students

The result is improved student outcomes in nearly all the cluster schools in only a few short months—less time than ever thought possible. These positive outcomes are having a profound effect on all schools in Metro Region and beyond.

Lessons Learned: Successful Improvement Strategies Using the 14 Parameter Framework

Kenworthy used the 14 Parameters aligned with the region's high-impact strategies, and she and her staff have learned the power of the following:

1. Having high expectations: A shared belief that every student can achieve, and an unwavering focus on teaching, learning, and knowing the curriculum (Parameter #1)

2. Using data: Knowing every student, knowing what s/he can and cannot do, and knowing what the teacher needs to teach for the student to make progress (Parameters #5 and #6)

3. Ensuring needs-based Professional Learning: An unrelenting focus at all cluster Professional Learning sessions on data, reading and writing, and the shared responsibility for this work by all members of the school staff (Parameters #4, #7, #14)

4. Differentiating support: The assistant regional director's ability to genuinely know and understand each school and each principal and then tailor support in a differentiated manner based on this knowledge (Parameter #1, #14)

5. Orchestrating collaborative learning: Through Learning Walks and Talks in each other's schools, observation and sharing of intervention strategies, collaborative discussion groups, and working together with the assistant regional director as a colleague in the work (Parameter #11)

All school leaders and teachers in the cluster of schools now know and can articulate the focus of the work and the moral imperative to make a difference in the lives of all students.

The focus for the coming years is to stay the course; the work has only just begun, with very positive results. The goal is to sustain the focus on data and deepen instructional practice to embed consistent high-impact practices in every classroom in every school (Parameters #1, #3, #6, #14). Plans are in place to focus on

- using assessment data in planning (Parameter #3),

- ensuring assessment is aligned with the achievement standards in the curriculum (Parameters #1 and #14),

- undertaking the power of teacher collaborative assessment of student work (Parameter #8) both within schools and across school groups to affirm teachers' judgment and determine Descriptive Feedback on student work,

- planning for future Professional Learning sessions focused on improving student learning (Parameter #7),

Kenworthy will continue to

- participate in the learning and leading,

- focus on working as an instructional leader with school leaders and teachers,

- enhance collaborative learning opportunities between leaders and teachers in and across schools.

This cluster of schools and the entire Metropolitan Region will continue to focus on putting FACES on their school and student data. It's an exciting journey that's making a difference!

Lessons Learned: From Working in the Field and at the Center

Lessons I have learned from being "in the field and at the center simultaneously," working alongside leaders and teachers:

1. The 14 Parameters are powerful when considered in concert— woven together and not necessarily in lock step.

2. The case management approach (Data Walls and CMMs) is an impactful course of action and a system nonnegotiable.

3. Strategic leaders deliver clear and consistent messages.

4. System and school leaders are insistent in providing evidence that they are making a difference in the lives of their students.

5. System leaders are present and persistent in offering support and CLARITY of high expectations to ensure all schools participate and succeed.

Clearly, this CLARITY of expectation and support to uncover best practices is working. Successes are shared throughout Metro Region at dedicated times for knowledge mobilization that I call the "Learning Fair."

THE LEARNING FAIR: MOBILIZING AND CELEBRATING SMALL AND BIG WINS

How do you celebrate and mobilize the learning gained from implementing the 14 Parameters? Once you have completed your own assessment of the 14 Parameter matrix, developed a good understanding of the 14 Parameters, completed some staff capacity-building work in CI, and established agreed-upon, high-impact strategies including the case management approach, you will want to ensure that learning across your system and schools is shared, grown, known, and celebrated.

When your system has had success, as in the case study above, you are ready for sharing successes and failures, a key component of this improvement work. "Sharratt Schools" in Catholic Education Western Australia, which have been working on improvement for three years, recently participated in an outstanding sharing opportunity called the Learning Showcase, shown in Figures 1.9 and 1.10. A Learning Fair, symposium, or showcase is an opportunity to highlight, reflect on, and celebrate the CI journey using the 14 Parameters as the tool for the reflection.

Learning Fairs are designed for knowledge mobilization. The focus of the Learning Fair is to reflect on the successes and challenges of each school's journey and to share evidence of their actions, results, and learning, modeling what schools can continue to do internally, in learning clusters and Professional Learning Communities (PLCs). This is how transformative knowledge gained in one school is transmitted and may be transformative across many schools in a system. Each school is invited to produce a 30-minute presentation that begins with members of the school team using whatever presentation tools they choose, as depicted in Figures 1.9 and 1.10. The focus is on the narrative of the school's learning journey, not on the presentation tools.

Figure 1.9 Elementary Storefront From Learning Fair

Figure 1.10 Secondary Storefront From Learning Fair

Source: Lyn Sharratt, 2017.

For more detailed information about creating a learning event after using the 14 Parameters and inquiring into improvement, see **Web Resource 3: Organizing and Mobilizing a Learning Event—The Learning Fair.**

SYSTEM AND SCHOOL IMPROVEMENT REQUIRES TIRELESS COMMITMENT

The 14 Parameters are the product of initial research into the hard work that led a very large, underperforming school district to become a very successful school district—not just high achieving relative to its previous low-achieving status but against all other districts in the state. They have sustained that high achievement for more than a decade. The Ipswich cluster took the lessons learned and ran with them, developing their own meta-language. Whole states, like Ontario, or regions like Metro Region adapt the learning from integrating the 14 Parameters to create their own education powerhouses.

As we move into the next chapters on knowing the learners and professional CI, remember the impact of the 14 Parameters. Together, they are an evidence-proven toolkit

Web Resource 3:
Organizing and Mobilizing a Learning Event— The Learning Fair

to carry with you in your improvement work throughout your career. Specifically, in Chapter 2, I look at the CLARITY needed in knowing the many FACES of learners, with an understanding that will enable them to learn, adapt, and achieve.

Author's Note

After an introduction to the 14 Parameters, leaders of system and school teams that I work with make an ongoing commitment to move ahead together, using the 14 Parameters as their unifying framework. At the end of each chapter in this text are some of the commitments participants have made early on this journey. Of note, these are real system and school leaders who realized, as they worked alongside me, that *they must make the time to invest in using the 14 Parameters to support, focus, and align their whole-system improvement efforts.* Each Commitment section reflects the FACES and voices of my research participants who continue to contribute to my thinking and writing.

COMMITMENT

I commit to

● being part of the team to develop the plan to use 14 Parameters with all our teachers,

● sharing the learning about the 14 Parameters with all staff members back at school,

● moving students from being engaged to being empowered,

● shining the spotlight on not only struggling students but also stuck students and students needing extending,

● incorporating more opportunities for staff to co-plan using the 14 Parameters as the framework for improvement.

Given what you have read so far, what commitments could you make for yourself and with your team?

A DELIBERATE PAUSE
TO CREATE CLARITY

Can you envision your system or school team agreeing with you that they can accept the statements in Parameter #1 as part of your vision? According to your data, which Parameter after #1, #6, and #14 would be the next most important to implement to improve your student achievement results? Think about how you could get buy-in from your team to agree with your assessment. Take a few moments to note obstacles that you foresee in using the 14 Parameter framework as a self-assessment tool in your system or school. How will you solve those problems? Think about how Metro Region's leadership team created their "Precision" watermark for continuous system improvement. What would your watermark be? What evidence from the case study is there to show Helen Kenworthy's intention to move schools in her cluster along? Kenworthy had senior leader support and a systemic approach to the implementation. If you had that systemic support, can you imagine how it would roll out? What support do you need?

Visit the companion website at
resources.corwin.com/CLARITY
for videos and downloadable resources

CLARITY
Knowing the
FACES of Learners

1. How do we ensure shared beliefs are embraced by all members of our education community?
2. How do students know what they are supposed to learn and whether they are progressing or not?
3. What practices empower our students to own their learning?
4. How can we better engage/empower all of our teachers to come aboard?
5. Do we have the right structures and processes in place to support student and teacher growth?

What are you, the reader, wondering?

Amazing teachers know their students really well—they believe in them and when their students are not learning, that is, not exhibiting thinking, they look to their own practices and ask their students to reflect with them on what works and what does not work. They listen to the feedback and focus on meeting the needs of the students in front of them. (Pauline Beder, Ontario Ministry of Education, 2017)

ACHIEVING BECAUSE THEY BELIEVE THEY CAN

Educators believe they are capable of teaching all learners and believe that all learners can grow and achieve beyond what they ever thought was possible. These educators believe that knowing who their learners are is reflected in the teaching and learning in every classroom. In this chapter, I link these beliefs and data as compatriot forces, not as antagonists. I discuss data as something used to purposefully sharpen our focus to know students better, in order to instruct them at their point of need on their personal learning journey. This begins with relationship building within the school or system and becomes an intentional Collaborative Inquiry to put FACES on the data that enables educators to

- understand each student,

- find practices that suit each student's way of learning and needs on a growth continuum,

- move everyone forward, achieving at least one year's growth for one year at school (Hattie, 2011).

Being part of a school, regional, or system staff is "being in a relationship"—actually, multiple relationships. No relationship can accomplish anything unless the people in it have some determined or defined commonality and vision and maintain their integrity regarding those commonalities. The similarity is that as leaders and teachers, we must continuously demonstrate the CLARITY of our beliefs in teaching and learning through our actions. Open-to-learning conversations about shared beliefs and understandings strengthen our relationships and build a common language and vision, with collective CLARITY. With these relationships in place, systems and schools can advance the learning and

Figure 2.1

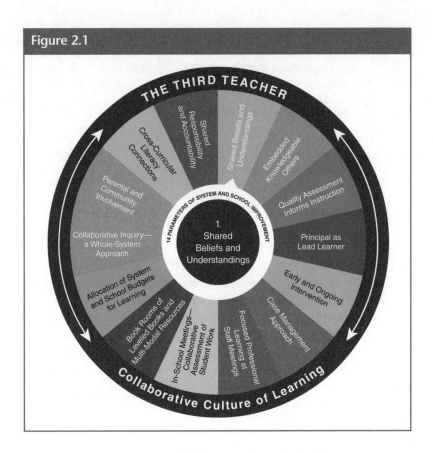

improvement work together. *Learning and improving together* is our critical work and *is* putting FACES on the data.

PARAMETER #1: SHARED BELIEFS AND UNDERSTANDINGS

Improvement begins with knowing each FACE, hearing each voice, and having sufficient knowledge about each student or teacher to apply agreed-upon differentiated supports as required. It is a whole-school and community approach to knowing how students learn best that leads to developing precise instructional strategies. This is CLARITY and precision in practice.

> The best thing about being a teacher is that it matters. The hardest thing about being a teacher is that it matters every day. (Todd Whitaker)

Key questions for self-assessment surface from this:

- What evidence of learning do you collect to decide whether or not each learner is engaged, is learning, and is being empowered?

- Do you know 10 things about each learner beyond academics? Do *they* know that you know those things about them?

- How are your teachers articulating the high expectations that you have agreed are basic understandings of how you do things around here?

- Are there barriers to developing a culture of learning?

Parameter #1, then, implies and demands being able to articulate and put forward "evidence" to confirm that actions match beliefs and, as colleagues in often-stressful relationships, each is maintaining integrity to that belief. The good news is that with every noticeable increase in the degree of sharing of beliefs and understandings and with every open-to-learning conversation, relationships grow, taking collaborative professionalism (Sharratt, 2016) to new heights.

Parameter #1, shared beliefs and understandings, is about collaboratively breaking down the silos of beliefs until we are all in agreement with its four dimensions:

The Four Dimensions of Parameter #1

1. **All students** can achieve high standards, given the right time and the right support.

2. **All teachers** can teach to high standards, given time and the right assistance.

3. High expectations and early and ongoing interventions are essential.

4. **All leaders, teachers, and students** can articulate what they do and why they lead, teach, and learn the way they do. (adapted from Hill & Crévola, 1999)

The biggest knot in our work is believing that all students can learn. It can take time to demonstrate to some colleagues that students with differing abilities, from different parts of town, and from different language backgrounds or cultures can and will learn.

In primary education, the responsibility is to take students to their optimum potential—every one of them—before they are transitioned to secondary. Similarly, in secondary, the responsibility is to take students to their optimum potential before they are transitioned to post-secondary education, work, apprenticeships, or other programs.

Another huge knot was recently defined for me when Michael Fullan asked me, "Do you really believe that all teachers can teach?" My response immediately went to three levels. First, a very real sense of urgency that this belief *might not* be valid. Second, and in the longer term, a feeling that we need to assure ourselves that we have the necessary Professional Learning (PL) in place so that all teachers *can teach*. And finally, a pause to restate the question: "Can all teachers *learn to* teach literacy, numeracy, and critical thinking skills to high standards, given sufficient time and support?"

Our work is urgent. We cannot lose a single day of focused teaching and learning. My answer to Fullan's question was and is unequivocally, "Yes, all teachers can *learn to* teach to high standards, given time and the right assistance." Our entire education system and school improvement work is predicated on a deep belief that teachers can, will, and must teach to high standards and that all students can and will learn. The "how" it can happen is the stuff of this book, *CLARITY,* developed from the 14 Parameter Framework (see Chapter 1) researched from schools in systems that are doing it extremely well.

WHAT IS THE EVIDENCE THAT ALL TEACHERS CAN TEACH?

Recently, colleague Tracey Petersen wrote to me:

> Today I worked alongside a teacher in an instructional coaching cycle. When the day was finished, I asked for her reflections. She said that I had created cognitive dissonance for her; that is, everything she thought teaching should be was "flipped on its head" in a day because of the way I worked alongside her and from the evidence of learning that we collected from teaching together. It demonstrated to her that there is a better way.

Tracey's comment is a strong example of bringing beliefs closer together in schools and classrooms and being responsible to co-labor to support and advance teachers' skill level to teach all students. For Tracey and for me, that teacher is now responsible to teach another and that one to teach another until they all have similar beliefs, as well as consistent and continuously improving practices.

We must believe that all students can learn and all teachers can teach. The leaders and teachers I work with make a difference in increasing students' achievement by working on changing classroom practice together.

PARAMETER #14: SHARED RESPONSIBILITY AND ACCOUNTABILITY

Believing as we do in Parameter #1, we must also agree that we are all responsible for every learner within and across our schools. Then it follows that everyone knows and can articulate system, school, and classroom priorities that align to each other with clear, precise, intentional, evidence-based language. Similarly, teacher-leaders, principals, and leadership teams must agree they are responsible to ensure that every teacher receives the supports required to improve practice.

Sharing and accepting responsibility and accountability is the first step in knowing every learner—and knowing where every learner is compared to where he or she should be at each point in the school year. One way of accomplishing both objectives is by creating a Data Wall (see Chapter 7) and having conversations about students with teachers around the Data Wall, as shown in Figure 2.2.

Figure 2.2 At the Data Wall Walk Looking for Evidence of Students' Improvement

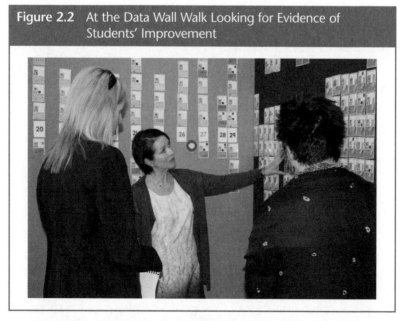

Source: Tricia Ward, St. Laurence Catholic School, Wilcannia-Forbes Diocese, 2017.

Where educational systems have developed their collective capacity and worked collaboratively, the achievement of students has increased more than in schools that have worked individually (Sharratt & Fullan, 2009, 2012; Sharratt & Planche, 2016). When leaders and teachers own all the FACES together, all students, teachers, and leaders become empowered by each other to continuously improve, as success not only breeds success but a continually growing appetite for success. Success is multiplicative. Success goes "viral," as described in the following secondary school narrative.

CASE STUDY: GETTING TO SHARED BELIEFS IS CHALLENGING—ESPECIALLY IN SECONDARY SCHOOLS!

As Allen and Madden mentioned to me recently, change in practice is not easy, and getting to a "fail fast" mindset (trying, getting fast feedback, determining success or not, feeling safe in order to get right back up to give it another go) is not easily attained and requires a change in culture and thinking. In working with staff, this leadership team helped them to recognize, through example, that they *are* responsible for all students' learning and that leading learning to engage every student was a necessary mindset change—not an unfamiliar story in many school settings during the change process.

These leaders worked to change the culture and build capacity so that staff could take ownership. They did this by co-constructing a vision and mission that was readily adopted by their whole community, and through that co-development, they were able to identify what does and doesn't work, what they needed to implement, and their priorities. They purposefully built in time for PL to discuss the way they collectively

- delivered lessons;

- reinforced assessment "for," "as," and "of" learning in every lesson;

- built positive relationships in every classroom.

They developed a schoolwide pedagogy and an online resource that specifies how lessons are to be taught, using deconstructed Learning

(Continued)

(Continued)

Intentions, co-constructed Success Criteria, intentional instructional practices, and rigorous performance tasks that reflected the need for student collaboration.

Resulting from this CLARITY, many teachers have bought in and are now feeling empowered. They are working hard to build their capacity, where needed, so that they can work toward the college vision of personalizing learning for their students. They have recently created a distinctive style so that the students are now using a common language across their school and subject areas. They are considering using a team of staff instead of one individual to fill the new head of learning position to be responsible to "value add" for their students. It is a work in progress, and staff are excited with the positive results to date.

Source: Jeff Allen, principal, and Roseanne Madden, deputy principal teaching and learning, Servite College, personal communication, 2017.

The above narrative is a reality check about how difficult this work of developing shared beliefs and understandings is, in spite of the urgency. However, it is possible, as Allen and Madden demonstrate. We know that

- challenging assumptions about personalizing pedagogy,

- owning all FACES, and

- being willing to model taking risks to change practice

Web Resource 4: One Principal's Thoughts on Building Capacity in Secondary Schools

opens doors for getting staff buy-in to share responsibility and accountability for their own learning and that of their colleagues and students (Parameters #1 and #14). To do this, students need to play a pivotal role in the teaching/learning process. To augment this case study, see **Web Resource 4: One Principal's Thoughts on Building Capacity in Secondary Schools**.

As in any relationship, once beliefs and understandings become aligned, they form a cultural foundation for co-learning, in which members of the school or system staff can co-labor, with the strength of the group commitment, permitting them to "stay the course" and "hold their nerve" until they get the results that students deserve. (Pam Betts, Executive Director, Brisbane Catholic Education, 2017)

PUTTING FACES ON THE DATA

Data sources come in many shapes and sizes. For example, I believe that student work is powerful data. We must scrutinize student work to reflect on what skills students will need to reach their true potential and become contributing citizens. Two examples follow in which school staffs have done just that in creative and resilient ways. The first is a secondary school account of a change process that personalizes where students are and what they can become when given multiple opportunities to experience success. The second is an elementary example of precision in practice as a whole-school approach.

CASE STUDY: PUTTING FACES ON THE DATA AT THE SECONDARY LEVEL

Groves Christian College, consisting of 1,100 students from more than 70 nationalities, is located in a low socioeconomic area in Logan, Australia. Students from refugee backgrounds make up 20% of the school's population. Many students are from single-parent homes or from large families with little income, which means parents and caregivers work long hours. To help form community and family groupings, school staff created vertical, gender-streamed home classes.

Prior to a turnaround, Groves experienced persistent symptoms of school ineffectiveness, including poor school culture, low attendance, underachievement, and frequent staff issues. High disengagement was exhibited, with only 69% of students receiving a Queensland Certificate of Education (QCE) qualification. The QCE is a certificate achieved for completion of five subjects at the end of Grade 12.

(Continued)

(Continued)

The Turnaround

School leaders felt that they needed to raise staff and student expectations by focusing on a moral purpose and mindset that every student can achieve given the right opportunities, voice, and choices (Parameter #1).

Collaboratively, all staff created the Groves Teachers' Creed:

- I believe that every child can succeed and can achieve their personal best.

- I know all my students' stories and personal learning journeys.

- I believe I am a key role model and can have positive or negative influence on my students.

- I build and maintain authentic relationships within Groves and the wider community.

- I have a moral purpose and responsibility to ensure that each student flourishes, particularly academically, and that my students will achieve or exceed our established benchmarks.

By intentionally creating industry, community, and university partnerships, students had a voice in discussing their hopes and dreams (Sharratt & Harild, 2015). Subsequently, the school was able to offer Senior Phase Pathway packages, which consisted of a combination of Queensland Assessment and Authority subjects, vocational subjects, certificates, diplomas, traineeships or apprenticeships, and workplace experience. The curriculum was customized into five packages: Traditional Pathway, Academic Intensive Pathway, Workplace Connect Pathway, Life and Work Skills Pathway, and Recreation and Leisure Pathway.

A full-time teacher was assigned as the senior phase student performance coordinator, working with teachers to track students to ensure they reached their goals and achieved agreed-upon outcomes. Consequently, within 12 months, an impressive 100% of the senior students received a QCE!

Vertical Home Classes

Vertical home classes were created to support the pastoral care program, meaning that each home class had a mix of students, gender streamed, from each grade level. Vertical home classes allowed for leadership development and pastoral care to take place across the grade levels. Within these classes, students became big sisters to little sisters, or big brothers to little brothers. The vertical home classes were 20 minutes every day, and the students moved up to the next grade level in the same vertical home class, to develop a continued sense of community and leadership potential.

It has been inspiring and insightful to see students mixing at break times across the grade levels. Students have been co-mentoring and sharing their educational, cultural, and social journey with each other. Students initiated and ran lunch-time clubs such as robotics, Spanish, media, social justice, and sporting.

The outcome of having a vertical home class structure in the school has been a greater sense of belonging and connectedness for students and staff. For some students, the vertical home classes provide an extended family. Student attendance was a low 70% prior to the vertical home classes and is now above 95%. The strength of this approach is demonstrated in a tiny example that has had a huge impact: one girl who became homeless and was at risk of dropping out of school was taken in by a family of an older girl who had connected with this at-risk student in her vertical home class. She now attends daily, empowered to graduate.

Source: Roshea Buksh, head of school, Groves Christian College, personal communication, 2017.

In this powerful case, data that the leaders reviewed to understand student achievement took many forms. In addition to understanding the potential impact of creating community in the school that the students otherwise did not have, their first-order structural changes led to empowering second-order changes that resulted in incredible benefits to students, staff, and the broader community.

CASE STUDY: PUTTING FACES ON THE DATA AT THE ELEMENTARY LEVEL

I began my long-term work in Darling Downs South West Region (DDSWR) over 10 days in 2017, with principals and school teams who were early adopters in wanting to increase all students' achievement. At one of those schools, Geham State School, the principal and leadership team asked all teachers to set a five-week SMART Goal, as in Figure 2.3, for students at risk of not getting a least a "C" standard in English.

> **Figure 2.3** Sample SMART Goal at Geham State School
>
> By the end of this unit, all Grade 5 students will be able to adapt a poem using descriptive language to create a mood and an image. The student will present this poem to an audience using tone, pace, pitch, volume, eye contact, and rhythm.

Staff used specific, precise assessment data to design instructional strategies in every classroom. As the first layer of intervention, teachers used data to analyze individual student performance and provide relevant and targeted instruction in every classroom. Staff were asked to consider how they would identify prior knowledge when introducing a new concept and how they would track progress throughout a unit of work. Their many intentional instructional strategies included the following:

- concept maps
- mind maps
- "show me" boards
- KWL anchor charts (What I know, What I want to know, What I learned)
- anchor charts displaying higher-order verbs to use for questions and answers

Teachers were asked to choose one student at risk of not getting a "C" or above in English at the end of the Semester 1 reporting period and to present the case to a small group in a regularly scheduled Case Management

Meeting (see Chapter 7). Teachers were asked to keep pictures of these "at-risk" students in the front of their diaries and bring them to each staff meeting for regular check-ins and reviews throughout Semester 2.

As a focus for PL, the staff looked at the assessment "for" and "as" learning, particularly Descriptive Feedback, as a specific area of improvement. Together they built quality assessment practices that informed instructional approaches across the whole school. Their moral imperative was realized after they put their pre- and post-data on their co-constructed Data Wall, shown in Figure 2.4.

Figure 2.4 Data Wall of Students' Performance at Geham State School

Source: Shelley Tompson, principal, Geham State School, Darling Downs Southwest Region, 2017.

IMPACT!

Did this "putting FACES on their data" and precision in practice make a difference? Impactful results displayed in Figure 2.5 indicate that in Semester 2

(Continued)

(Continued)

- 100% of students on support programs made progress using reading assessment data

- 65% of students on support programs reached or surpassed regional benchmark targets in reading

- 83% of students achieved at least a "C" standard or above in English—an increase from 64%

Importantly, from Semester 1, 2016 to Semester 1, 2017 impressive results occurred, with all but one grade level achieving 90% or more of the students receiving a grade of "C" or better.

Figure 2.5 Results of Students Who Achieved a "C" Standard or Above in English

English A–C	Prep/K	Grade 1	Grade 2	Grade 3	Grade 4	Grade 5	Grade 6
Semester 1, 2016	13%	44%	79%	73%	54%	86%	59%
Semester 2, 2016	100%	95%	73%	87%	78%	81%	76%
Semester 1, 2017	100%	93%	91%	76%	90%	90%	90%

Figure 2.5 displays very impressive results in most cases and, of course, they are not finished. But they were highly successful in getting many of the students "over the line" in a short time due to their laser-like focus on knowing every learner and on co-determining CLARITY in their practice. These staff members realize, as do so many others in this work, it takes the collective capacity building and co-laboring of all staff to make a difference in one student's life. The multiplier effect is shown when there is a positive moral imperative, co-written by staff, that directly relates to Parameter #1: Shared Beliefs and Understandings. Leaders and teachers at Geham State School are not there yet, but they continue to make impressive gains. They believe they can do even more—and they definitely will, as staff continue to ask questions to move their thinking and learning forward together.

POWERFUL QUESTIONS TO GET TO KNOW LEARNERS AND LEARNING

Leaders, principals, and Knowledgeable Others can go literally another step in knowing each learner by engaging in daily Learning Walks and Talks to observe student achievement gains against curriculum expectations and simultaneously note teacher capability and support needed. Learning Walks and Talks are more thoroughly reviewed in Chapter 9, but a key component of each Learning Walk and Talk undertaken— asking the 5 Questions—is germane to the content in this chapter.

How well do you know the FACES of your learners: students, teachers, leaders, and parents? While gains in student achievement occur inside the classroom and are directly influenced by the effectiveness of the teacher, large system change, in owning every student, is only possible when everyone in the organization sees himself or herself as responsible for the success of each student—their own and others. Each class contributes to the school targets, each school contributes to the system targets, each system contributes to the state targets, and each parent wants to know how his or her child is doing. Everyone must know the answer by having a "line of sight" to every student.

5 QUESTIONS TEACHERS CAN ASK STUDENTS

A highly focused snapshot is taken of how a teacher is making a difference for each student by asking students five critical questions that check for the ongoing use of assessment "for" and "as" learning (see Chapter 4):

1. What are you learning? Why?

2. How are you doing?

3. How do you know?

4. How can you improve?

5. Where do you go for help?

School leaders who conduct daily Learning Walks and Talks (Sharratt & Fullan, 2012; Sharratt & Harild, 2015; Sharratt & Planche, 2016) gather evidence of teachers' intentional teaching and of students' improvement when they ask students the 5 Questions above. Student answers make teachers aware of how explicit their teaching is and often necessitate unpacking the questions with students, as shown in Figures 2.6A and 2.6B. Leaders, teachers, and students who can accurately describe their learning and how to improve, close the achievement gap. After many

Figure 2.6 Where Do You Go for Help?

Source: Anthony Lucey, principal, St. Williams School, Grovely, 2017.

Source: Melissa Marquis, principal, 2017.

walks, conversations with teachers ensue. The 5 Questions assist in knowing more about our learners, how they learn, and what further instruction and support they may need.

5 QUESTIONS TEACHERS CAN ASK THEMSELVES

Similarly, there are essential questions that leaders should ask teachers to reflect on, ensuring teachers have time together to think through the answers. The 5 Questions for teachers are as follows:

1. What am I teaching?

2. Why am I teaching it?

3. How will I teach it?

4. How will I know when students have learned it or not?

5. What is next . . . if this works? If it doesn't work? Where do I go for help?

They are a tool to reflect on

- the firm foundation necessary to instruct all students in the mastery of reading, writing, oral language, mathematics, and critical thinking;

- the problem-solving skills needed to incorporate learning skills into the curriculum content areas;

- more precise instructional strategies needed in every classroom.

As teachers, we learn best from other teachers and leaders to curate the work alongside us. Teachers who feel they have a strength in one area can self-nominate to be helpful to other teachers or leaders, as shown in Figure 2.7. This Data Wall has "I Can Assist You" envelopes in which teachers identify their areas of expertise so that colleagues can go to them for assistance and insights.

The answers to the 5 Questions for teachers provide the data collection necessary to craft relevant PL sessions and match up teachers as Knowledgeable Others with teachers who are not quite there yet.

Figure 2.7 "I Can Assist You" Envelopes at the Data Wall

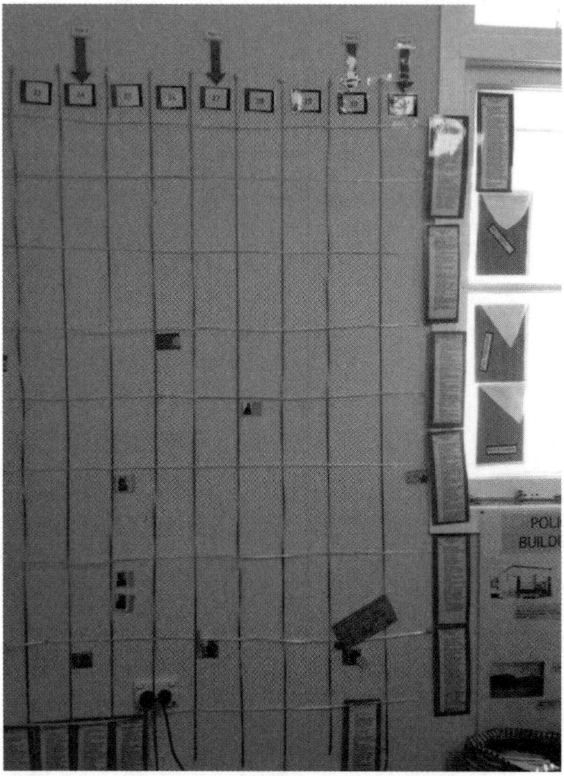

Source: Karen Buckley, Indigenous Curriculum and Pedagogy, principal project officer, Darling Downs South West Region—Toowoomba Office, Department of Education and Training.

5 QUESTIONS LEADERS CAN ASK THEMSELVES

The questions for teachers also work for instructional leaders, with some adjustments:

1. What am I leading?

2. Why am I leading it?

3. How will I lead it?

4. How will I know when teachers have learned it?

5. What is next . . . if this works? If it doesn't work?

Darling Downs South West Region leaders have developed their own very detailed and thought-provoking questions and probes for leaders:

1. What is your sharp and narrow focus for improvement?

    Does everyone know what the focus is?

    What is your signature pedagogy to support this focus?

    What support processes are in place for teachers?

2. What is your approach to leading improvement?

    What is the evidence base of this approach?

    Are roles and expectations crystal clear?

3. What data source is informing your decisions?

    Which school data?

    Which research?

4. How will you know if it is working?

    By when?

    What monitoring processes are planned?

    What are the success indicators?

5. What's next . . .

    If it works?

    If it doesn't?

Source: Leanne Wright, regional director, Darling Downs South West Region, personal communication, 2017.

PARENTS ARE CRITICAL PARTNERS IN KNOWING EACH LEARNER

Parents are our learners' first teachers. They can be hugely influential players in the learning for, with, and beside each student. Systems leaders interrogate data, discern directions, model expected practices, monitor change, and adapt as change unfolds to ensure optimal conditions for student success. System leaders are listeners; they engage in dialogue and *participate as learners*. They know and value the key stakeholders—teachers, leaders, students, and parents—who have important roles in improving student learning outcomes. By being open and attentive to the many voices at play, system and school leaders draw widely on expertise and are better informed to paint the clear horizons and bring about system reform (Pam Betts, personal communication, 2017).

As Pam Betts reminds us, "parents and the broader community are important stakeholders, with parents and caregivers having roles critical to their children's success. More often than not, they don't know the questions to ask their children or to ask the teachers when they want to know more about how their child is doing in school. So, we give them a script" (personal communication, 2017).

Recently, I wrote to colleagues in Manitoba saying that giving parents this tool is a key communication strategy for teachers and leaders. We discussed that the 5 Questions for parents were closely related to those for students, only addressed to the teacher:

5 QUESTIONS PARENTS CAN ASK TEACHERS

1. What is my child learning?

2. How is she or he doing?

3. How do you know (how she or he is doing)?

4. How can she or he improve?

5. What supports can I provide and can you provide if she or he is struggling? When will we check in again?

Source: Developed with Mike Borgfjord, chief superintendent, Seine River School Division, Manitoba, Canada, personal communication, 2017.

Consultant colleagues in Sydney Catholic Schools feel that their 5 Questions for Parents cause "deliberate pause" for teachers and students and are a highly effective tool in measuring learning progress. They realize that questioning has been an important strategy in building teacher efficacy to improve learning. There has been an increased use of these questions by teachers and students in the Sydney schools, with resulting heightened teacher effectiveness as they have learned how to flexibly change their instructional responses according to what they hear in the students' answers. This questioning process is now being embedded in the school learning culture, in the classroom, and in collaborative planning. Together, they designed the following 5 Questions to assist parents in engaging with their child's learning:

5 QUESTIONS PARENTS CAN ASK THEIR CHILDREN

1. What did you learn today?

2. How did you do?

3. What did you do if you didn't understand?

4. How can you improve on your learning?

5. What are you most proud of?

Sydney schools have made parents aware of these questions at parent forums, in school newsletters, and during parent workshops in reading and mathematics. Parents have found using these questions has created opportunities for informative conversations with their children. It has provided a script for discussions with their child's teacher. This is

Figure 2.8

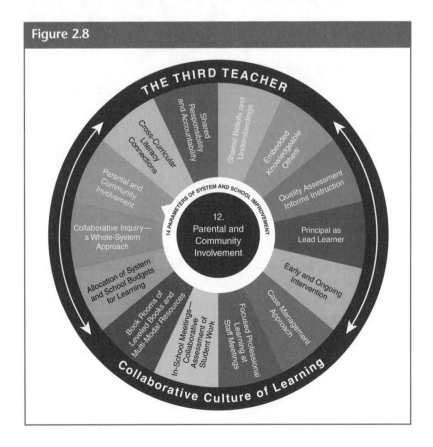

another way of changing school culture and building collective efficacy (Tosca Galluzzo, curriculum consultant, personal communication, 2017).

It works elsewhere, too. In Finland, for example, there is a culture of trust where "education authorities and political leaders believe that teachers, together with principals, parents, and their communities, know how to provide the best possible education for their children and youth" (Sahlberg, 2011). In the following case study, Marisa Kelly, who I have worked with for many years, wraps her narrative around this notion that learning and doing on behalf of our students' growth and achievement is everyone's business.

PARAMETER #12: PARENTS AND THE COMMUNITY ARE CRITICAL PARTNERS IN LEARNING

CASE STUDY: PARENTS MAKE RICH CONTRIBUTIONS TO KNOWING THE FACES

Marisa Kelly is the director of a special center that brings together grandparents, parents, children, and community members to support the work of owning all the FACES in a school-based center. Her narrative is a powerful example of inviting families to be partners in learning.

Our Child and Family Center and Early Learning Center (child care) are new additions to an existing primary school and preschool. Each service is located on the campus like a point on a compass, with shared gardens at the heart [see Figure 2.9]. The pathways that join us represent the dry riverbeds of the central Australian desert town we live in: Alice Springs. Families with young children can now access a range of early childhood services, and the education and care professionals collaborate across the precinct. We share a vision that "every child must have the best start to life."

Larapinta Child & Family Center works with families with young children from pre-birth to 5 years of age. We support families to access quality, culturally responsive services to strengthen health, well-being, and education outcomes for their children. We have a strong priority to support vulnerable, disadvantaged, and indigenous families. Alice Springs has a significant indigenous population,

Figure 2.9 Larapinta Child & Family Center

Source: Marisa Kelly, 2017.

and the local indigenous peoples have rich and diverse languages and cultures. However, health, education, and life outcomes for indigenous children are poor in this remote region of Australia. Our town is also home to many refugee and migrant families from all over the world.

Children and their families are at the center of all we do [Figure 2.10]. If we are to improve outcomes for the most vulnerable children in our community, we believe that respectful and trusting relationships with families are vital. We have worked to create a place of belonging, where families with young children feel welcome and respected. We tell them directly, "This is your place. It's for you and your children." Some of the women we work with have experienced domestic violence and are living in poverty. Many factors impacting on children in this region are now intergenerational and multifaceted. Building trust with families is an essential first step in breaking this cycle.

(Continued)

(Continued)

Figure 2.10 Children Are at the Center

Source: Lyn Sharratt, 2017.

We connect with families who are already involved in the school and preschool, and we also receive referrals from other services in town. Our indigenous coordinator has extensive family and community connections, and she has been instrumental in connecting families to our center. We have families dropping in, we host playgroups, and we also partner with other health and community service agencies who run family support and early childhood programs in our center. We have a special program for young mums and are starting a study group to assist mothers to access training and return to work. Our center is friendly and open—the kettle is always on and families are encouraged to come and see us whenever they want.

We have had five generations of one family sitting around a young mother and her newborn baby, with a great-grandmother singing songs to the baby in her traditional indigenous language. One mother has recently been reunited with her children who were taken into care over a year ago. Another mum who has survived years of domestic violence has recently returned to work, with her youngest child accessing our child care service. We have heard the voice of a young boy whose mother was severely isolated and had not taken him out of the house before coming to our center. If we are to empower families to have a positive impact on their children's learning and development, we need to build faith and confidence that we want to work in partnership with families, walking alongside them as their children's first teachers.

Of our many goals and aspirations, a key one is that student attendance at the main preschool and primary campus will increase. We feel that with the quality of service we can offer families, we can overcome some of the fear of school and build expectations of daily attendance among the adults that will become student habits.

We feel we are using whatever we can learn about the families, whatever data we can gather, to work with the families and their students for their benefit together.

Source: Marisa Kelly, CEO, Family Center, Larapinta Center, Alice Springs, Australia, 2017.

Kelly's inspirational account of the Center's foundational belief that families are children's first teachers and how, as a leadership team, they have diligently listened to and heard the voices of the families, again underscores the importance of ensuring parental and community involvement (Parameter #12). Schools must be models to the surrounding communities of what community life can be—of what a society can aspire to be. Educators as architects not only educate students; they create possibilities for families. In communities where children seldom see a wider world beyond their corner of the block, the safety and quality of their community centers, housing, schools, parks, recreation, and infrastructure are of critical importance (Mark Gibson, principal, Toronto, Canada, personal communication, 2018).

In the next chapter, I build on learning and knowing each learner, to explore how it is possible to develop that passion for truly knowing each FACE through professional Collaborative Inquiry and how that is most effectively implemented in dedicated Professional Learning Community time—when teachers and leaders use data to inquire about precision in practice.

COMMITMENT

I commit to

● knowing and understanding the needs of my learners—staff and students,

● using data to inform the selection of resources and to differentiate PL,

● using the group to move the group toward shared beliefs and understandings by all,

● asking students the 5 Questions to reflect on my precision in practice,

● including parents and community as active participants in our improvement process,

● providing the 5 Questions from parents to children and answers they should listen for from their children,

● providing the 5 Questions from parents to teachers that parallel the questions they would ask their children,

● going more deeply into my community to ask about parents' expectations for their children's education, their level of understanding about the system/school, and their comfort level in coming to the school to speak with the teacher.

Given what you have read so far, what commitments could you make for yourself and with your team?

A DELIBERATE PAUSE TO CREATE CLARITY

Identify a powerful team learning experience that you have participated in as a teacher or a leader. What contributed to the success of that experience, and what was the impact on student learning? How might the ideas in this chapter extend the impact of the outcomes for your staff members and for students?

Visit the companion website at
resources.corwin.com/CLARITY
for videos and downloadable resources

CHAPTER 3

CLARITY

Collaborative Inquiry
With Teachers and Leaders

1. Are my students and colleagues engaged? How do I know?
2. What is the evidence that I listen to every voice and learn from each?
3. What elements of inquiry feel chaotic?
4. How do I know I am the most effective practitioner I can be?
5. Where do we find the time to get better at what we do?
6. What is impactful practice in a digital age?

What are you, the reader, wondering?

Figure 3.1

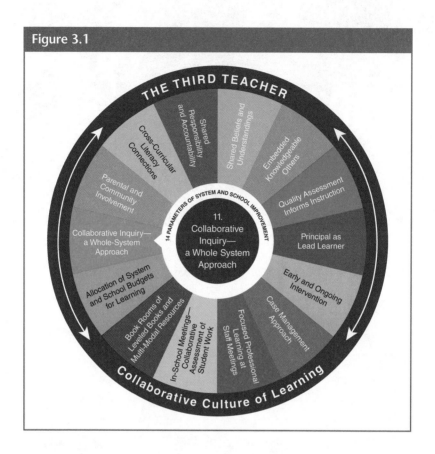

PARAMETER #11: COLLABORATIVE INQUIRY

Teacher and leader data-informed professional Collaborative Inquiry (CI) is the subject of Chapter 3 and provides CLARITY in how to strengthen and refine expected, effective practices that empower all learners and learning.

CI is a structured, collaboratively planned approach (Sharratt & Harild, 2015; Sharratt & Planche, 2016), often initiated when an issue is identified by reviewing student achievement data at the Data Wall (see Chapter 7) or when teachers and leaders come together to focus on a question of pedagogy to improve their practice. An impactful CI is iterative; that is, the CI question is reviewed and tweaked as the research progresses toward creating one or more solutions to the initial question. The CI cycle is a tri-level, whole-system approach to improvement, as shown in Figure 3.2. It is tri-level because it is about leaders and teachers at all levels inquiring to improve their practice. They model the inquiry process that is impactful to achieve all students' critical thinking and understanding, as illustrated in Figure 3.2. Thus, professional CI is a continuously refreshing quest for teachers and leaders to examine high-impact strategies, including assessment that differentiates instruction to meet the learning needs of each and every student. The CI cycle, Figure 3.2, includes opportunities for midcourse corrections and insights that can inform the current or define the next CI.

CI benefits teachers, school leaders, and system leaders by building collective efficacy as teams persevere in examining seemingly complex questions focused on persistent issues of practice. They never give up. There is always a solution.

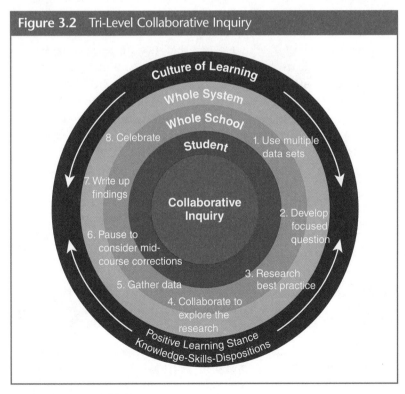

Figure 3.2 Tri-Level Collaborative Inquiry

Source: Sharratt & Harild (2015).

CI is an ideal knowledge-building approach at system and school levels as it promotes the following:

- sharing and clarifying beliefs and understandings
- analyzing specific data to uncover student achievement and well-being issues
- wrestling with problems of practice together
- trialing practices in a safe, fail fast environment
- learning what works and what doesn't work at every level, in order to experience collective efficacy

In emerging research, Dr. Howard Youngs, Maggie Ogram, and Dr. Patsy Stringer describe how teachers acknowledge relational trust as a central component of all collaborative practice. Teachers associate this trust with open interaction to reveal their own vulnerability, especially when developing new practices. As one teacher stated, "A mindset that has changed for me . . . is learning to appreciate what other people bring to the table and having that trust in other teachers that they are doing their best for their students and releasing that control of learning to their students. That's huge and it's so difficult to do. Probably the biggest mindset change is that we all have collective responsibility for every single student." Teachers in this network now openly discuss how changes in their mindsets have led to shifts in their Collaborative Inquiry practice. (Maggie Ogram, international consultant, New Zealand, personal communication, 2017)

In this chapter, there are CI examples from system, school, and classroom teachers and leaders. These examples are meant to challenge you to reflect and build on your own knowledge and current practice in maintaining an inquiry stance every day.

FUNDAMENTAL CHALLENGE

As you read the case studies and narratives in this chapter, connect, compare, and contrast them with your prior knowledge—a strong, values-laden force—*and* your current lived experiences.

COLLABORATIVE INQUIRY OPERATING NORMS

Co-construction of operating norms for engagement that leads to empowerment for everyone is critical. Similarly, every CI begins by codeveloping operating norms; some examples follow:

- Everyone's voice is important. We listen respectfully.

- Being respectful in our engagement builds strong working relationships that lead to empowerment.

- We make the time to reflect on our work as we learn with and from each other.

- We empower our own learning and the learning of our colleagues.

- We build and facilitate learning capacity together.

- We build confidence and success through collaborating authentically.

- We persevere. We believe all students can learn and all teachers can teach with rigor and impact, given the right time and support.

- We believe in our interdependence to achieve each student's Learning Goals.

- Our work is guided by shared beliefs and understandings about our collective capability to increase all students' achievement.

The following narrative outlines a protocol for collaboratively planning and teaching a lesson, beginning with the above operating norms, to ensure shared decision making and ownership in the inquiry process and the achieved outcomes.

THE POWER OF USING CO-LEARNING PROTOCOLS

CI is a co-learning process. In *Leading Collaborative Learning: Empowering Excellence* (Sharratt & Planche, 2016), we describe several methodologies that allow involvement in co-learning processes, such as lesson study, CI, collaborative assessment of student work or, in this case, the Co-Teaching Cycle. The following protocol is designed as a sample. It demonstrates how a protocol can be used to deepen our understanding of how to improve a lesson plan by observing student responses to a lesson planned collaboratively with three or four participants (Sharratt & Planche, 2016).

PLANNING A LESSON USING STUDENT WORK AS THE DRIVER FOR CO-LEARNING

This protocol works well for members of a teaching division or grade partners and does not require release time during the school day.

Step One: Collaborative Planning Before Teaching

- Establish an area of common teaching concern, asking, "What do the student data sources reveal as an area of focus?"

- Plan a lesson collaboratively with all voices heard around the table.

- Choose a specific curriculum Learning Intention(s) as the focus within a predetermined subject area.

- Determine how the big ideas, essential questions, and Success Criteria will be co-constructed with students (see Chapter 4).

- Develop a rigorous performance task that directly relates to the Learning Intention and Success Criteria as a culminating event. Ask, "In what variety of ways will students demonstrate their learning?" (see Chapter 5).

- Determine how the student work will be assessed against the curriculum standards/Success Criteria.

- Determine together how students' prior knowledge will be assessed as part of the planning process.

- Develop the instructional strategies to be taught during the lesson.

- Schedule time for the team to reconvene.

Step Two: Individual Teaching and Choosing Pieces of Student Work to Share

- Teach the lesson, observing the students' responses and thinking.

- Within no more than two days of teaching the lesson, each member of the collaborative group chooses three pieces of student work from the rigorous performance task to bring to share and discuss.

- Choose pieces of student work that represent different levels of student thinking and understanding.

Step Three: Collaborative Debrief

Remembering that effective questions and facilitation of the discussion about the student work samples deepens the learning, each participant debriefs his or her teaching experience and shares one piece of student work at a time. Collaborators listen to each other and ask questions for clarification, such as,

- How do each of the pieces of student work relate to the Success Criteria?

- What do we see as evidence of student thinking?

- What are the next steps for our students' learning based on the evidence we see in their work?

- What specific feedback will we give the students?

- Which students can be grouped together for guided practice and mini-lessons in response to our data?

- How will what we observed in teaching and is evidenced in student work impact our future teaching?

Collaborative debriefing ends with a reflection on the process of professional co-learning.

Step Four: Collaborative Reflection and Next Steps

A valuable component of co-learning is reflection and asking self and others questions:

- What did we learn from listening to our colleagues as we shared student work?

- What new perspectives did we gain from the experience of co-learning?

- What will we take back to our classrooms to try, amend, or refine?

- How will we build on the learning?

- What will we change about our planning, assessing, and instructing?

- What would we change about the co-learning process and what would we keep?

- When will we meet again to plan another lesson and co-assess students' work samples? (Dr. Beate Planche, personal communication, 2017)

As illustrated above, collaborative learning is a powerful tool for staff when it is purposefully focused on ongoing assessment that informs instruction, shown in the planning, teaching, debriefing, and reflecting process used in this protocol. There are certain essential elements of CI that must be present in order for it to work. Videoing the lesson, using a "swivel camera," for example, enhances this experience.

Lessons Learned: The Essential Elements of Collaborative Inquiry

Some important lessons learned while working alongside teachers and leaders include the following:

1. **Time.** If collaborating to improve practice is "the work," then we must restructure the time we have to make room for it.

2. **Knowledgeable Other.** The absence of a Knowledgeable Other is detrimental. It is essential that we have Knowledgeable Others with strong interpersonal skills and assessment and instructional knowledge to work alongside teachers and leaders.

3. **Training in Facilitation Skills.** These skills are fundamental to ensuring co-constructed operating norms, Learning Intentions, Success Criteria, and appropriate protocols to follow.

4. **Attendance.** The absence of the leader in a group of colleagues learning together dooms the process to failure. The leader and leadership team must see themselves and be seen in the work. This means not only must they show up but they must work alongside staff members, learning together.

When beginning any new collaborative cycle with colleagues, it is vital to clarify the CI cycle and the eight steps to be followed, as shown in Figure 3.2. The CI process is not lock-step but iterative and fluid, always focused on evidence of impact on increasing all students' growth and achievement. When demonstrable impact of the team's collective process is uncovered, the collective efficacy of the team increases. Hattie (2016b) lists "collective teacher efficacy" as the top influencer of learning, noting an **effect size** of +1.56. Collective efficacy results when leaders and teachers find multiple, sustainable solutions to "wicked problems of practice" by using a structured approach to investigate what works best for students.

One of the key elements of creating collective teacher efficacy is successful experience as a group of teachers, often in collaborative engagement (Hattie, 2015). Learning through CI that leads to collective teacher efficacy is our work. We carry our mind frames to our work every day; the 10th mind frame we need to capture and embrace is "I collaborate" (Hattie, 2016c).

The case studies and interviews that form the CI lessons that follow in this chapter demonstrate the importance of establishing group norms, protocols, and clear steps in the ongoing reflective cycle of CI, as shown in Figure 3.2.

THE VALUE OF COLLABORATIVE INQUIRY

CI is based on harnessing the power of the data and the learners' own curiosity about a concept or challenge of practice to drive learning. Typically, collaborating in groups supports unpacking problems of practice in teaching and learning within the context of social communication and an open-to-learning stance. Offering a disciplined approach to CI permits and encourages participants to

- wonder,
- research,
- reflect on the possibilities that could deliver greater results,
- empower leaders and teachers at every level to accept the challenge of the new learning and the new personal responsibility and accountability for using it where appropriate.

This results in a 1 + 1 = 3 level impact on individual and group learning and on their individual and group professional practice. More significantly, the improvement results in a collective sense of increased professional capability and self-esteem; that is, an increase in the group's collective efficacy. This is a virtuous cycle that is both completed and re-energized when the group initiates another CI. The following two case studies, A Whole-System Collaborative Inquiry and A Whole-School Collaborative Inquiry, feature my work with both of them in using the 14 Parameters and the CI model in Figure 3.2. The use and extension of the elements investigated result in a significant positive impact on student achievement—our core business.

CASE STUDY: A WHOLE-SYSTEM COLLABORATIVE INQUIRY

Cluster 5, consisting of 14 primary schools in the Inner Western Region, a low socioeconomic area within Sydney Catholic Schools, is considered one of the most diverse clusters in the diocese. Within Cluster 5 there are 3,990 students, of whom 68 (1.7%) students are Aboriginal or Torres Island descent; 2,820 (70.6%) have a language background other than English; 2,314 (58%) have English as their second language; and 235 (5.9%) students have been identified with a disability. The schools range in size from single stream (seven classes) to three stream (21 classes).

Cluster 5 Data

Figures 3.3, 3.4, 3.5, and 3.6 show how Cluster 5 performed in the National Assessment Program Literacy and Numeracy (NAPLAN) compared to the national test results and against the other clusters in Sydney Catholic Schools at the beginning of the study. When analyzed, the data in these tables demonstrate that in Grades 3 and 5 reading, writing, and numeracy, Cluster 5 had more students in the lower two bands than the other Sydney Catholic Schools and had fewer students in the upper two bands than the other Sydney Catholic Schools, thus the need to improve student achievement.

Figure 3.3	Percentage of Students in the Bottom Two Bands, NAPLAN, Grade 3, 2014		
	Australia	**Sydney Catholic Schools**	**Cluster 5**
Reading	13.1	6.22	8
Writing	11.2	4.06	5
Numeracy	13.4	7.57	11

Figure 3.4	Percentage of Students in the Bottom Two Bands, NAPLAN, Grade 5, 2014		
	Australia	**Sydney Catholic Schools**	**Cluster 5**
Reading	16.3	10.5	18
Writing	21.4	6.9	10.6
Numeracy	18.1	10.9	19.3

Figure 3.5	Percentage of Students in the Top Two Bands, NAPLAN, Grade 3, 2014		
	Australia	**Sydney Catholic Schools**	**Cluster 5**
Reading	46.2	56.74	47
Writing	39.1	63.61	57.4
Numeracy	36.2	51.49	43

Figure 3.6	Percentage of Students in the Top Two Bands, NAPLAN, Grade 5, 2014		
	Australia	**Sydney Catholic Schools**	**Cluster 5**
Reading	34.5	38.9	29.6
Writing	15.5	24.4	17.8
Numeracy	25.9	33.9	27

(Continued)

(Continued)

After reflecting on the above data, reviewing the literature about improving literacy and numeracy, and researching best practices, teachers realized there was a need to provide greater support for students in learning English as a second language (ESL) and support for all teachers in explicitly teaching ESL students. However, wondering about the current in-class support, staff funding, and levels of expertise offered to ESL students in Cluster 5 led to an inquiry focused on building *all* teachers' capacity in applying collaboratively designed assessment and instructional approaches in the teaching of English for *all* learners.

The Collaborative Plan

Supported by system leaders, the wonderings and research within Cluster 5 were distilled to a simply-stated CI question: *How can Cluster 5 leaders and teachers enhance teacher efficacy, capacity, and responsibility in the teaching of literacy and numeracy skills to all students across all key learning areas?* Although this question became the focus of a three-year improvement plan for Cluster 5, it was applicable to all Sydney Catholic Schools and was guided by the following inquiries:

1. How should Sydney Catholic Education Office (SCEO) resource equity programs to enhance student learning?

2. How should SCEO monitor success and report on progress?

3. How can SCEO allocate resources to ensure the focus is on improving student learning outcomes for all students by building teacher and school capacity?

Based on the *Budget 2013–14: National Plan for School Improvement* (Commonwealth of Australia, 2013) and further reviews of system change processes, the following principles were defined as underpinning the Cluster 5 CI:

- Ongoing Professional Learning (PL), collaboration, and leadership development support effective literacy and numeracy instruction.

- Literacy and numeracy are the responsibility of every teacher in every classroom.

- Explicit literacy and numeracy instruction is planned and takes place within and across syllabi, classrooms, and schools.

- Assessment drives instruction. Use of system, school, classroom, and individual literacy and numeracy achievement data direct ongoing instructional decisions and actions.

- Effective literacy and numeracy instruction motivates, engages, and supports all students in their learning.

- Literacy and numeracy instructional practices are monitored, regularly reviewed, and refined to ensure that the needs of all learners are met (both teachers as learners and students as learners).

- School, home, and community partnerships enhance literacy and numeracy instruction.

With these principles to guide decision making, the project began by establishing clear expectations that this was to be cluster work rather than 14 individual schools working independently and that the improvement work was everyone's responsibility. Three areas of baseline data were sourced:

1. Teachers' levels of efficacy, capacity, and responsibility in teaching literacy and numeracy

2. Schools' organizational practices

3. Students' reading, writing, and numeracy levels

Resourcing to Build Capacity and Efficacy

The key to the Cluster 5 CI was to develop the capacity, and therefore the collective efficacy, of teachers and leaders to address students' learning needs in literacy and numeracy across all schools in the cluster. Previously, students were withdrawn for specific English lessons at least twice a week for half an hour each time. It was deemed imperative that *all* teachers in Cluster 5 be upskilled to be able to teach *all* students who have English as their second language.

(Continued)

(Continued)

The initial use of funding for withdrawal support was evaluated, and those funds were reallocated and mobilized to place an additional 0.5 of a full-time equivalent teacher in each of the 14 schools as a literacy and numeracy coach. According to their PL work with Sharratt, withdrawing students for support was not effective and selecting the Knowledgeable Other as coach in each school was critical. Therefore, in 11 schools, the .5 was added to the .5 assistant principal position, and another person was engaged in the other three schools.

Getting the Instructional Coach Role Right First

The CI began by developing the role descriptors and accountabilities of the literacy and numeracy coaches. It took six months to confidently define the role as "teacher coaches" using Sharratt's research (Sharratt & Fullan, 2009, 2012, 2013; Sharratt & Planche, 2016) of high-impact approaches:

1. co-planning, co-teaching, co-debriefing, co-reflecting

2. co-creating assessment practices that inform instruction

3. using the Case Management Approach

4. developing data analysis methodologies

Each of four PL sessions with the literacy and numeracy coaches was spent reviewing the 14 Parameters (Sharratt & Fullan, 2009, 2012, 2013) as the improvement lens, sharing practice, reflecting on research, evaluating how the cluster was working together, and setting the goals for the next level of work to be done. Learning Walks and Talks (Sharratt, 2008–2018) were a critical part of this work. The regional school consultant, the cluster coach, and all school leadership teams worked closely together in partnership, challenging and engaging in critical discourse about what they saw and heard during the Walks and Talks (see Chapter 9).

Aligning School Practices

Using the 14 Parameters as a guide to determine what important practices supported consistent literacy improvement, the following key documents were identified as necessary to understand the baseline for consistency and precision in practice across all Cluster 5 schools. It was an expectation that by the end of the 2017 school year, the practices in these documents would be consistent across the 14 schools.

1. Reading plan K–6

2. Home reading guidelines

3. Benchmarks for reading K–6

4. Running records plan

5. Data plan K–6

6. Assessment plan K–6

7. Writing editing process K–6

8. Class timetables K–6

9. Professional Learning plans K–6

10. Reading assessment data K–6

Student Learning as the Driver

After a year of working with the school literacy and numeracy coaches through focused PL exploring the 14 Parameters (Sharratt & Fullan, 2009, 2012, 2013), expanding on the use of appropriate data, and establishing methodology for the co-construction of Data Walls, the 14 schools began to share the vision of improvement. Agreed practices began to be developed and understood. Both the cluster culture as a Professional Learning Community (PLC) and culture within the schools were revitalized by increased teacher and student learning.

Reading and writing data were collected to determine where each student was on the literacy continuum, K–10 and within the English as an additional language/dialect learning progressions, considering both growth and achievement of each FACE. Schools' Data Walls demonstrated leaders' and teachers' deep knowledge and understanding of the use of data. Throughout the life of the CI, the Data Wall designs and Case

(Continued)

(Continued)

Management Meeting methodologies used grew to truly represent where individual students were and to specifically highlight the need to progress in reading and writing.

Instructional Coaching Is Key to Teaching and Leading

Since the CI began, the regional school consultant and the Cluster 5 coach have met regularly with each school leadership team, beginning at the Data Wall, sharing knowledge during regular Learning Walks and Talks (Sharratt, 2008–2018), looking for evidence of learning and discussing the impact of their focused culture of learning in the school. The Cluster 5 coach has been instrumental in maintaining focus and orchestrating insightful conversations at the Data Wall. Triads or quads of school-based literacy and numeracy coaches have met regularly to discuss their data and the culture within each school. The Cluster 5 coach has been the motivator for the cluster's school-based literacy and numeracy coaches, keeping them focused on the learning agenda and providing them with thoughtful provocations to stimulate ongoing CI discussions. This practice has been critical to maintaining the high expectations for literacy and numeracy practices that have built the collective capacity of teachers and leaders across the 14 schools.

The regional school consultant has coached and challenged the Cluster 5 coach and modeled the CI process with the school leadership teams by providing gentle pressure, asking provocative questions about the data and the culture in the school, and always maintaining the focus on the FACES of learning. This practice has begun to build collective capacity of leaders and teachers in each of the 14 schools, ensuring that students who are not reaching the expected growth are the center of the work.

Leadership to Do This Work

School principals who implement the 14 Parameters in their schools understand the importance of collective capacity building alongside teachers and colleagues. They enthusiastically share their expertise

(Parameter #4), whole-heartedly support the presence of the literacy and numeracy coaches as Knowledgeable Others (Parameter #2) across the schools and, as required, challenge and support each other in leading the improvement process. They demonstrate that they care for the success of each other's schools as much as their own (Parameter #1 and #14).

The regional school consultant worked with principals and assistant principals on the strategic side of CI delivery to ensure they were upskilled in literacy and numeracy specifics, as needed. Together, they diligently committed to

- making use of the precious time available to enable teachers to work alongside each other,

- raising expectations about student learning and classroom practice,

- knowing the syllabus and ensuring that it is every person's responsibility to also know it.

The 14 Parameters Align Leaders' and Teachers' Collective Work

The use of the 14 Parameters within Cluster 5 was an enabler that caused the key people in the schools to sustain the focus on improvement. For example,

- The two bookends—Parameter #1: a shared vision of learning in the school and across the cluster and a shared understanding of the high expectations of both student and teacher learning and Parameter #14: a shared responsibility and accountability—are evidenced in the behaviors of the leaders.

- The ongoing process of CI (Parameter #11) and the explicit expectations of common documentation and procedures across the 14 schools supported the focus on learning. The concept of sharing resources across the schools, such as home reading guidelines, PL plans, and the K–6 reading plan meant that the schools were constantly engaged in dialogue about agreed high-impact practices.

(Continued)

(Continued)

- Continuous dialogue meant that the documentation took longer to develop; however, it has resulted in both clear expectations and shared responsibility for all students (Parameters #1 and #14).

- As teachers and leaders experienced, the **Gradual Release and Acceptance of Responsibility** model worked in their classrooms (Parameter #3). In parallel, they guided other schools in similar processes. In this way, they codeveloped an across-schools shared Google document to sharpen the original documents.

Having these expectations at the beginning of the CI meant leadership teams knew how to begin the processes of change. The impactful practices came from paying close attention to the details of the 14 Parameters for System and School Improvement (Sharratt & Fullan, 2009, 2012, 2013).

Recent recognition of three Cluster 5 schools for achieving the highest student growth in external testing attests to this focused, continuous improvement work using the 14 Parameters as the self-assessment tool. The increased capacity of teacher-leaders also shows that future leaders will work with each other to achieve high expectations for all.

Source: Kate O'Brien, Tosca Galluzzo, and Sybil Dickens, personal communication, 2018.

IMPACT!

The evidence of impact in Cluster 5 is that the language of improvement is consistent; the inquiries across all schools are focused on student growth; and teacher knowledge, expertise, and performance are improving. The data from NAPLAN in 2017, just 24 months into the project, showed improvement in students' learning in literacy and numeracy, as shown in Figures 3.7 and 3.8.

Figure 3.7 Percentage and Number of Students in the Bottom Two Bands, NAPLAN, Grades 3 and 5, 2014–2017

	2014 yr 3	2017 yr 3	2014 yr 5	2017 yr 5
Reading	8 (53 students)	6.4 (41 students)	18 (82 students)	11 (58 students)
Writing	5 (32 students)	1.7 (11 students)	10.6 (46 students)	8.6 (43 students)
Numeracy	11 (68 students)	7.2 (46 students)	19.3 (84 students)	9.9 (49 students)

Figure 3.8 Percentage and Number of Students in the Top Two Bands, NAPLAN, Grades 3 and 5, 2014–2017

	2014 yr 3	2017 yr 3	2014 yr 5	2017 yr 5
Reading	47 (282 students)	58 (367 students)	29.6 (129 students)	42 (207 students)
Writing	57.4 (344 students)	64 (407 students)	17.8 (77 students)	22 (109 students)
Numeracy	43 (258 students)	53 (335 students)	27 (117 students)	34 (170 students)

The NAPLAN 2017 assessment suggests that continuous improvement is happening at all levels in Cluster 5 schools. Most important, the learning culture is continually developing with a shared understanding of what is expected at every level. All teachers share a common understanding of the learning that is required to have every student succeed. This balanced improvement across all schools in reading, writing, and numeracy is shown more dramatically in Figure 3.9.

The "Z" scores for Grade 3 Cluster 5 (Figure 3.9) show that all NAPLAN assessment tasks—reading, writing, spelling, grammar, and numeracy—are impressively heading upward together. This is an indicator that classroom pedagogy is changing to reflect CLARITY in all key learning areas. The impact of the CI on teaching in Cluster 5 has not

(Continued)

(Continued)

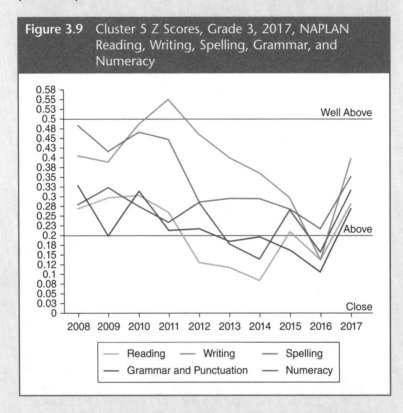

Figure 3.9 Cluster 5 Z Scores, Grade 3, 2017, NAPLAN Reading, Writing, Spelling, Grammar, and Numeracy

been limited to ESL; it has expanded to include increases in the language and numeracy assessments for all students. And, rather than having an impact on only one key learning area, the "Z" score data have a brilliant upward trajectory in every area, demonstrating that the CI question has been clearly answered. All "Z" scores are "above" expected scores; they are not yet "well above," but significantly better than in previous years and, as noted, consistent across all key learning areas.

Because of the very nature of constant change experienced in these school communities, the CI is always being refined, refocused, and renewed. The evolving framework for change in Sydney Catholic Schools continues to include the following:

- the 14 Parameters
- leaders who support each other

- CI that builds on the research in this text of what works
- the sharing of expertise
- encouragement to stay the course
- a cycle of PL with all students' achievement in literacy and numeracy at its core

Lessons Learned: Whole-System Collaborative Inquiry

This informative narrative of system improvement focused on student growth and achievement from Sydney Catholic Schools substantiates my work and underlines the importance of the following:

1. **Commitment.** All system leaders need to be fully committed and invested in the details of system and school improvement work, aligning the work throughout the organization as co-learners. Kate O'Brien, Tosca Galluzzo, and Sybil Dickens modeled the process and content by working right alongside school leaders.

2. **Structure.** The 14 Parameter framework provides focus for improvement that allows leaders to say "yes" to what fits inside the improvement agenda and "no" to distractors that bombard and derail it. When the bookends, Parameters #1 and #14, are constantly visible at every PL session (Parameter #7) to remind everyone of their shared beliefs, improvement occurs. When the structural changes are made to support the plan and when resources are similarly reallocated, outstanding things happen.

3. **Knowledgeable Others.** Instructional coaches act as Knowledgeable Others and are carefully selected for their relational and content skills (Parameter #2). When coordinated by the system, Knowledgeable Others offer capacity building and upskilling for teachers that is transferable across schools, ensuring sustainability of best practice and interchangeability of staff (that is inevitable), with minimal new-hire training required.

4. **Presence.** Leaders like O'Brien, Dickens, Galluzzo, and the principals in Cluster 5 make a powerful difference in their own schools, in other schools, and in entire systems because they

attach Knowledgeable Others to their sides and are present in the work, leading and learning simultaneously.

5. **Data Collection.** Data Walls showing growth and achievement, Case Management Meetings to find solutions to identified instructional challenges, and Learning Walks and Talks are key approaches in putting FACES on the data and taking timely and precise action. Experiences on Learning Walks and Talks become data to be shared with the school staff and with the schools from which walkers have come. The cross-sharing in Cluster 5 due to PLC meeting time and Learning Walks and Talks contributed to the cluster-wide adoption of the strategies that resulted in the impressive improvement displayed in Figure 3.9.

6. **Inquiry.** Ongoing CI cycles cause deep reflection on and changes to classroom practice that result in increased student achievement (Sharratt, 1996). CI is not an "initiative" nor a "project." CI is a continuous cycle and an approach to reflective improvement in our craft of teaching and learning.

This system CI case study demonstrates that when system and school leaders authentically co-labor, triage problems using data, reallocate resources, and follow an agreed CI process, they create a culture of constructive debate, new shared knowledge and practice, and decision making that makes a difference. "Leaders at every level have a responsibility to improve an organization's decision-making ability by identifying the prevalent biases and using the relevant tools, [such as the 14 Parameters], to shape a productive decision-making culture" (Lovallo & Sibony, 2006). What follows moves us from a system CI case study to consider the impact of CI within one Cluster 5 school to get a "close to the ground" view of the importance of CLARITY in the school improvement process.

CASE STUDY: A WHOLE-SCHOOL COLLABORATIVE INQUIRY

Sharratt and Planche (2016) describe collaboration as an approach in which system and school leaders build collective capacity; create new knowledge together; and move schools from places "of plans and good intentions to centers of purposeful practice." As we began the Cluster 5 work, Sharratt's ongoing work with us caused me to think about how I could best provide leadership within the team and teaching staff at St. Martha's Strathfield School.

The Cluster 5 initiative required collection and analysis of data to inform our next level of work. As the school's instructional coach in Cluster 5, I proposed that we use the cycle of CI (Figure 3.2) found in Sharratt and Fullan (2012, p. 131) to improve our effectiveness as instructional leaders. Specifically, team members adopted this cycle of CI to collectively deepen their analysis, evaluation, and monitoring of the school's English and mathematics data. This team decision informed an area of inquiry for the whole school to undertake, and it became the driver for the school's collective Performance Growth in Action school goal aimed at improving student learning and directing personal professional growth. When we aligned this strategy with our school's annual improvement plan, it seemed natural that Parameter #1, with its emphasis on developing shared beliefs and understandings of teaching and learning, would be a good starting point for the work. Then, we began our work of building a culture of inquiry through collaboration to drive improvement for all students.

In implementing and participating in this cycle, we codeveloped operating norms that focused on creating a "no-blame" environment. This action freed all teachers and the leadership team to

- work collaboratively with each other
- question their practice
- interrogate their data
- reflect on what was working and what was not
- decide what could be done differently to have an impact on student learning

The strategy aimed to develop personal as well as whole-school efficacy. The following notes describe how the cycle of CI, Figure 3.2, was implemented as a whole-school approach to improvement:

1. Multiple data sources were used to triangulate student data to identify an area of inquiry to improve student outcomes. They included reading records, writing samples, pre- and post-assessments in mathematics, standards-based NAPLAN assessment, and PAT assessments for reading and mathematics.

(Continued)

(Continued)

2. Based on the data, teachers collaborated with each other to develop a focused question concerning school and classroom practice to improve student achievement.

3. Teachers researched best practice to improve students' outcomes in literacy and numeracy.

4. At staff meetings, teachers shared their research about best practices. This research and student data informed their planning for targeted intervention.

5. Teachers collected post-intervention data on their targeted area of inquiry.

6. At staff meetings, teachers were asked to use a "deliberate pause" question to identify the need to modify the intervention.

7. Teachers collaboratively wrote up their findings.

8. Teachers celebrated the final report by presenting their research at a Sydney Catholic Schools Authentic Learning Symposium.

This process has built collective capacity and synergy of action that empowered teachers and students to act to meet students' needs and move our school to become a center of "purposeful practice" (Sharratt & Planche, 2016). Our collective impact demonstrates that staff members made solid progress in evidence of learning. Most students accomplished one year's growth for one year at school.

Source: Caroline Boulis, assistant principal, St. Martha's Stratfield.

IMPACT!

All students were assessed, including all English language learners. The reading growth improved throughout the year in all grades, with the exception of Grade 2. Three examples of impact were: 27% more Kindergarten students were "at or above" level from Term 1 to the end of Term 4; Grade 3 improved significantly, from 45% "at or above" level in Term 1 to 91% in Term 4—a 46% improvement; and in Grade 6, there was a 35% increase in number of students "at or above" expected level from Term 1 to Term 4.

Their work is not over; however, these impressive student results demonstrate the power CI brings to collective CLARITY and precision in practice.

Lessons Learned: A Whole-School Collaborative Inquiry

The whole-school approach to CI builds on the system CI lessons and highlights the importance of the following:

1. **Data.** Under the right conditions, teachers and leaders must use multiple sources of data, including student work samples and evidence-proven research, to develop meaningful inquiries.

2. **Operating Norms and Protocols.** The right conditions for learning together include ensuring teachers and leaders are offered blame-free operating norms and clear protocols to which they can refer during the CI cycle. The work is not linear; it is messy, and having touchstones to create structure is critical.

3. **Focused Leadership.** Every inquiry needs a champion and Knowledgeable Other who are willing to focus, stay the course, and keep the learning cycle enjoyable and moving forward.

4. **Reflective Practice.** Champions who lead need to model taking "deliberate pauses" to step back, reflect, and ask questions, then move forward again toward a goal while it is still being defined. This is the messy bit.

5. **Thinking.** The work of CI is focused on the FACES of real students and their thinking in classrooms. CI is also focused on the FACES of teachers who, by thinking about their wonderings and findings, with the freedom to relinquish their biases toward current practices, can grow and extend their professional capacity.

6. **Iterative.** CIs must focus on questions arising from the data, on being flexible in going where the findings take staff, and on evidence of students' thinking as feedback of changed practice. Teachers must ask, "What worked?" "What didn't?" and "What will we do differently next time?" The cycle of inquiry causes teachers to experiment with and reflect on their learning. As new challenges arise, the cycle begins again, from the new starting point of what has been learned thus far. It is an iterative process. However, the cycle of inquiry is not abandoned for a "new adventure" when the going gets tough.

7. **Fail Fast.** The only way to change practice is to be given the opportunity of time to try new approaches in a safe, fail-fast learning environment of co-planning, co-teaching, co-debriefing, and co-reflecting but within a short time cycle: "Did it work?" is a quick turnaround question. Then reflect: "Let's modify and try it again."

8. **Small Wins.** Accountable Talk (see Chapter 5), writing up the findings collectively, mobilizing the knowledge gained across schools, and celebrating small and big wins are key components of the CI cycle—not to be omitted! They are the stuff of building capacity, of maintaining history in all environments (especially those with rapid staff turnover), and of building individual and collective efficacy.

9. **Provocations.** Although all components are critical, CI is not a lock-step recipe; it is an approach that tests our assumptions and biases, often using provocations (if/then statements) in order to investigate what can make a difference to increasing all students' attainment and then knowing why it did.

10. **Learning**. Learners at all levels of the system see learning with, alongside, and on behalf of each other as "the work" of teaching and leading.

When CI, as described in the previous case study, is the focus of staff meetings that establish them as PLCs (Parameter #7), the work is recognized as hard, dedicated work in which context and culture inevitably influence and shape professional practice (Harris & Jones, 2015).

WHEN DO WE INQUIRE COLLABORATIVELY? PROFESSIONAL LEARNING COMMUNITIES AT WORK

PARAMETER #7: FOCUSED PROFESSIONAL LEARNING AT STAFF MEETINGS

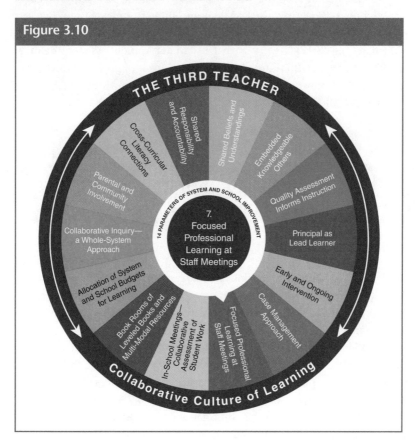

Figure 3.10

The work in PLCs is the serious work that makes a difference to increasing all students' achievement. PLCs are known to contribute to improved school and system outcomes (Harris, Jones, & Huffman, 2017). The key cross-cultural features of successful PLCS are teacher agency, teacher leadership, teacher voice, and, alongside these, the facilitating role played by combinations of system and school leaders and university colleagues—all people who work at the interface of policy and practice (Harris et al., 2017).

University partners bring the research, knowledge, support, and facilitation needed to intertwine policy and practice for system and school leaders. They are effective when they work in partnership PLCs that focus on putting FACES on data to increase all students' achievement. My experience in working with university, system, and school leaders at Michigan State University (MSU) amplifies the message in *Teachers Leading Educational Reform: The Power of Professional Learning Communities* (Harris et al., 2017). I work with Dr. Barbara Markle, assistant dean of education, MSU, who leads a highly trained team of professors and practitioners to support system and school improvement through CI, across the state of Michigan. Their narrative is told in the following case study.

CASE STUDY: MICHIGAN STATE UNIVERSITY PARTNERSHIPS REFLECT PLC WORK

Setting the Context

The MSU K–12 Outreach model has always been one of research-based support connecting faculty members to K–12 leaders and practitioners in the field. It is a model that integrates the collective capacity and ability of the university to bridge the gap between the university level and the K–12 school level and to apply research to practice in situ. MSU's K–12 Outreach program has proven to be a vital source of support to schools and districts that through stronger compliance and metric-driven reforms coupled with financial setbacks have lost the internal institutional ability to apply research to practice, harness or build the capacity of their own staff to be the leaders of change, or to research and evaluate their own programs. School leaders have found themselves as "content experts" in a process-based environment where understanding, interpreting, and applying data to changes in teaching and learning is key. This is where the larger outreach role of the MSU K–12 Outreach makes a difference for K–12 students.

Twenty Years of Service in the Spirit of Collaboration

During her tenure, Markle has brought together researchers, administrators, and policymakers in a spirit of collaboration to better understand continuing policy reforms and to draw on best practices in other countries. MSU's K–12 Outreach has provided essential leadership development services to policymakers, superintendents, principals, and teachers through various incarnations of programs, such as Emerging Leaders, Coaching 101, Policy Forums, International Study Tours, and the Fellowship of Instructional Leaders (FIL), training thousands of leadership and instructional coaches, school and district leaders, and teachers. MSU K–12 Outreach has also been an important partner of Michigan's professional education associations and a founding member of the Education Alliance of Michigan.

No Silver Bullet!

However, the core of MSU K–12 Outreach's mission has been support for disadvantaged schools. From its beginning, Markle and her team have had a sharp focus on the pressing challenge of providing educational opportunities to high-needs students. Among the fruits of MSU K–12 Outreach's decades-long involvement with Michigan schools are some hard-won insights about effective ways to improve those schools. Anyone who works in the area of school reform is aware of its challenges and complexity, and there is a very strong temptation to cut through those difficulties by identifying a "silver bullet" solution. It is clear that this temptation needs to be resisted. But just because there is no simple or universal model for improving underperforming schools does not mean that no good model exists or that good structures can't be moved between situations. Comprehensive school reform is complex and multifaceted, so any strategy to improve education must also be complex, multifaceted, and ready to import high-impact strategies.

Dynamic Tension

University and K–12 school partnerships are an often-studied solution to the challenges of school and district improvement efforts (Eddy, Amey, &

(Continued)

(Continued)

Bragg, 2014; Lieberman, 1992; Smith, 1992; Zetlin & MacLeod, 1995). However, a limited number of studies have focused on the processes that form and sustain these partnerships and the results that can be realized from thriving partnerships (Beverly, 2017). In this age of high-stakes accountability, policymakers who have a role in developing school reform programs that encourage or mandate university and K–12 school partnerships often do so without a full understanding of the practical implications (Zimpher & Howey, 2004). Partnerships between universities and schools include dynamic tensions of interdependency (Shafritz, Ott, & Jang, 2011), and it becomes necessary to understand the degree of impact of these tensions within and between partners (Beverly, 2017).

The Fellowship of Instructional Leaders

The Fellowship of Instructional Leaders (FIL) provides intensive PL that is customized to the specific needs of each school in the district. Before working with a district, MSU K–12 Outreach FIL staff work with district leadership to examine the educational community's specific strengths and weaknesses. The FIL has worked with nearly 100 principals and more than 1,000 teachers and their instructional coaches to help MSU's K–12 Outreach participants understand the importance of leadership teams in schools, as well as the interplay between schools and their contexts within districts. This is highlighted by the need for stronger PLCs and instructional program coherence throughout a district. The Fellowship program has previously worked with several schools from Detroit, with a grant from the Skillman Foundation. This intensive program brings together cohorts of instructional learning teams to identify and work on their specific school needs and to learn from turnaround experts and from one another. One particular example of the important partnership role MSU takes on with local school leaders to foster educational improvement is discussed here.

Focused Work in One District

The FIL began a partnership with a local district near the MSU campus in 2014. Several meetings and communications with the district's central office staff led to the development of a memorandum of understanding that outlined the expectations and responsibilities of each partner and required approval at the administrative and policymaking levels for each institution. In order to introduce the program to the schools, a meeting was held with all 12 of the district's school principals to convey an overview and to outline expectations (Beverly, 2017). The focus of the work, reached by consensus, was to build the professional capacity of district teachers in three key areas:

- collaborative leadership
- school culture and personalized learning environment in PLCs
- curriculum, instruction, and assessment

The three areas were not imposed by "outsiders" applying a cookie-cutter model but were identified as essential by the district to meet the needs of their teachers and leaders to improve student achievement.

A Framework to Focus the Partnership Work

The FIL Professional Learning model is based on MSU's Leadership for Coherence Framework (Figure 3.11), which draws on the best research for school and organizational improvement.

Figure 3.11 Leadership for Coherence Framework

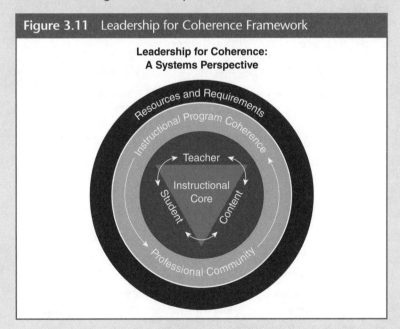

(Continued)

(Continued)

The heart of the Leadership for Coherence framework is the instructional core (City, Elmore, Fiarman, & Teitel, 2009), which focuses on the interactions of teachers and students in the presence of content. The layers outside the instructional core describe the context necessary for effective teaching and learning to take place. It is MSU's and Sharratt's conclusion that improving the quality of assessment and instruction is the only route to sustained student learning (Parameters #3 and #13).

The high level of attendance at the district PL sessions demonstrated the commitment of the district's educators to the PL model that the FIL used (Figure 3.11) and the value they derived from their own participation.

The FIL's teamwork with this district blended the hard-won lessons of decades of professional experience as K–12 teachers and administrators with the fruits of MSU's cadre of cutting-edge researchers. The FIL's model of PL is based on rigorous research, as shown in Figure 3.12. These attributes were woven into their successful PL program and include the following:

- a focus on reform designed specifically for this district

- sustained PL over at least the course of one school year

- collective participation of teachers and leaders in forming effective leadership teams

- active learning by focusing on relevant problems of practice

- an emphasis on system coherence among planning, resources, and instruction

- combined efforts of MSU's FIL and leadership coaches, who supported improvements in the district's student achievement

As well, the FIL and district staff worked together to identify goals and specific plans of action for each school, implementation of which was also supported in the schools by MSU leadership coaches. All of these components make for a sustained, coherent strategy to strengthen assessment and instruction in the schools.

Figure 3.12	Changes in Teacher Capacity and Classroom Practice Based on Type of Professional Learning		
	Professional Support Outcomes		
Professional Support Components	**Total Knowledge Acquisition**	**Total Skill Acquisition**	**Total Classroom Implementation**
Level 1	Presentation	10%	5%	0%
Level 2	Plus Demonstration	30%	20%	0%
Level 3	Plus Practice	60%	60%	5%
Level 4	Plus Feedback	95%	95%	95%

Source: Adapted from *Student Achievement Through Staff Development* by B. Joyce and B. Showers (2002).

Feedback is Critical to Move Forward

The value of the FIL can also be seen in the reflective feedback offered by the program participants. At the conclusion of each session, 100% of participants indicated that they had gained knowledge and skills in the specific topics that were covered at each session. In addition, as part of MSU K–12 Outreach's evaluation process, participants were asked to describe what they gained during each session and what they planned to implement in their schools. MSU's team of trained evaluators conducted a content analysis of these anonymous, open-ended responses. FIL participants stated that they had greater skills and efficacy for school improvement and how to apply the strategies in their schools. Of the 236 coded responses, five broad learning themes emerged:

1. Increased understanding and use of processes, structures, and systems of school improvement and culturally responsive practices

2. Implemented methods for monitoring, evaluating, and assessing progress being made to increase student achievement

3. Built individual and team skills focused on collaboration to improve student learning and teaching

(Continued)

4. Used data to differentiate instruction to improve student outcomes

5. Learned and applied school improvement strategies and developed school goals and action plans

While the participants made many notable gains throughout their work with the FIL, the strongest gain cited by participants was in the first category, which related to change in practice, understanding systems of school improvement, and a strong focus on cultural responsiveness.

Goals in Moving the Work Forward

The Fellowship will build and expand on the successes of the previous year. As a result of the PLC work, the continuing growth in the capacity of the district's instructional leadership teams makes it possible to expand the scope of this reform effort. After consultations with district leadership, the Fellowship will place greater emphasis, in the coming year, on promoting the following:

- student engagement
- teachers' use of learning targets
- more effective PLCs
- creating a culture of high expectations

The MSU FIL will continue to play an integral role in helping the schools in Michigan achieve their mission of becoming "the educational asset."

Source: Dr. Bryan Beverly, Dr. Brian Boggs, and Dr. Barbara Markle, Michigan State University, 2017.

IMPACT!

As presented in Figure 3.13, Continual Growth Indices data suggest that students in this district have made substantial academic progress in 2016–17. In three cohorts in each subject area, students improved at a faster

Figure 3.13 Conditional Growth Indices (CGI): Overall District Results

Cohort	Grade 15–16	Grade 16–17	Math CGI 15–16	Math CGI 16–17	Difference	Reading CGI 15–16	Reading CGI 16–17	Difference
3–4	3	4	−0.41	−0.68	−0.27	−2.39	0.14	2.53*
4–5	4	5	−1.11	0.6	1.71*	−1.37	1.58	2.95*
5–6	5	6	0.3	1.4	1.1*	−1.08	1.31	2.39*
6–7	6	7	−0.5	−0.21	0.29	−0.36	−0.35	0.01
7–8	7	8	−0.88	1.43	2.31*	−2.78	−2.85	−0.07

*Significant positive change

(Continued)

(Continued)

rate in 2016–17 than they did in 2015–16. In no cohort was there a meaningful decline in relative student progress. For four of five cohorts in both mathematics and reading, students improved at a faster rate than in the previous year. For most cohorts, students actually improved more quickly than other students in both math and reading nationally. Compared with 2015–16, when four grades in math and all five grades in reading saw subpar growth, the 2016–17 findings represent appreciable progress by the district's students.

Clearly, a major component of the MSU FIL work, and one of many reasons for notable successes in this district (see Figure 3.13), is training and supporting each school's leadership teams in the use of data. Teams are trained in the Data Dialogue Cycle, in which data sources are used to identify, plan, monitor, and assess student learning. The Data Dialogue Cycle is critical to developing data-driven instruction that changes teaching practices based on the individual needs of the students.

Lessons Learned: Partners in System and School Improvement

It is apparent from the data in Figure 3.13 that regardless of context, there are many lessons that university and school district partnership leaders can apply:

1. **No Silver Bullet.** Note that there is no magic, prepackaged program to fix system and school improvement, only carefully crafted programs that work when they are tailored to suit each district's context, culture, and concerns arising from the data, as the MSU example clearly illustrates.

2. **Knowledge Mobilization.** Employ a diffusion model in which members of instructional leadership teams are expected to share what they have learned and help build the capacity of other educators at their schools. This diffusion model is also supported by MSU leadership coaches active in the schools.

3. **Ownership of Learning.** Apply the principles of effective K–12 classroom instruction to teachers themselves. Just as students

learn best when they are engaged, set their own goals, and are in charge of their learning, so teachers learn when they are able to work collaboratively and are self-directed.

4. **Sustainability.** Note that it is critical for all schools in the district to participate in the FIL approach, creating a community of practice so that teachers, administrators, or students who transfer schools have a smoother transition as cultures, expectations, and practices are similar.

5. **PL Model.** Integrate all four levels (presentation, demonstration, practice, and feedback, as shown in Figure 3.13) that exemplify a strong delivery model of PL, leading to greater teacher knowledge and skill that changes classroom practice.

6. **The Heart of Educational Reform.** Use data assessment to inform instruction.

7. **Host a Learning Fair.** Celebrate small wins!

I have always noted the sensitivity that MSU faculty portray in their work with system and school leaders in the United States. They know what it takes to build sustainable PLCs.

SUCCESSFUL PLCs MANAGE CHANGE SENSITIVELY AND POSITIVELY

It is important to understand the complex and often fragile processes of building and sustaining PLCs, especially in light of central government reforms that are often dominated by the influences of external assessments. The importance of being able to change the culture of schools and systems includes the need for teachers to

- mediate and internalize externally instituted change,

- move from routines to adaptive expertise,

- realign their professional identities in changing practice landscapes (Harris et al., 2017).

The ability to manage the tension between pressure to be more academically competitive and accountable and the drive for more creativity and collaboration within and between schools and systems will ultimately result in gains for students (Harris et al., 2017). As these authors rightly point out, without positive management and leadership, there can be no guarantee of "authentic, effective collaboration," as "deep collaboration" requires time and trusting relationships that cannot be achieved without changing the culture of schools.

The following case study, also from the United States, flows from the previous one and highlights what Harris et al. (2017) address. Here, district leader and Assistant Superintendent Greg Upham and I dialogue about his experiences in leading PLCs that align developing a culture of learning and finding time for leaders and teachers to inquire collaboratively—learning together that results in student gains.

CASE STUDY: PROFESSIONAL LEARNING COMMUNITIES IN HELENA PUBLIC SCHOOLS, MONTANA

"Staff in Helena Public School District believe in collaborative communication and are strongly committed to Professional Learning Communities," says Assistant Superintendent Greg Upham. With 8,000 students K–12, more than 1,000 staff members, and 40% free and reduced lunches, student learning must come first.

This wasn't always the case. Under his leadership over several years, Upham says that the focus on learning in PLCs has become the norm rather than the exception. Not easy to accomplish, but incredibly rewarding when achievement results soar.

As an assistant principal, Upham could see that other districts in similar challenging circumstances were beating the odds. As a coach with a belief in his players—leaders, teachers, and students—Upham began to investigate what might make a difference.

In scrutinizing the data, now–secondary principal Upham discovered that only 67% of students graduated from Helena High School and the rest dropped out. When looking further, he found that about 80% of those students who dropped out began losing ground by third grade.

Four years ago, as assistant superintendent, Upham knew that something had to change structurally as he delved further into their alarming data trends. With his central office colleagues, he took action in three ways:

1. He went on a Red Line Tour to every school, presenting the big picture data and facts about high numbers of students performing below expectations and positively expressing to teachers and principals, "We are better than this" and "Our kids deserve better" (Parameter #1).

2. He sought expert advice and guidance from practitioner and consultant Janelle Keating, who had experience in her own district using PLCs as the vehicle to bring about change in practice (Parameter #2).

3. He collaboratively set three targets for the district, focused on students (Parameter #14):

   o 80% "proficient" (at/above expected level); color-coded green on the Data Wall

   o 15% "strategic" (almost proficient); color-coded yellow

   o 5% "intensive" (below expectation); color-coded red

Upham and his team made many heroic decisions that caused structural change in the organization and resulted in positive outcomes for students. They met with union leaders, principals, and teachers and communicated clearly with parents why they were implementing "PLC Mondays," weekly, in every school—a time when students go home from school 70 minutes early so that teachers and leaders can meet collaboratively in PLC groups to explore high-impact practices in every classroom. These PLC meetings include the following:

- co-constructed operating norms

- a clear purpose

- a glossary of terms, to develop a systemwide common language

- a process for examining practice

- principals and other leaders consistently attending

- a report written to the principal on the proceedings and findings from each meeting

(Continued)

(Continued)

During PLC time, teachers in grade teams or subject area groups begin with student work samples, for example, as data conversation starters. Teachers and leaders now work from the essential curriculum standards as they plan units of study together, K–12; develop formative assessments; and create summative assessment tasks to evaluate how students are doing and to determine the impact of their teaching.

The PLC sessions are lively as teachers discuss ways that they will differentiate their instruction to meet the needs of every learner—sometimes a challenge in secondary schools. However, these teachers and leaders are rising to that challenge and have made impressive gains reversing the drop-out rate and increasing attendance in every school.

> As an elementary school principal in a high-poverty school, I lie awake at night and worry about my students. All I want for them is a chance: a chance to find success in school; a chance for their education to open life's doorways. The PLC process has helped my students get *their* chance. As teachers are reaching more students, students are learning more and their lives are changed forever. It's not about teaching; it's about kids. (Tim McMahon, principal, Warren Elementary School, Helena School District, Montana)

Teachers and leaders are always learning. Upham and his team conduct Principals' Book Studies, selecting books by internationally acclaimed authors on leadership work in PLCs. In fact, teachers and leaders in this district return from summer holidays to attend their annual PLC Summer Conference. Beginning four years ago with fewer than 300 participants, the conference now enjoys more than 420 attendees who make this a priority during their summer break. This impressive piece of data reflects that teachers and leaders alike appreciate learning together and making a collective difference for their students. Success breeds success!

> I have been a teacher in the Helena School District for 23 years. When I first started teaching at the Project for Alternative Learning (PAL) school, I never had students taking geometry. The majority of the students at that time were taking pre-algebra and basic math. In the 2004–2005 school year, I had only one

student taking geometry. Then, in the 2015–2016 school year, I had nine students taking geometry and two taking Algebra 2 (the first time, ever, having students at this level). This year, there are 17 students currently enrolled and doing well in a geometry class! The changes our district has made at all levels, through the work accomplished in PLC groups, have had a tremendous impact on our incoming high school students' readiness for math education in general and in algebra, specifically. The results of our most recent math assessment show that 67% of PAL students are achieving above the 50th percentile of our district benchmark. That statistic would have been unheard of 10 years ago. (Kathy Collins, math instructor, PAL School)

The learning from this case study aligns with our 14 Parameter research and field work (Sharratt & Fullan, 2009, 2012, 2013). Success breeds success, and this district has the intentionality and drive to continue its impressive learning journey to reach its initial three targets. Teachers and leaders reflect that CLARITY in practice is about knowing the FACE of every student and targeting each action. As Upham says, "None of our successes would ever happen without a great team!"

Source: Greg Upham, assistant superintendent, Helena Public Schools, personal communication, 2018.

IMPACT!

Elementary data in Figure 3.14 and secondary data in Figure 3.15 show the district's impressive improvement over four years of dedicated PLC time during the school day to improve practice.

From the fall of the 2013–2014 school year to the spring of the 2016–2017 school year (4 years and 8 months), teachers and leaders successfully increased the percentage of elementary students who were proficient in math with a 40th percentile ranking or above by 16%. With approximately 3,000 students taking the Renaissance Benchmarking Assessment in the spring of 2017, the 16% increase is equivalent to more than 450 additional students performing at a proficient level. Similarly, from fall of

(Continued)

(Continued)

the 2014–2015 school year to the spring of the 2016–2017 school year, Helena School District increased the percentage of students who were proficient in reading by 16%. With approximately 3,350 students taking the assessment in the spring of 2017, the 16% increase is equivalent to more than 530 additional students performing at a proficient level (see Figure 3.14).

Figure 3.14 Elementary Student Improvement Over Four Years of Implementing PLCs

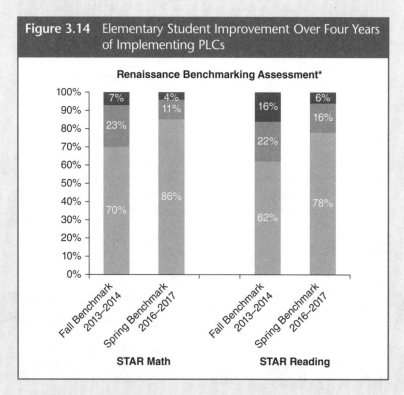

Similarly, results for Grade 11 secondary students in Helena Public School District are displayed in Figure 3.15. ACT stands for American College Testing assessment and is an assessment of readiness for college entrance. The ACT benchmark assessment scores for English, math, reading, and science identify the level of achievement necessary to prepare students for success in their first-year college courses.

Helena School District completes an internal ACT analysis. Comparing the 2014 cohort to the 2017 cohort, the percentage of students in the

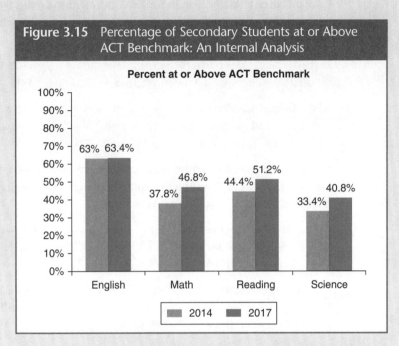

Figure 3.15 Percentage of Secondary Students at or Above ACT Benchmark: An Internal Analysis

Percent at or Above ACT Benchmark

English: 63%, 63.4%
Math: 37.8%, 46.8%
Reading: 44.4%, 51.2%
Science: 33.4%, 40.8%

2014   2017

*ACT is the registered trademark of ACT, Inc. Academic rankings and designated terminology are also the property of ACT. Helena Public Schools is not affiliated with ACT, Inc.

Helena School District meeting the ACT benchmarks increased in all four subject areas. The most significant gains are evident in math (9%), reading (6.8%), and science (7.4%).

Lessons Learned: In Implementing Professional Learning Communities

To what does Upham attribute these successes in Helena Public Schools? "Leaders and teachers make the difference," he says, "when they roll up their sleeves, in dedicated PLC time, and work collaboratively." I have taken away many insights from this case study, as listed in the following Lessons Learned.

1. **Vision.** Articulate daily a compelling vision that this is "the work," and that all students can and will learn beyond what was ever thought possible (Parameter #1).

2. **Commitment.** Ask principals for a commitment to do this work in PLCs, to be present in the work, and to stay the course when the work gets tough and energy gets low (Parameter #4).

3. **Data-Driven Decision Making.** Use data to provide the rationale for change, as data are irrefutable (Parameter #6).

4. **Risk Taker.** Be a coach who is not afraid to ask people what they think and to stroke those who are working tirelessly to support teacher and leader learning (Parameter #2).

5. **Time!** Provide dedicated learning time during the school day for PLCs to focus on learning together about high-impact assessment and instruction in every classroom (Parameters #7 and #8).

6. **Clear, High Expectations.** Have some nonnegotiables—the line drawn in the sand—with a comprehensive rationale to which everyone can commit (Parameter #14).

7. **Knowledgeable Others.** Train three to five Knowledgeable Others from each school, focusing on the format of and facilitation skills needed in PLCs (Parameter #2).

8. **Differentiation.** Create strategies to differentiate support to all learners. For example, Upham is creating Math Labs for the 5% of students who need intensive, laser-like support. Reports indicate that teachers and students are appreciating this innovation (Parameters #1 and #14).

9. **Amplify Every Success.** Celebrate small wins (Parameters #4 and #14).

These lessons learned reflect the power of the 14 Parameters working in unison when we take an open-to-learning, inquiry stance in PLCs.

LEAD IN ORDER TO LEARN AND LEARN IN ORDER TO LEAD

Through CI, educators work together to improve their understanding of what learning is (or could be), to generate evidence of what's working (and what's not), to make decisions about next steps, and to take action to introduce improvements and innovations. And then they start again on emerging new issues and challenges (Ontario Ministry of Education, 2015b). Notably, CI positions educators to be key participants in understanding how to achieve excellence and equity in education—our collective goal. CI is an innovation that creates a profound shift in how we think about, talk about, and value learning (adapted from Ontario Ministry of Education, 2015a). This shift from teaching and teacher-centered practice to learning and learner-centered practice applies to system and school collaborative inquiries as well as to how we must teach in every classroom.

The strength of the multi-leveled CI approach, often taken in PLC time, is captured in Figure 3.16. Here, Tracey Petersen aptly describes CI in her powerful visual as an opportunity to "learn in order to lead and lead in order to learn" at every level of the organization. The direction of and text in the arrows are key to achieving CLARITY in collaborative learning.

CI, an impactful, ongoing process, often led by teachers and leaders together in PLCs, leads to increased empowerment, achievement,

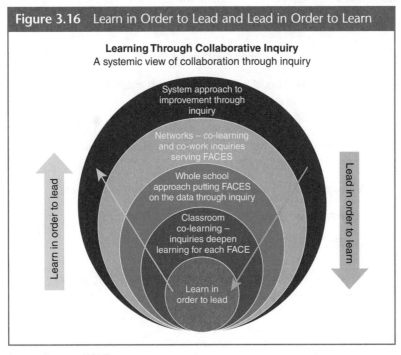

Figure 3.16 Learn in Order to Lead and Lead in Order to Learn

Source: Petersen (2017).

and learning growth for participants, as seen in the case studies in this chapter. Successful CIs within systems and schools self-propagate into higher self- and collective efficacy for all.

Thus far, each chapter has built on the previous one, starting with a framework for system and school improvement: the 14 Parameters (Chapter 1), progressing to knowing the FACES of learners (Chapter 2), and, finally, to understanding how CI in PLCs (Chapter 3) builds teacher and leader knowledge and appreciable skill to reflect on and to improve classroom practice. Although these big ideas are not clear cut, for purposes of organizing my thoughts, these chapters forming *Part I: Learning* seem to me to be a clarion call for changes in practice. In *Part II: Teaching*, I examine practice. That is, how an open-to-learning stance in investigating high-impact assessment and instructional approaches, how modeling CI with students, and how understanding the tools we have available to us when students aren't learning, make a difference to all students' growth and achievement.

COMMITMENT

I commit to

- demonstrate an open-to-learning, inquiry stance;
- create and model a risk-free environment to encourage CI in all of my work as a leader and team member;
- set up, communicate, and model operating norms, protocols, and a questioning environment to encourage opportunities to fail fast and move forward together;
- move intentionally from engaging to empowering others;
- learn in order to lead, and lead in order to learn;
- find dedicated, regular time to conduct CI in PLCs.

Given what you have read so far, what commitments could you make for yourself and with your team?

A DELIBERATE PAUSE
TO CREATE CLARITY

Identify the ideas and examples in this chapter that may challenge your own knowledge and current practice of CI in PLCs. Which concepts can you capitalize on and share with others to move your system and school forward?

Visit the companion website at
resources.corwin.com/CLARITY
for videos and downloadable resources

PART II
Teaching

CLARITY IN TEACHING
Assessment

CHAPTER 4

Wonderings...

1. Where do I start when planning for students' and teachers' learning?
2. How do I get teachers and students to own their own improvement?
3. How do I move forward when some teachers and students "get it" and some don't?
4. How do I get staff involved in understanding the process of co-construction of meaning?
5. Where do I find elementary and secondary examples of strong assessment practices?

What are you, the reader, wondering?

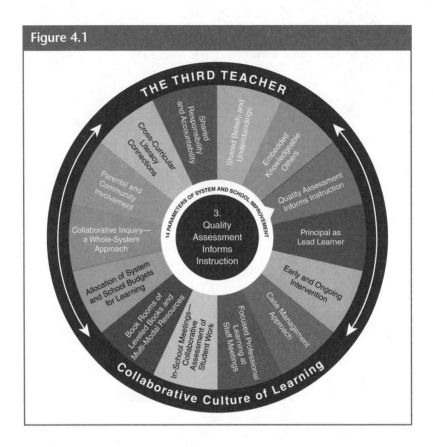

Figure 4.1

THE THIRD TEACHER

14 PARAMETERS OF SYSTEM AND SCHOOL IMPROVEMENT

Shared Responsibility and Accountability

Cross-Curricular Literacy Connections

Parental and Community Involvement

Collaborative Inquiry—a Whole-System Approach

Allocation of System and School Budgets for Learning

Book Rooms of Leveled Books and Multi-Modal Resources

In-School Meetings—Collaborative Assessment of Student Work

Focused Professional Learning at Staff Meetings

Case Management Approach

Early and Ongoing Intervention

Principal as Lead Learner

Quality Assessment Informs Instruction

Embedded Knowledgeable Others

Shared Beliefs and Understandings

3. Quality Assessment Informs Instruction

Collaborative Culture of Learning

PARAMETER #3: QUALITY ASSESSMENT INFORMS INSTRUCTION

Nothing else matters in teaching and learning as much as quality assessment, that is, data that inform and differentiate instruction for each learner in a never-ending cycle of inquiry to discover what works best. This is the power of Parameter #3: get right what happens in large blocks of instructional time, and improvement accelerates across the school and schools.

In Chapter 3, I discussed what contributes to knowing our learners if we all have a responsibility to inquire into how each learns best. In this chapter, I consider assessment approaches that ensure knowing and owning all the FACES and lead to changed or refined teaching practices. **Assessment literacy is the heart of system and school improvement.**

The word *assessment* comes from the Latin *assidere* ("to sit beside"), and assessment literacy means to begin with a clear vision of what is possible for every learner. Knowing the end game and working alongside every student help to define where teaching begins and how it flows through an ever-improving cycle of plan—assess—instruct—assess—interpret (differentiate/guide/refine)—instruct—evaluate, as shown in Figure 4.2. This is the art and science of teaching. "To sit beside" is the continuous process of co-construction necessary in every classroom to ensure that students and teachers are building meaning, together, through the learning process. Assessment literate teachers and students know where they are heading and how they can orchestrate learning together along the way. Importantly, leaders must know what that assessment and instruction cycle of improvement looks and sounds like in every classroom.

Beginning with the end in mind in learning is a well-established, impactful assessment practice (Sharratt & Planche, 2016). Teachers planning together begin by knowing the destination or outcome from the curriculum expectations that all students will master. Students must experience

- the critical language literacy and mathematical literacy skills embedded in every lesson,

- time to reflect on their learning,

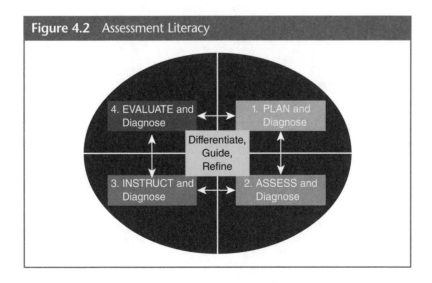

Figure 4.2 Assessment Literacy

- ways to articulate how to improve,

- opportunities to demonstrate their personal best—to date—and to do this collaboratively within groups, pairs, and on their own.

Figure 4.3 lists the questions that are foundational to clarify during the assessment planning process. The answers to these teacher and student questions lead teachers to plan using their knowledge of formative and summative assessment.

Figure 4.3 Planning With the End in Mind	
Teachers Ask	**Students Ask**
1. What are my students expected to know and be able to do? What can they already do? (Unpack curriculum expectations)	1. What am I learning?
2. How will I know my students are learning? (Gather the evidence through ongoing assessment data collection)	2. Why am I learning it?
3. How will I help my students learn and respond if they are not learning? (Teach and reteach in a new way for some who didn't get the concept)	3. How do I know how I am doing?
4. How will I determine the level of my students' learning and report on it? (Ongoing assessment, evaluation, and reporting)	4. How can I improve?
5. How does my evaluation inform my diagnostic next steps for every student? (Cyclical nature of assessment that informs instruction)	5. What are my next steps?

FORMATIVE AND SUMMATIVE ASSESSMENT

Formative assessment takes place before (assessment *for* learning) and during (assessment *as* learning) teaching; summative assessment (assessment *of* learning) takes place after the teaching. They are defined as follows.

Assessment for learning involves teachers determining where students are in their learning, through assessment of prior knowledge, and also using the information collected from ongoing, daily assessments and observations to plan for differentiated instruction, thinking about the needs of the whole class, small groups, and individual students.

Assessment as learning involves teachers using their ongoing assessment information during teaching to flexibly group for instruction, reteaching some concepts, when necessary, in a different way. Assessment as learning involves students using clearly articulated, co-constructed Success Criteria (SC); visible classroom prompts; and feedback from teachers and peers to articulate their next steps in learning. Importantly, students become reflective of their own capabilities and own their improvement. Ultimately, gradually increasing the autonomy of learners leads to self-regulation and metacognition, or knowing how one learns best.

Assessment of learning involves teachers summarizing, judging, and evaluating student work against the SC, providing a summation that must inform next steps for their teaching and student learning. Thus, it is a never-ending cycle of teaching and learning as assessment of learning becomes diagnostic and informs assessment for learning.

In this chapter, I describe ongoing assessment for and as learning as the drivers of change in every classroom. **Fair, equitable, and clearly understood assessment practices are at the heart of learning for students and for educators in every system and school. This is equity and excellence—the heart of educational improvement.**

The Assessment Waterfall Chart in Figure 4.4 depicts all the components of assessment for and as learning. No amount of instruction will work unless it is informed by transparent teacher and student self-assessment practices. These practices, details of which are unpacked below, must *all be present* in every classroom to make a difference for each student's learning growth and achievement. We need CLARITY in understanding that the components all weave together to form robust classroom practice.

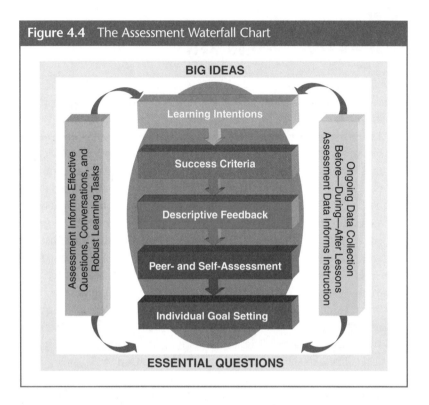

Figure 4.4 The Assessment Waterfall Chart

BIG IDEAS

Learning Intentions

Success Criteria

Descriptive Feedback

Peer- and Self-Assessment

Individual Goal Setting

Assessment Informs Effective Questions, Conversations, and Robust Learning Tasks

Ongoing Data Collection Before—During—After Lessons Assessment Data Informs Instruction

ESSENTIAL QUESTIONS

DEBRIEFING EACH COMPONENT OF THE ASSESSMENT WATERFALL CHART

BIG IDEAS AND ESSENTIAL QUESTIONS

The twin notions of *big ideas* and *essential questions* envelop the Assessment Waterfall Chart, Figure 4.4, and answer the question, "Why are we learning this?" The big ideas are at the very core of teaching and learning. They make concepts understandable, so they must be woven throughout the teaching and learning cycle. Developing big ideas alongside students demands the explicit teaching of the higher-order thinking skills of analysis, interpretation, evaluation, and synthesis of a text or curriculum unit. **It is critical that teachers and students make the links to real-world relevance so that students not only know what they are learning but why they are learning it.** Delving into real-world issues through big ideas and essential questions moves students from just being engaged to being empowered to make a difference, as discussed in Chapter 6.

Thus, the term *big idea* does not mean naming a theme unit, such as "friendship," and selecting a bunch of books and activities that go along with the friendship theme, but rather modeling higher-order thinking skills for students and giving them opportunities to think through text or essential questions critically, bringing them to levels of deep understanding, creativity, and new learning about what characterizes "friendship," for example (Greenan, in Sharratt & Fullan, 2012).

Essential questions are thought provoking and cognitively demanding. Students always want to know how the world works, so topics and questions that capture students' interest and create academic controversy, using evidence, are directly related to multiple, interdisciplinary curriculum expectations. For example,

- Sustainability of our planet: Can everything be conserved? Should it be?

- Impact of global warming: How do we predict the future?

- History repeats itself: Defend which is better, self-interest or the greater good.

- Nutritious food versus junk food: Which is better and why?

Essential questions are developed from discussions of the big ideas that we want students to know and be able to do. They are developed at the beginning of a unit and added to as learning in the unit evolves:

What do you already know about X?

What do you want to know more about X?

Where could we go to find out more about X?

What are you wondering about?

Together students and teachers create anchor charts of wonderings for ongoing reference. Big ideas and essential questions can be addressed by reading individual texts or during a unit of study, but they need to cause and stretch students' thinking by highlighting what is essential in the text or learning experience and connecting these ideas meaningfully to students' lives and the world (M. Greenan, personal communication, 2017).

LEARNING INTENTIONS

Learning Intentions (LIs), shown in Figures 4.5 and 4.6, flow from the conversations with students about big ideas and essential questions. LIs are derived directly from state standards or curriculum expectations and also answer the question, "Why are we learning this?" The LI must make sense, be meaningful to students, be purposefully unpacked, and then be communicated in student-friendly language. It is a statement of what students are learning and why, *not* what they are doing. Referring back to our initial discussions, teachers must also ponder whether and why it is worth learning and make that clear to students.

LIs become most meaningful to students when teachers pull together several curriculum expectations from across the learning areas. Classrooms filled with anchor charts of prompts for students' use make the learning visible for them. Further, in order for students to understand why they are learning and what they are learning in the unit of study, teachers must deconstruct the words in the LI with their students and

Figure 4.5 Anchor Charts Support Students in Answering "What Am I Learning?" and "How Am I Doing?"

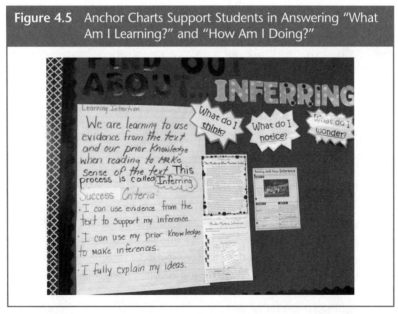

Source: Elaine Lochhead, assistant superintendent, Seine River School Division, Manitoba, Canada, 2017.

> **Figure 4.6** Sample Anchor Chart of Learning Intentions and Success Criteria

Learning Intention:

We are learning to select evidence from the text to analyze and explain how language choices and conventions are used to influence an audience.

Success Criteria:

I can:

- use evidence from the text to explain my thinking,
- use considered vocabulary choices,
- identify and apply ways to improve my responses using our annotated strong and weak examples,
- reflect on our Bump-It-Up Wall to move my writing to the next level.

put these prompts on charts that are visible for all students to use to support their thinking. Figure 4.5 from a Grade 7 and 8 class at Ste. Anne Elementary School, Seine River School Division, Manitoba, Canada depicts useful anchor charts co-constructed by teacher and students.

Interestingly, by ensuring CLARITY with easily understood prompts (Figures 4.5 and 4.6), every teacher, regardless of subject area, becomes a literacy teacher.

Teachers must ensure the right LIs are selected so that rigorous performance tasks (see Chapter 5) reflect the LIs and can be assessed against the SC.

Anchor charts show students the specificity of the learning but can also show how teachers and students have deconstructed the words to make the vocabulary of the learning and the expectations very clear in student-friendly language. From explicit LIs, deconstructed with students, teachers and students can co-construct the SC, as shown in Figure 4.6.

If the LI is "We are learning to infer to be able to read between and beyond the lines," then the SC should reflect the key components of a good inference:

I can

- understand the vocabulary,
- use my own schema,

- deduce clues in the text, and

- combine these three elements to draw a conclusion that makes sense about what is happening in the text to extend my understanding.

(SC are added as unit of study progresses.)

These will be scaffolded, and additions made to the list, as the focus on inference continues during the large block of instructional time. This anchor chart is visible for all students to see and access the information as a self-assessment tool.

> Success Criteria

SUCCESS CRITERIA

SC must be clear, visible in classrooms, and easily understood by students. Most important, SC must paint an accurate picture of what is truly the essential learning that will be assessed in the LI. When LIs and SCs are co-constructed collaboratively and added to continuously as learning unfolds throughout a unit of study or exploration of a "wicked problem," students understand, in detail, how to be successful. Experiencing scaffolded instruction that supports attainment of the SC moves students from being engaged to being empowered. This occurs when teachers incorporate evidence-proven teaching practices, such as the following:

- making deconstructed LIs and co-constructed SC visible

- posting them in classrooms

- updating them as learning grows and the unit of study or inquiry progresses

- having students use SC in an active way to articulate and own their next steps

As John Hattie (2015) reminds us, when students are confident, assessment-capable learners, there is a significant effect size of 1.33 on students' learning and achievement. Teachers become more confident in their professional practice with positive student responses to their very specific, "precise in practice" assessment tools. Student success breeds success for teachers, too, meaning that both teacher and student empowerment occurs. When that individual teacher efficacy is raised to have a collective staff impact, the effect size of the collective efficacy is 1.56 (Hattie, 2016b). This is the impact of CLARITY!

As shown in Figure 4.7, the first step in classroom practice is planning with the end in mind, to know what students are expected to learn; only then can teachers begin to co-construct the SC with students. With every teacher using this process across the school(s), students learn that understanding and executing language skills is not exclusive to English class; as Figure 4.7 illustrates, it is key to understanding in every class. The following science example is color coded to show that each curriculum expectation in the LI corresponds to each SC. The instructional teaching points, Descriptive Feedback, peer- and self-assessment, and individual goal setting are based on these co-constructed SC.

Figure 4.7 Linking Learning Intentions and Success Criteria Using Color Coding

Learning Intention:

We are learning to write a generalization about the patterns of reflected rays and light refractions in convex and concave mirrors to explain everyday occurrences.

Success Criteria:

I can

- write a broad statement using provided information, observation, and experience;
- identify and describe the regular or repeated form of reflected rays;
- locate, label, find examples of convex and concave mirrors.

Source: Principal Jill Maar, Ontario, Canada, 2017.

CO-CONSTRUCTION

Co means *with*. When we add the prefix *co* to educational practices, it implies that leaders, teachers, and students are working together to achieve learning that would not be possible in isolation. Co-construction is the operative word in accomplishing CLARITY of assessment and instructional practices.

The co-construction process is vital to students' understanding of what success looks like and their ability to articulate how they are doing and how can they improve. When teachers use strong and weak examples to co-construct SC, they can subsequently hear students' voices comparing and contrasting what makes a strong piece of work versus a weaker sample, allowing them to understand the curriculum expectations more deeply.

Steps in the Co-Construction of Success Criteria

Part 1: Teachers Prepare Through Detailed Planning

Teachers:

- plan to provide opportunities for students to discuss and engage in the development of SC that are clear, detailed, focused, and aligned to the curriculum expectations;

- provide concrete models, anchor charts, and exemplars that clearly define the attributes of *both* strong and weak work, based on co-constructed SC (see Bump-It-Up Walls, Figures 4.13, 4.14, 4.15, later in the chapter);

- model the use of SC to analyze and critique *anonymous* student work samples;

- teach students to use SC as tools for peer- and self-assessment (see below).

Part 2: Teachers and Students Co-Construct the Success Criteria

Teachers and students:

- identify and clarify the LIs to ensure understanding;

- analyze examples of strong and weak work for strengths and weaknesses;

- generate a list of possible indicators based on the analysis;

- organize the indicators into related categories to develop criteria;

- record, on chart paper, the general categories and the SC indicators;

- critique the SC and revise them for CLARITY;

- add to them as students discover more SC needed to bring CLARITY to the curriculum expectations;

- conclude the development of SC prior to beginning the summative performance task;

- use the SC to evaluate their final products. There should be no surprises, that is, undeclared SC!

SC are detailed elaborations on the outcomes that will be assessed formatively along the learning journey and/or summatively at the end of a unit or Collaborative Inquiry (see Chapter 6). Students must be able to choose how to demonstrate their learning at the summation of a study, using the SC to guide them. Students must be able to achieve an "A" if they proficiently accomplish all the SC.

An Example From Grade 5
Science Curriculum Expectation

Learning Intention: We are learning about maintaining a healthy body (systems, nutrition, health) to be able to live life to the fullest.
    Success Criteria:
    I can

- identify the main purposes for the six body systems (digestive, skeletal, muscular, nervous, respiratory, circulatory);

- demonstrate and describe how the systems of the body work together to maintain a healthy body;

- evaluate media information for science content and bias about body image and health.

An Example From Grade 9
Science Curriculum Expectation

Learning Intention: We are learning how electric circuits work in order to understand how the world works.

Success Criteria:

I can

- measure voltage, current, and resistance;

- explain the role of voltage, current, and parallel circuits in a simple electric circuit;

- explain how all of the above create light and brightness;

- explain and show safety considerations when working with electrical equipment;

- construct electric circuits from schematic diagrams (on an anchor chart).

Source: Monica Biggar, assistant superintendent, Seine River School Division, Manitoba, Canada, personal communication, 2017.

In the following case study, secondary teacher Bradley Powers and Principal Regina Menz illustrate the importance of teachers and students being explicit by co-constructing what quality work looks like in all classrooms.

CASE STUDY: SECONDARY STUDENTS CO-CONSTRUCT SUCCESS CRITERIA

Bradley Powers (first-year teacher) and Regina Menz (principal) have been co-planning, co-assessing, and co-teaching a Grade 11 chemistry course. They meet once a week to plan, debrief, and reflect. Their aim has been to consistently use formative assessment (for and as learning) and reflection to provide students with opportunities for deep learning. One of the key areas for success in the High School Certificate exams at the end of Grade 12 is the ability to write coherent, concise long-response answers using correct chemistry and technical language. The low statewide data for these responses point to the importance of explicitly teaching scientific literacy skills.

Throughout the year, Powers and Menz give many opportunities for students to attempt to answer questions and, using the Gradual Release and Acceptance of Responsibility model, the students have begun to improve their scientific writing. As a lead-in to the Grade 11 chemistry final summative assessment, they planned a series of lessons to really hone all the skills that students needed to answer questions successfully.

They gave students a sample question that they might be asked: Describe the properties of one allotrope of carbon and link the properties to its bonding.

Then the co-constructing began. The students were told explicitly that the SC they developed must be an "A" response. The students had experience in reading quality responses and identifying what high-level responses include. The students were divided into groups of four or five students, with chart paper and markers. They then proceeded to develop group SC, as illustrated in Figure 4.8.

After drafting a set of SC in their group, a representative student from each of the original groups then worked with the class to create the class SC (Figure 4.9).

Figure 4.8 Collaborative Group Work in the Progressive Development of Success Criteria

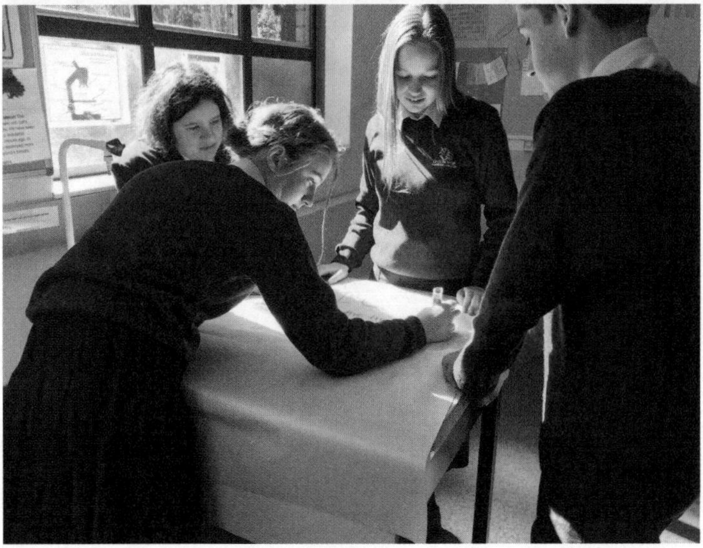

(Continued)

(Continued)

Source: Regina Menz, secondary principal, Diocese of Armidale, 2017.

Figure 4.9   Co-Constructed Success Criteria

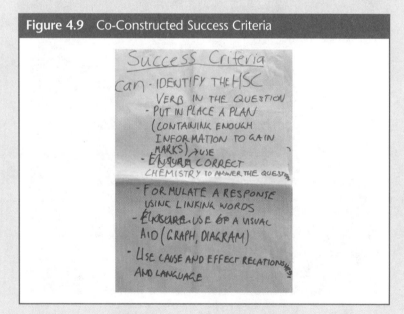

Source: Regina Menz, 2017.

Figure 4.10 Co-Developed Answer Using Co-Constructed Success Criteria

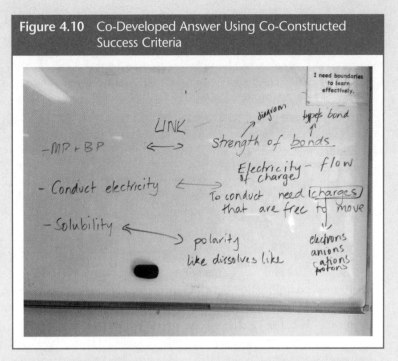

Source: Regina Menz, 2017.

Students then revisited the original exam question—Describe the properties of one allotrope of carbon and link the properties to bonding—using the co-constructed SC to break down and scaffold the answer, as shown in Figure 4.10.

The students worked with a learning buddy to co-construct an answer to their question. Each pair's response was given to a different pair to provide Descriptive Feedback using the SC. The two pairs then had a learning conversation during which verbal feedback was given to each pair by the other pair. The students then had an opportunity to rewrite their response using the feedback given.

The quality of the responses was very rich; it was evident that students had achieved higher-order, critical thinking. By using the SC, students understood clearly what was expected of them when writing their responses. As a result of co-constructing the SC, the students really owned the work and were very capable of providing accurate feedback

(Continued)

(Continued)

to each other and of constructing coherent, concise responses. These successes were also evident in their written responses in their final Grade 11 exam. Teachers and students had achieved collective efficacy. The co-construction of SC will continue to be used and the process modified by Powers and Menz as the students progress through Grade 12. Due to the CLARITY that students gained, their co-teachers, Powers and Menz, have decided that co-constructed SC will now form the basis of any work that they do in chemistry.

Source: Regina Menz, secondary school principal, Diocese of Armidale, 2017.

The CLARITY of the co-construction process and the use of the Gradual Release and Acceptance of Responsibility model to scaffold students' understanding highlight not only the teaching skill developed by the beginning teacher and the principal as co-learners, but also the power of the Co-Teaching Cycle and the positive effect on student learning. This case study precisely illustrates how students, at any grade level, use Descriptive Feedback against their co-constructed SC as an integral and powerful component of ongoing, daily assessment.

Descriptive Feedback

DESCRIPTIVE FEEDBACK

Explicit Descriptive Feedback is the ongoing, daily element in assessment that informs instruction and is provided to students in a timely, meaningful way. It is best used when students articulate what next steps they will take to improve their learning—always prior to a summative point in their learning. Teachers base their feedback to students only on the co-constructed SC. Descriptive Feedback must be in the moment, precise, and clearly understood by students.

To be precise, in each verbal or written piece of feedback, teachers state at least one way students have met the SC, and at least one (age- and level-appropriate) instructional point. Teachers facilitate assessment by ensuring the Descriptive Feedback is recorded and transferred into student learning and thinking. Descriptive Feedback is cognitive nourishment. As the example in the secondary case study above illustrates, students must have opportunities to practice and learn to offer Descriptive Feedback to other students based only on the SC, to ensure more accuracy and rigor.

It is essential that students receive feedback *during* the learning, and it's equally important that they are provided with sufficient *time to implement* what they have learned from the feedback. Both are critical steps in actually enhancing student learning.

Hattie (2012) states that feedback is most powerful when the nature of the feedback is related to the student's degree of proficiency (moving them from novice to proficient). Hattie (pp. 96–98) also reminds us that how well students are progressing (or not) is invaluable feedback for teachers in how well their teaching is increasing students' achievement— and how they must craft lessons to achieve the next level of proficiency. Skilled teachers see their role as evaluating their effect on students' learning, which places a key responsibility on teachers to understand the impact of their teaching on students' achievement and to respond with instructional precision to students' learning gaps.

Figure 4.11 demonstrates the power of the Venn diagram as a tool to provide teachers with ongoing assessment information that provides immediate feedback to differentiate instruction. For example, on the left in Figure 4.11, teachers record which students are getting the concept being taught (using the SC as a guide); in the middle, teachers record

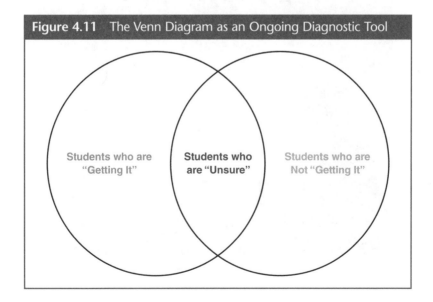

Figure 4.11 The Venn Diagram as an Ongoing Diagnostic Tool

Students who are "Getting It"

Students who are "Unsure"

Students who are Not "Getting It"

who is wobbly and uncertain; and on the right, teachers record students who aren't getting the concept. First, teachers invite those not getting it to gather in a small group for a mini-lesson to learn the concept in a clearer way—in other words, to reteach the concept because students are not getting it using the present method. Next, teachers take a small group who are wobbly to review and cement the concept, allowing those who grasp the concept to move forward. Assessment today becomes instruction tomorrow.

Supporting Students' Work Using Collective Feedback

There is power in giving students individual feedback and also in giving a class collective feedback. Collective feedback occurs when teachers observe that all students need to go deeper into a text or in understanding a concept. In Figure 4.12, Jennifer McGie, Ballarat Clarendon College, is literally and figuratively "sharing the pen" with her Grade 6 class as they deconstruct an anonymous piece of student writing. Using a document

Figure 4.12 Supporting Students' Writing Using Collective Feedback

Source: Lyn Sharratt, 2017.

camera, McGie and her students are "thinking aloud" as she examines the text with her students. Together they note important aspects of the writing and also try to revise sections that they all feel need improvement, always referring to their co-constructed SC as described above. Students most often need to see "what we're talking about" unfold explicitly in front of them. As such, students discuss improvements to the writing with McGie and also with each other, often getting into academic controversy—which is where the collective feedback makes collective learning happen!

PEER- AND SELF-ASSESSMENT

Building the capacity for students to peer assess and self-assess is an important goal in teaching. Student self-assessment is the process by which students gather information about and reflect on their own learning; that is, the *student's own assessment of personal progress in knowledge, skills, processes, and attitudes*. The ability to self-assess begins to develop in Kindergarten and forms another basis point for self-regulation. It demands that students use the SC as a reference when assessing their own work and the work of their peers. This leads to students' ability to reflect on and evaluate how to improve their own and others' work.

Bump-It-Up Walls Are a Peer- and Self-Assessment Tool

One way to provide students with a visual scaffold of expected practices is to co-construct Bump-It-Up Walls that allow students to improve their work by comparing it to exemplars and by following explicit next steps to achieve it. Bump-It-Up or Performance Walls are visual displays of rich performance tasks that explicitly show what low-level (Level 1) work might look like compared to what Level 2, Level 3 (expected), and Level 4 (the highest level) work looks like.

In Figure 4.13, the reader can see that the visual art work, in this secondary school example, progresses from a low Level 2 piece of work, to more detail in a Level 3 piece of work, to then become an intricate Level 4 piece of work. Teacher and students collaboratively discuss ways

Figure 4.13 Bump-It-Up Walls Show Students What It Takes to Get to the Next Level

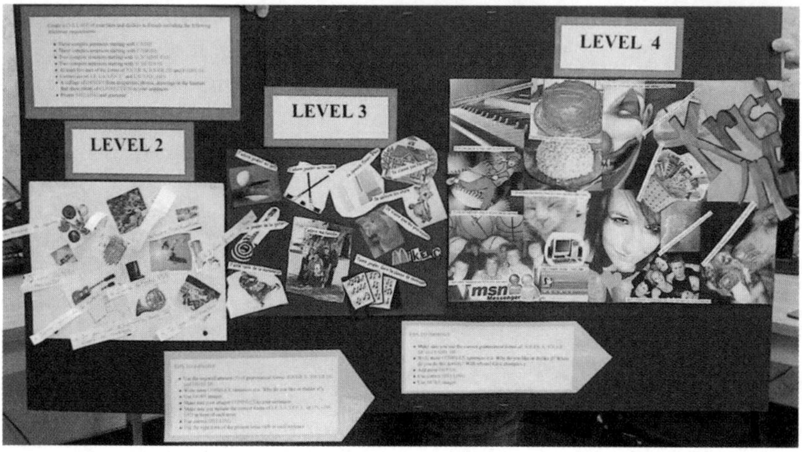

Source: Lyn Sharratt, York Region District School Board, Ontario, Canada, 2008.

to improve Level 2 and 3 work samples, then specifics are placed on the yellow cards between the levels to which students can refer. The yellow cards reflect the scaffolded thinking that occurs to attain the SC for this performance task. The SC are on the card in the top left corner of the photo in Figure 4.13. As seen in Figures 4.13, 4.14, and 4.15, the components of the SC need to be visible and understood by students, but students' finished work doesn't need to be the same as the exemplars—a teachable moment when Bump-It-Up Walls are co-constructed and discussed as opportunities to achieve excellence.

The purpose of Bump-It-Up walls is to show students that through self-assessment

- learning is iterative—it gets better with feedback and successive attempts,

- improvement is possible,

- work can always get better,

- students look for ways to improve and never settle for the first attempt.

Bump-It-Up Walls help teachers communicate clear expectations and help students develop the thinking skills required to become evaluators of their own work. They provide students with a visual reminder (and visual Descriptive Feedback) of what the SC look like and how to get there. Bump-It-Up Walls provide guidance for students to use in self-assessment and goal setting. They anchor the learning and ensure a common vision of the LIs and SC.

What it takes to get to the next level is shown on the wall and discussed often in class. Students and teachers co-construct what is required to move the piece of work from a low to high level. As shown in Figures 4.14 and 4.15, Bump-It-Up Walls allow students to see what their next expected level of work is and to discuss with teachers and each other how they will reach it.

Figures 4.14 and 4.15 show that these exemplar-based Bump-It-Up Walls take self-assessment to a higher level of student and teacher agency when teachers and students co-construct them. The self-assessment process leads students to a greater self-awareness and understanding of themselves as learners. Explicit peer- and self-assessment, against the SC, leads to individual goal setting by students.

Figure 4.14 Example of a Primary Classroom Bump-It-Up Wall

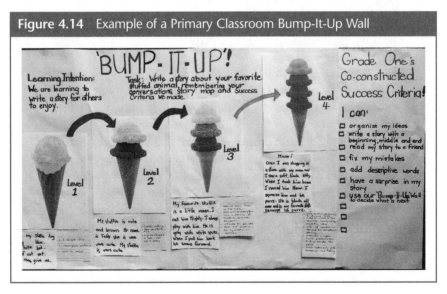

Source: Lyn Sharratt, 2018.

Figure 4.15 Example of a Grade 11 Bump-It-Up Wall—Moving From a "C" to an "A"

Source: Lyn Sharratt, Brisbane Catholic College, 2017.

Individual Goal Setting

INDIVIDUAL GOAL SETTING

The ultimate destination of assessment for and as learning in the Assessment Waterfall Chart (Figure 4.4) is developing the capacity for individual goal setting by students, in collaboration with other students, or with teachers and students conferencing together. When students achieve CLARITY from deconstructed LIs, co-constructed SC, and Descriptive Feedback to amend or revise their own work, there are no surprises for anyone when summative evaluation takes place. Students and teachers can judge for themselves how well they have done.

Teachers must continuously ask, "Can my students apply what has been learned to new situations?" This can occur only when co-constructed SC are used so that students can assess their work or when they use teacher Descriptive Feedback to self-assess and improve their work, thereby becoming independent learners—taking ownership of their learning. In Figure 4.16, students have determined the questions they must ask themselves at each step of the goal-setting journey.

Figure 4.16 The Cycle of Student Self-Assessment

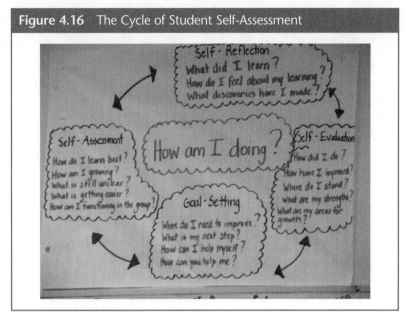

Source: Lyn Sharratt, 2009.

Beginning with self-assessment:

- How do I learn best?
- How am I growing?
- What is still unclear?
- What is getting clearer?
- How am I functioning in the group?

Progressing to self-reflection:

- What did I learn?
- How do I feel about my learning?
- What discoveries have I made?

Moving to self-evaluation:

- How did I do?
- How have I improved?

- Where do I stand?

- What are my strengths?

- Where are my areas for growth?

and finally, finishing with a clear picture of the questions to ask when individually setting goals:

- What do I need to do to improve?

- What is my next step?

- How can you help me?

- How can I help myself?

This completes the discussion of each component of the Assessment Waterfall Chart.

How is this individual learning using formative assessment captured by teachers for whole-class learning? Developing Learning Walls, as a critical component of the Third Teacher, is one way of recording class learning progress, as well as individual progress.

LEARNING WALLS CAPTURE THE ONGOING ASSESSMENT JOURNEY

Whereas a Bump-It-Up Wall focuses on the micro level of a specific rigorous performance task, a classroom Learning Wall looks at the big picture, macro level of the big ideas and concepts that are being taught in the classroom and reflects assessment for, as, and of learning. The Learning Wall is a concrete, visual, and pedagogical documentation complete with LIs and SC. Classroom Learning Walls are formative (How are we individually progressing and what will each of us need to do next in our learning?) and summative (Here's what we have learned—how did it go?).

When Learning Walls are routinely used by teachers and students, they give students opportunities to articulate how they are doing and enable them to identify what they understand, are starting to understand, or where they may be in between or unsure. Once students have accurately self-assessed, teachers then can take small groups of students who are unsure or not getting it to the guided table, or in small groups for mini-lessons, to teach the concept in a new way. It is critical to understand that teaching in a new way is not teaching in the same way but louder and longer; it is about finding a new approach that is suited to a student's specific needs.

To use a Learning Wall successfully, the classroom environment must be safe and encourage risk taking. Students need to be comfortable to say that they didn't understand a concept when it was taught or introduced. Students' voices regarding their understanding offer clear feedback for teachers about the success (or not) of the lesson. Students must not be made to feel guilty when they don't understand. Teachers must treat this self-assessment as an opportunity to differentiate their instruction, in response to student self-review.

Figure 4.17 shows the progressions on the Learning Wall that Grades 4, 5, and 6 teacher Daniel Farrawell has constructed with his students. Because this is a blended classroom, there are two parallel Learning Walls: the bottom Learning Wall is for Grades 4 and 5; the top is for Grade 6. Using the Learning Wall as a discussion starter, students self-assess how well they have done in meeting the SC they developed together as they progressed through the unit.

Figure 4.17 The Classroom Learning Wall

Source: Lyn Sharratt, Hamilton Island State School, Australia, 2017.

GETTING STARTED WITH
CLASSROOM LEARNING WALLS

The most important prerequisites to employing this strategy are building Accountable Talk (see Chapter 5) among students and ensuring robust SC on visible anchor charts.

1. Start with the curriculum expectations for a unit of study or a Collaborative Inquiry.

2. Note the alignment among content, standards, or assessment guides; select the expectations that can be grouped together to form the big idea(s) and promote essential questions, as discussed above.

3. Co-develop the LIs and SC for a unit of work and display them on a Learning Wall in the classroom (note in Figure 4.17 the water theme of the Learning Wall, to coincide with the classroom unit of study).

4. Discuss the Learning Wall concept with students. Teacher to student: "Where would you put yourself on the wall: 'I didn't get it'; 'I'm unsure in learning this concept'; or 'I got it, so let's move on'?"

5. Listen to student voice in the development of the Learning Wall. For example, one student places herself on the wall and clearly uses evidence to support why she placed herself at the top. (It is really important that the student articulates her evidence in line with the SC to clear up any misconceptions.) In this example, one student voiced that she was hesitant in her learning of the concept, which gave her teacher a clue about what the next steps would be for her at the guided table. This is an important stage in gathering evidence to inform the next steps in differentiating the teaching and learning.

6. Chat about the learning and discuss with students where they are and how they can improve using the SC and exemplars displayed in the classroom.

When classroom Learning Walls move from teacher-made to student-owned walls, the learning is transformational. When we listen for and really hear the voices of the students self-assessing their understanding in classrooms, we can celebrate success. This only occurs when students have CLARITY because teachers have been precise about their expectations.

Lessons Learned: When Assessment Becomes the Heart of the Matter

The following impactful characteristics are in place wherever assessment for and as learning have become central to system and school improvement.

1. **CLARITY:** Students and teachers are empowered when they know the learning destination with scaffolded signposts along the way.

2. **Empowerment:** Engagement moves to empowerment when teachers and students give and get feedback related to the SC.

3. **Co-Learn:** Teachers and leaders need to unpack the Assessment Waterfall Chart and apply each component to their own contexts and curriculum expectations.

4. **Assessment Literacy**: Planning with the end in mind and knowing where each learner is and how to move him or her way beyond is both an expectation and an outcome of quality teaching.

5. **Teachers Make It Happen**! Teachers need time to work together as co-planners, co-teachers, co-debriefers, and co-reflectors to implement and embed assessment practices that are transparent to and meaningful for students.

This is CLARITY: precision in action that doesn't happen accidentally. Intentional structures creating co-learning experiences move collaboration from being rather abstract, unrelated events to tangible, ongoing, trial-and-error investigations about learning. Having covered the aspects of the Assessment Waterfall Chart here in Chapter 4, I will next look at the other arm of the Waterfall Chart—Instruction—in Chapter 5 because assessment and instruction are inextricably linked.

COMMITMENT

I commit to

- using data to begin every meeting and every planning session,

- using assessment data to flexibly group students for differentiated instruction as needed,

- having an open-to-learning mindset in order to develop students' wonderings about big ideas and essential questions,

- deconstructing LIs and co-constructing SC,

- using SC to give and receive Descriptive Feedback to and from students,

- using SC to teach students how to peer- and self-assess,

- circulating during independent time and using the Venn diagram to bring students to the guided table who are not getting the concept,

- engaging in teacher-student conferences on an ongoing basis to establish individual goals for learning.

A DELIBERATE PAUSE TO CREATE CLARITY

What are the strengths and opportunities presented in this chapter that would be most beneficial if implemented in your school or system? Where might you start? Assess your practice using the Assessment Waterfall Chart components as the expectation. How can Bump-It-Up Walls be co-constructed with your students? How could Learning Walls be developed for the Grade 11 chemistry class? How is the assessment information in this chapter linked to the 5 Questions for students you ask in Learning Walks and Talks (refer to Chapters 2 and 9)?

Visit the companion website at
resources.corwin.com/CLARITY
for videos and downloadable resources

CHAPTER 5

CLARITY IN TEACHING
Instruction

Wonderings...

1. How do teachers use assessment information to inform the next steps in instruction?

2. How do classroom teachers differentiate instruction to meet all students' needs?

3. How do we ensure that our instruction equips students with the fundamental literacy skills needed in an ever-changing world?

4. What is the repertoire of high-impact strategies needed by every teacher to meet the needs of all students?

5. What is the evidence that teachers use to show students' growth and achievement?

6. What actions do leaders take to demonstrate instructional leadership?

What are you, the reader, wondering?

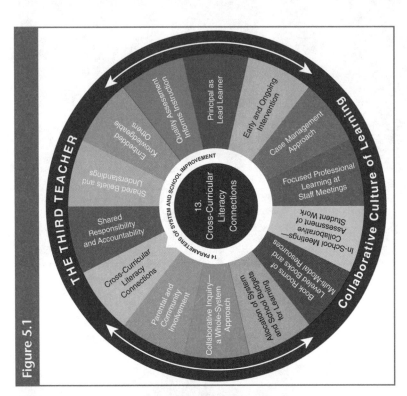

Figure 5.1

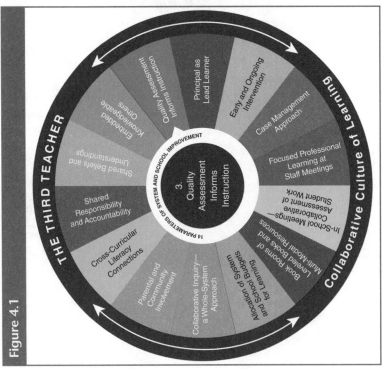

Figure 4.1

PARAMETER #3: ASSESSMENT INFORMS INSTRUCTION AND PARAMETER #13: CROSS-CURRICULAR LITERACY CONNECTIONS

In this chapter, I focus on Parameter #3: Assessment Informs Instruction and Parameter #13: Cross-Curricular Literacy Connections because literacy is everyone's business; it must be evidenced in every K–12 classroom. This discussion of instruction focuses on literacy, that is, language and mathematical literacy, as it underscores the vital importance of fundamental literacy skills required not only in student-centered classrooms but also in ensuring literate graduates across the globe (see Preface for discussion of illiteracy).

It is difficult to separate assessment and instruction. They are two sides of the same coin. You cannot have one without the other, and they are equally important in that you can never make a coin so thin that there is only one side. When you hold a coin between your fingers, you can feel both sides. You *know* both sides are there. In the same way, Figure 4.4: The Assessment Waterfall Chart could just as easily have been labeled The Instruction Waterfall Chart (see Figure 5.2). The real strength of the two sides—assessment and instruction—is when they work together.

This chapter looks at the other side of the coin—instruction—following on from the purpose of assessment for and as learning. Assessment's greatest power is its two-sided strengths.

Assessment side of the coin: By demonstrating their learning in the assessment for and as learning and by the questions they ask teachers and the answers they give, students provide powerful feedback to teachers about where they are in their learning and what they need next. When students can articulate and become accountable for their own improvement, they give teachers valuable insight into the instruction needed next.

Instruction side of the coin: By providing feedback to students during the course of learning about the gap between where they currently stand and the co-understood desired performance, teachers can determine what instructional approaches they will use with one student, with small groups of students, and with a whole class.

Is this complex? Not really. Two sides of the same coin. In considering instruction, we can build on the premise from Chapter 4 that *all* students can

- co-determine assessment Success Criteria with the teacher,

- provide accurate Descriptive Feedback to self and peers,

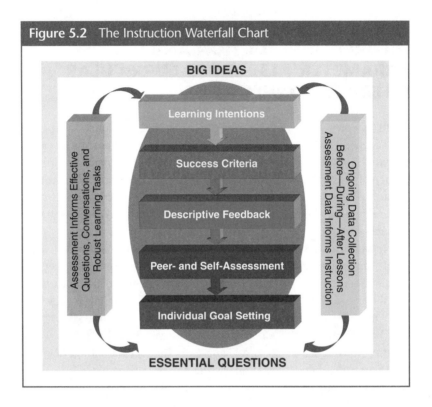

Figure 5.2 The Instruction Waterfall Chart

BIG IDEAS

Learning Intentions

Success Criteria

Descriptive Feedback

Peer- and Self-Assessment

Individual Goal Setting

Assessment Informs Effective Questions, Conversations, and Robust Learning Tasks

Ongoing Data Collection Before—During—After Lessons Assessment Data Informs Instruction

ESSENTIAL QUESTIONS

- define strengths and areas for personal growth,

- set personal learning goals and work toward them,

- monitor their progress and be accountable for their improvement.

LITERACY LEARNING IS THE FOUNDATION OF ALL INSTRUCTION

Literacy instruction underpins this discussion as its importance surpasses any moral imperative we individually or collectively may have. Literacy is freedom and the foundation of democracy. I believe it is every student's right to learn to read, write, do mathematics, and think critically—to become a critically literate graduate (see Figure 5.3). These skills must be developed and reinforced as students become skilled within 21st-century pedagogies such as Collaborative Inquiry, knowledge building, and integrative thinking, discussed in Chapter 6.

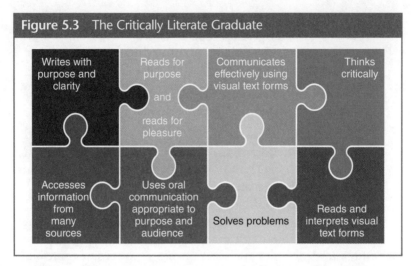

Figure 5.3 The Critically Literate Graduate

Writes with purpose and clarity	Reads for purpose and reads for pleasure	Communicates effectively using visual text forms	Thinks critically
Accesses information from many sources	Uses oral communication appropriate to purpose and audience	Solves problems	Reads and interprets visual text forms

Source: Adapted from York Region District School Board, Ontario, Canada; and Sharratt & Harild, 2015.

The following eight literacy principles extend the Shared Beliefs and Understandings of Parameter #1 and the Shared Responsibility and Accountability of Parameter #14. They underpin everything that must be done in improving system, school, and students' achievement in teaching and learning.

LITERACY PRINCIPLES

1. Literacy learning transforms students' lives.

2. The goal of all cross-curricular literacy instruction is to enable students to make meaning from and in the wide range of texts and media that they will encounter and produce at school and in the world.

3. All students can develop as literate learners when they receive scaffolded support that prepares them for higher-order thinking and growing interdependence.

4. Students are motivated to learn when they encounter interesting, diverse, and meaningful texts on topics that matter to them.

5. Teachers continually assess the literacy learning of their students in order to design classroom instruction that will promote critical thinking for each student.

6. Teachers and leaders continually develop their professional knowledge and skills, drawing on lessons from research, experience, and each other to improve their intentional teaching of a literacy skill in every subject-area lesson.

7. Leaders and teachers value the importance of literacy as the foundation of their students' future successes.

8. Successful literacy learning is a team effort, requiring the support of the whole learning community—including teachers at all grade levels, school leaders, support staff, system leaders, parents, and community members.

While most educators would nod approval at these understandings, for some it becomes more difficult when they realize teachers must have time with Knowledgeable Others (see Chapter 8) to become consciously skilled in literacy instruction; that is, all teachers must see themselves first as literacy teachers, K–12, and then as subject specialists. Consciously skilled (discussed in Chapter 8) teachers are able to talk about their practice, and work alongside leaders to explain why they do what they do, with confidence (Parameter #1). They aren't accidentally competent or sometimes competent. All teachers need to understand and be able to use the following component parts of literacy development that cross all content areas to contribute to developing critically literate graduates:

1. Oral language

2. Reading comprehension

3. Critical literacy

4. Writing

5. Accountable Talk

6. Gradual Release and Acceptance of Responsibility model

7. Differentiation

8. Higher-order thinking and robust performance tasks

These eight big ideas form a substantive foundation and a varied repertoire of instructional approaches that each teacher needs at the ready in order to meet all learners' needs. Oh, these are not primary school–only strategies. Far from it. They are unlimited and unlimiting. They are unpacked in sequence in this chapter.

EIGHT COMPONENTS OF HIGH-IMPACT LITERACY INSTRUCTION

1. ORAL LANGUAGE

Oral language is the pillar of the critically literate graduate. It is the driver of all social interaction and, hence, learning. As Bandura (1977) said, learning is a social process. Embedding oral language strategies in every lesson, K–12, is just **good first teaching** that supports what we know from neuroscience and experience. We know that all students learn in many different ways and that each student learns in many unique ways. Oral language is one way everyone learns, to one degree or another. And all teachers can learn very quickly, using oral language techniques, just how well students are learning and what they, as teachers, may need to do to improve the learning. Teachers use oral practice/rehearsal in the following ways:

- using participation prompts, such as Think Alouds (Modeled Reading), Think-Pair-Share, Say Something

- using skilled questioning to promote critical thinking

- providing wait time to allow students to process and increase participation

- using inclusive, inviting language that respects the learner

- checking for understanding—often

Oral language is not just for students in the early years, although importantly it begins there. Oral language evolves into productive Accountable Talk (see #5 below). It is critical to continue to embed oral language by intentionally teaching students to talk accountably, beyond the early years.

2. READING COMPREHENSION IS THE LYNCH PIN

Vocabulary building, letter-sound recognition, using the three cueing systems (see Figure 5.4), decoding, and making sense of print are where we begin in learning to read. Figure 5.4 illustrates how all three cueing systems work together and must be analyzed to determine student needs in learning to read.

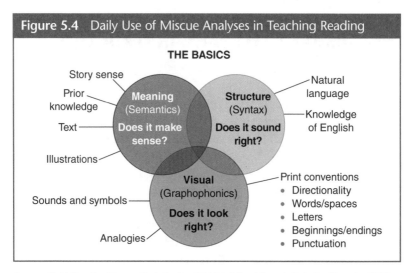

Figure 5.4 Daily Use of Miscue Analyses in Teaching Reading

THE BASICS

Story sense
Prior knowledge
Text
Illustrations

Meaning (Semantics)
Does it make sense?

Structure (Syntax)
Does it sound right?

Natural language
Knowledge of English

Sounds and symbols
Analogies

Visual (Graphophonics)
Does it look right?

Print conventions
- Directionality
- Words/spaces
- Letters
- Beginnings/endings
- Punctuation

Source: *Guidelines for Literacy,* York Region District School Board, Ontario, Canada, 2007.

However, our goal in moving to reading to learn, as proficient readers can, is for students to be able to read fluently with comprehension using all the techniques that highlight each comprehension strategy listed in Figure 5.4. We know that reading without meaning is not reading. Reading must become an integrated process that is best applied in a context that students see as meaningful and that encourages them to think creatively and critically about what they are reading. When all components of comprehension, shown in Figure 5.5, are deeply embedded as a metacognitive skill, then students relish the opportunity to become critically literate.

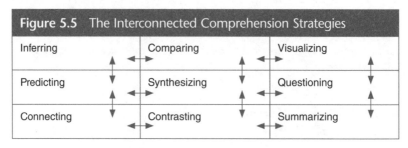

Figure 5.5 The Interconnected Comprehension Strategies

Inferring	Comparing	Visualizing
Predicting	Synthesizing	Questioning
Connecting	Contrasting	Summarizing

I am completely convinced that all teachers must be reading teachers in every subject area and at every grade level because of the power it brings to teaching practice, as indicated in Parameter #13: Cross-Curricular Literacy Connections. Here, Assistant Principal Kerry Faichney (personal communication, 2017) has outlined (1) what struggling readers may do and (2) the Success Criteria readers demonstrate when they can navigate text independently.

Struggling Readers:

- view themselves as poor readers and writers (lack confidence)
- are unaware when they aren't comprehending and keep on reading without understanding
- doubt their ability to understand text, often before reading begins
- allow their minds to wander during reading
- don't see connections between texts or personal experiences/prior knowledge
- demonstrate limited prior knowledge of content material
- approach all texts in the same way
- avoid reading long enough so it causes low fluency
- have relatively weak vocabulary

Effective Readers:

- make text-to-self, text-to-text, and text-to-world connections to understand the text by activating a schema
- determine the important details or facts to understand the text
- predict by thinking ahead while reading and anticipating information and events in a text
- ask questions as they read
- make inferences as they read
- visualize by creating pictures in their minds
- synthesize their reading by combining the new ideas from the reading with what they already know
- use fix-up strategies when their comprehension breaks down (re-read, ask clarifying questions, think of something they know that is similar, find a part they know and make inferences)

SCAFFOLDED TEACHING

Scaffolded teaching is carefully provided step-by-step, targeted instruction to take students from where they are to where they need to be in the next level of learning and acquisition of knowledge and skills. Teachers must recognize student needs and interpret them accurately to craft the next steps for instruction.

What must change in teacher practice to move students from "struggling" to "effective" readers?

Teachers must consider scaffolded instruction, best determined using the Gradual Release and Acceptance of Responsibility model (discussed below), in providing texts that are leveled and start where the student is, and then are increasingly demanding in their use of specialist language, technical features, jargon, precision, density—that is, **scaffolding** the greater cognitive demands placed on the struggling reader. After the early years, most students receive little or no ongoing instruction to help them negotiate meaning with increasingly challenging texts. All teachers must weave literacy instruction, intentionally scaffolded, into all subject areas to make meaning explicit not only for struggling literacy learners but for all learners, to stretch them beyond their present performance levels (Kerry Faichney, personal communication, 2017).

3. CRITICAL LITERACY

QUESTIONS TO ASK IN DETERMINING CRITICAL LITERACY SKILLS

- Knowing what we know about who created this text, how do we expect the author to treat the subject matter?
- Why are we reading or viewing this text?
- What do we already know about the text based on what we can see?
- What do the images suggest? What do the words suggest?
- What kind of language is used in this text? What is its influence on the message?

- What do you interpret to be the author's intent? Explain.

- With whom do you think the author wants us to identify or sympathize?

- Who is the target audience? How do you know?

- How might different people interpret the message of the text?

- How are children, adolescents, or young adults represented in this text? How are boys or girls represented?

- What has been left out of this text that you would like to have seen included?

- Is the text fair? Does it treat the subject matter/sides/parties fairly?

- Who benefits from this text? Who does not?

- What does the reader/viewer need to know ahead of time in order to really understand this text?

- What is real in the text? What is not real? How is reality constructed?

- How might the creator of this text view the world? Why do you think that?

Source: Compiled by Michelle Sharratt, University of Toronto, 2015.

Critical literacy is the capacity for a particular type of thinking that involves looking beyond the literal meaning of text to observe what is present and what is missing, in order to analyze and evaluate the text's complete meaning and the author's intent. Critical literacy goes beyond conventional critical thinking in focusing on issues relating to fairness, equity, and social justice (Ontario Ministry of Education, 2006).

Helping students acquire, practice, and invent critical literacies means that teachers must make the time for students to

- take analytical stances by understanding and identifying where a problem or issue exists,

- research how things are, how they got to be that way, and how they might be changed for the better,

- produce texts that represent the under- and misrepresented (adapted from National Council of Teachers of English, 2001).

Many local and world issues are relevant to students at different stages of their learning. Social justice issues engage the critical thinker in taking analytical stances. This begins with learning to read between and beyond the lines. The skills of critical literacy need to be intentionally and explicitly taught across the curriculum, in every subject area, as highlighted in Parameter #13 and illustrated in Figure 5.6.

A powerful way of embedding critical literacy, especially for struggling learners, is to use the 3 R structure: retell, relate, and reflect.

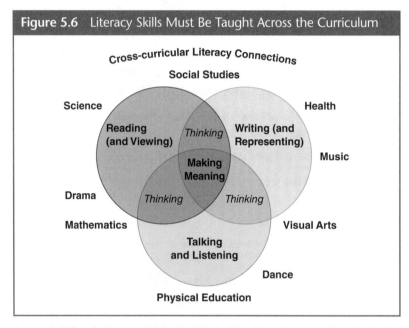

Figure 5.6 Literacy Skills Must Be Taught Across the Curriculum

Source: *Guidelines for Literacy,* York Region District School Board, Ontario, Canada, 2007.

A VISION OF CRITICAL LITERACY FOR THE ADOLESCENT LEARNER

By secondary school, all students must be equipped with the literacy skills to be critical and creative thinkers, effective meaning makers and communicators, collaborative co-learners, and innovative problem solvers in order to achieve personal, career, and societal goals. All students, individually and with others, develop abilities to

Think

Access, manage, create, and evaluate information in order to think imaginatively and critically, to solve problems and make decisions, including those related to issues of fairness, equity, and social justice.

Express

Use language and images in rich and varied forms to read, write, listen, speak, view, represent, discuss, and think critically about ideas.

Reflect

Apply metacognitive knowledge and skills, develop self-advocacy, a sense of self-efficacy, and interest in life-long learning (Edugains, 2016).

Reflective Thinking Is Critical Literacy

Reflection as a habit of mind facilitates thinking and problem solving. It demands self-assessment (the ultimate), goal setting, and problem solving on one's feet—all ways of being that we want for all learners (Schwartz & Bone, 1995). Too often we see students merely retelling or recounting teacher ideas in classrooms. The teaching of reading must move beyond remember, recount, or retell to intentionally plan for relate and reflect!

The 3 R's Framework Explicitly Supports Critical Literacy

When I taught Kindergarten to Grade 10, and now in teaching graduate students at the University of Toronto, I used and continue to use Susan Schwartz and Maxine Bone's 3 R's—the retell, relate, reflect framework—to enhance knowledge, generate questions, and develop metacognitive awareness. It is applicable at all levels.

I believe that explicitly teaching the 3 R's stretches students beyond lower-level thinking in retelling/recounting (*Describe your actions and the experiences they represent*) to the higher-level thinking demanded by relating (*Why is it meaningful to you? What connections can you make to your experiences, your school, articles, media, issues, other perspectives?*)

and reflecting (*What did you learn? What are your insights? What are your "aha" moments? How did you grow?;* Schwartz & Bone, 1995).

Sample questions and thinking prompts that are foundational to the 3 R Framework follow.

Questions for Retell

"What is the issue, concept, main idea, or area that I need to address in this answer?" "What do I know about it?" Retell questions such as these refer to descriptions of knowledge, understandings, and/or beliefs. They are lower-level comprehension questions.

Thinking Prompts for Retell

- The most significant part was . . .
- Something I especially liked, valued, enjoyed was . . .
- Something I would like others to notice about this entry is . . .

Teachers must intentionally plan to ask higher-order questions about texts that students are comprehending, like the following relate and reflect examples.

Questions for Relate

"What experience have I had in this area? What prior knowledge do I have about this topic? What connections can I make?" Relate questions refer to sharing students' experiences and expertise, as well as making important connections to situations or events in their lives. Relating their experiences allows the teacher to see the breadth of students' ability to make meaning from what they have read by connecting to prior knowledge, posing questions, and so on.

Questions for Reflect

The final part of the 3 R framework is when students ask themselves, "What would I do if I were in this role?" "What insights and understandings can I share?" "What do I believe about it?" "What is my philosophy?" Students need to project or envision themselves in the role. While in this new role, students wonder what they would do or say. They try to articulate how the actions they would take would have influenced others. Speaking from the point of view of another person is an important part of being a responsive, capable, and confident reader/ thinker. This allows the reader to evaluate what has been read and to then create and extend ideas through synthesis and posing questions (adapted with permission from Schwartz & Bone, 1995).

Reflection in three parts (retell, relate, reflect) provides the opportunity to make sense of, and learn from, any experience and apply the learning appropriately to new and similar situations another time. This powerful framework for critical thinking gives readers the chance to explore thoughts and feelings, work through difficult or painful experiences, develop self-awareness, and adopt fresh insights by making conscious, spoken-out-loud, informed decisions after weighing all aspects of the text. This scaffolded approach to becoming critically literate leads me to write about the other critical half of reading and consider the power of writing—as reading and writing are tightly woven together. That is, reading and writing have a reciprocal, symbiotic relationship.

4. WRITING IS A POWERFUL CRITICAL THINKING SECRET

The power of writing is not to be dismissed. After watching students as struggling readers come alive with daily opportunities to write—about the ordinary things that were important to them—I became a firm believer that if you can read you can write, and if you can write you can read. Too often we miss the opportunity to use writing to teach reading and vice versa. Most students can't wait to write about real-life happenings— that are only sensational to them, like David's "My New Hair Cut" or Jeffery's "We Went Tobogganing Last Night," and so on. The audience and purpose for writing across the subject areas has to be authentic and relevant to our student writers.

In science, geography, or mathematics, the ability to write detailed observations, stages of erosion, or steps in the solution to a problem depends on the ability to read and comprehend what is being read (see Parameter #13 in Chapter 1). Using writing in various subject strands informs teachers about the level of literacy as much as it informs teachers about the level of content knowledge developed. At that point, the teacher becomes a teacher of literacy—helping students to uncover the language of the discipline and to find their way in differentiated groups for instruction. The critical thinking skills used in writing (see below) must persuade teachers in every subject area to see themselves as literacy teachers first and subject-area teachers second.

CRITICAL THINKING SKILLS USED IN WRITING

questioning, hypothesizing, interpreting, inferring, analyzing, comparing, contrasting, evaluating, predicting, reasoning, distinguishing between alternatives, making and supporting judgments, synthesizing, elaborating on ideas, identifying values and issues, detecting bias, detecting implied as well as explicit meanings

The Power of Nonfiction Writing

The power of nonfiction writing is another secret to be uncovered. I have found that when teachers let students write about things they want to learn concerning how the world works, student engagement skyrockets and bursts into student empowerment. Students can't wait to share with a writing buddy or meet the teacher in a small group to find out when they can do a final proofread and then publish their masterpieces. It is a celebration not to be missed when the "published author" proudly presents her book before an audience of keen parents and caregivers, or to the principal and assistant principal. Then comes the special occasion when the published book is coded and placed in the school library for all to sign and comment on when they have finished the reading.

Using Mentor Texts in Teaching Writing

The process of using reading to teach writing offers all students authentic experiences through the eyes of real authors. For example, I use mentor texts (rich pieces of my favorite literature to highlight instructional points) to illuminate text forms, illustrators' detail, special effects, and new genres for students to explore. Mentor texts are first introduced as a read-aloud, giving the students an opportunity to enjoy and to comprehend the whole text. Don't think the use of mentor texts is limited to primary or elementary school. Secondary and even graduate students can be engaged readily when the methodology is introduced well. Teachers and students who use mentor texts

- build on the knowledge of reading like a writer,
- notice authors' craft techniques,
- point out aspects of texts they admire,
- label and describe what the author has done,
- search for other examples of that technique or genre,
- try to emulate that technique in their own writing.

Using mentor texts propels the discussion of reflective writing to go beyond description of events and associated feelings (retell) to become writing that relates to and reflects on experiences, emotions, and points of view to make meaning.

Assist Struggling Writers by

- sharing and deconstructing exemplars
- being explicit about purpose and audience
- modeling the use of the writing process and how to use graphic organizers to generate and organize ideas
- providing constructive and corrective Descriptive Feedback
- utilizing the writing continuum (featured in this chapter) to have focused conversations with each writer about next steps

Co-Constructing a Writing Continuum

Students need to understand the curriculum expectations, written for them in student-friendly language and called the Learning Intentions. To experience this, I have used this co-construction process with teachers and students at every grade level. I always get the same reaction: "This is so valuable; why didn't I know about this before?" The writing continuum is a high-impact instructional tool to assist students in self-assessing where they are and where they need to go—that is, being able to see the next level of attainment for them. The writing continuum process, across the subject disciplines, assists all students but begins with teachers and leaders first experiencing the development of a writing continuum.

Tips for Creating a Successful Writing Continuum, K–12

The steps in co-creating a writing continuum with students and teachers are sequentially laid out below by Elaine Krause, a teacher in Saskatchewan, Canada. She has refined the process over several years of practice. Note: Students need to be familiar with the process of writing paragraphs, for example, before creating a writing continuum.

1. Use anonymous writing samples from your grade level.

2. Choose samples from outside your current classroom.

3. Save students' work from year to year to use as writing samples.

4. Remember that continua can be used with all types of writing.

5. In order for all students to be on the continuum, ensure that you use 8 to 10 writing samples.

6. Create your continuum in such a way that every student is at least at the second or third exemplar so that each student can feel some success.

7. Have your students read all the writing samples.

8. Co-construct the attributes of the writing genre with your students and word the attributes in a positive manner. Post attributes along with the exemplars.

9. **Note: If your students cannot generate the attributes, you will need to review them.**

10. Take the time needed to look closely at the exemplars; it is well worth the effort, and it pays dividends for student learning.

11. Have students explain their thinking and point to evidence in the writing that supports their ideas.

12. Post the writing continuum where it is easily accessible, preferably at student eye-level so that students can easily assess their writing. You should refer to it many times during any

subject-area lessons, like science, with individual students as well as with the whole class.

13. The writing continuum should stay on the walls, be updated when necessary, and be used by all students in many content areas.

14. Allow students to choose their own starting point on the continuum based on the evidence of where they believe they are now.

15. Encourage students to verbalize where they are at on the continuum and talk about what they need to do to move forward. Give students verbal and written feedback on their self-assessments to ensure that students are genuinely working to improve their skills.

16. Add exemplars to the continuum as your students progress.

Krause's classroom is a lively place where students access the continuum as a matter of course, as shown in Figures 5.7 and 5.8. The photos reflect the Accountable Talk (discussed below) about writing that

Figure 5.7 Students Co-Creating and Using Their Classroom Writing Continuum

Source: Elaine Krause, teacher, Saskatoon Public School Division, Saskatchewan, Canada.

Figure 5.8 Students Discover Their Next Steps in Writing

Source: Elaine Krause, teacher, Saskatoon Public School Division, Saskatchewan, Canada.

empowers students to own their improvement and to know their next steps in writing.

Co-constructing a classroom writing continuum is exactly the CLARITY needed so that students can see how to become capable self-assessors—knowing and owning their next level of improvement. Developing a writing continuum has a place in classrooms across subject disciplines, K–12, as shown in Figure 5.9 from a Grade 7 classroom, Ballarat Clarendon College. To optimize comprehension and learning, every teacher must make literacy skills explicit in every subject area.

Deep literacy learning enables deeper thinking. Figure 5.5 (above) illustrates that literacy skills are the point of intersection in all subject areas and the commonality among all subjects that can assist students in making connections and meaning. This occurs in learning spaces that honor students' voice and choice and where making meaning is explicitly taught through Accountable Talk.

Figure 5.9 Secondary Co-Constructed Writing Continuum

Source: Lyn Sharratt, 2017.

5. ACCOUNTABLE TALK

This discussion of the importance of **Accountable Talk** builds on the foundations begun in the Oral Language section (see component #1 above). Learning to express oneself literately is often difficult enough one-on-one with a teacher, without adding the stress of having to express a thought, or to read one's thoughts to a class of peers. Reading and writing, and even presenting a point of view verbally, must always begin with talking about one's thinking with someone else, such as a talk partner. Learners, from young learners to graduate students and adult PL participants, appreciate the opportunity for oral rehearsal first before being called upon to answer.

Effective teachers create communities of conversation where students can test out their ideas and new learning alongside their peers. It causes a deliberate pause for us to ask and monitor, **"Who is doing the most thinking and the most talking in our classrooms?"** The answer is found in Figure 5.10. Student talk in classrooms must tip the scales and outweigh teacher talk.

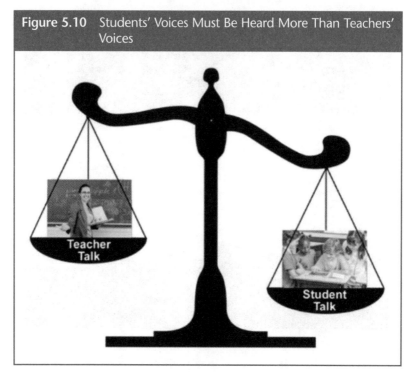

Figure 5.10 Students' Voices Must Be Heard More Than Teachers' Voices

Sources: iStock.com/bubaone; iStock.com/greyj.

By co-constructing operating norms and modeling what Accountable Talk looks and sounds like for speakers, listeners, and responders, teachers serve the instrumental role of creating and establishing the Third Teacher learning environment (see Chapter 1).

For example, teachers use and model

- attentive listening,

- think alouds,

- participation prompts,

- leading conversations,

- justifications of proposals and challenges.

Teachers have students practice these strategies, so they know how to own and present their own thoughts and learning and how to reflect on and respond graciously to the thoughts presented by their classmates. This is Accountable Talk.

A substantial portion of instructional time involves students in talk related to developing concepts, big ideas, and essential questions. To do this, teachers use instructional processes such as academic controversy, 4-corners, panel discussions, literature circles, case study exploration, mock trials, conferences, podcasts, presentations, interviews, debates, Think-Pair-Share, inside-outside circles, fish bowl, and so on.

Mathieson et al. (2007) propose that in order to create a learning environment that builds learning power, a teacher must create positive interpersonal relationships, honor student voice, and encourage perspective taking. Teachers can also nurture Accountable Talk by fostering a culture of learning and promoting an open-to-learning stance in the classroom where all responses are accepted, all students are respected, and mistakes are treated as rich opportunities for learning.

It is in this culture of learning that students learn from each other, through Accountable Talk. New knowledge is built together so that all students flourish. This is the goal. **Literacy learning that leads to critical literacy is the complex interaction of skills, resources, and thinking aloud that propels students to think critically and creatively.** In moving toward this goal, the learning must be scaffolded so that student learning is progressive, gradually releasing the responsibility of learning from the teacher to the student, who must accept it.

6. GRADUAL RELEASE AND ACCEPTANCE OF RESPONSIBILITY MODEL

The Gradual Release and Acceptance of Responsibility (GRR) model (adapted from Vygotsky, 1978) works effectively in any subject area, at any grade level. The approach allows teachers to differentiate instruction and flexibly group students with like needs for instruction, changing up groups on an ongoing basis and using in-class assessment data to inform the decision making. The scaffolding of instructional support from modeling to sharing to guiding and to becoming independent and culminating in applying new knowledge reinforces that one size doesn't fit all and ensures a gradual release of the ownership of learning. Releasing the learning to students and accepting new knowledge by students will be different depending on the readiness of students to accept that learning.

Many high-impact strategies, some discussed in this chapter, support this approach and accomplish the differentiation of instruction demanded in classrooms today.

The model moves on a continuum of *five* carefully planned scaffolds from high teacher support to low teacher support. This iterative model allows for differentiating the instruction for learners as follows.

1. **Modeled Practice:** Teachers explain, demonstrate, and think aloud. In reading and writing instruction, for example, teachers model, through think-alouds, what proficient readers and writers do while students listen and watch attentively (high teacher support)—teacher does and students watch.

2. **Shared Practice:** Teachers explicitly teach and teachers and students practice the strategy together. The student gradually assumes more and more responsibility for his or her learning (lower teacher support)—teacher does and students help.

3. **Guided Practice:** Students practice the skill or behavior with explicit coaching questions from the teacher to construct meaning, often at a quiet table in the classroom for guided support. Students return quickly to do the assigned work that is related to the skill/behavior practiced in the guided group (higher student participation)—students do and teacher helps.

4. **Independent Practice:** Students apply the skill/behavior on their own and receive teacher and peer feedback, taking ownership for their new learning, having opportunities to talk accountably with classmates (low teacher support and high student acceptance of responsibility for learning). Teachers are very engaged in this component of GRR as facilitators of small group and individual student conferences to ensure understanding—students do and teacher observes.

5. **Student Application:** Students apply previously taught skills to new genre, format, more difficult text, or another discipline, demonstrating a transfer of the learning to a new situation. Students can clearly articulate their thoughts and ideas about the new learning—students do on their own.

I find that many teachers model and then move swiftly to the independent stage of doing a hundred questions without taking time

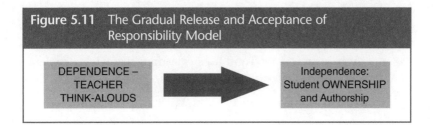

Figure 5.11 The Gradual Release and Acceptance of Responsibility Model

DEPENDENCE –
TEACHER
THINK-ALOUDS

Independence:
Student OWNERSHIP
and Authorship

to plan for sharing the learning, guiding the learning, supporting independent learning, and applying the learning in a different context. In any given classroom across all subject areas, there should be groups of students at many of these levels. When the GRR model of teaching is used, then thinking aloud, risk-taking, scaffolding, coaching and guiding, feedback, and reflection become habits of mind for learners. Ultimately, this approach to learning encourages students to become assessment-capable and know their expected next steps for learning.

Figure 5.11 demonstrates the GRR progressions when each of these five stages of development above is planned so that student learning is scaffolded over time. Unfortunately, this learning progression is not lock step but is scaffolded as determined by student needs. Thus, students will be working in small groups on like skills and move in and out of these groups as determined by assessment against the Success Criteria. Surely this approach is the art and science of teaching!

7. DIFFERENTIATED INSTRUCTION

The GRR model, explained above, offers a differentiated approach to instruction. Differentiated instruction allows teachers to extend the knowledge and skills of every student in every class, regardless of his or her starting point for instruction. Through differentiated instruction, teachers lift the performance of all students, including those who are falling behind and those who are moving ahead of grade-level expectations. Thus, differentiated instruction is a critical component of an effective classroom. Differentiating for instruction is based on students' strengths, needs, interests, and experiences, in order to ensure growth and achievement for all. Instruction is easily and fluidly differentiated when teachers follow the GRR model above. Teachers understand that students will be at every stage of learning at any time. Importantly, Learning Intentions and Success Criteria remain in place and unchanged while teachers differentiate the

- **environment**—the Third Teacher learning spaces (see Chapter 1) are co-created by teachers and students,

- **process**—varied instructional strategies,

- **resources**—varied levels of print and digital text forms reflect FACES in the class and the global community,

- **product**—various ways that students can demonstrate their learning to achieve the Success Criteria.

Use of diagnostics and assessment for and as learning and knowledge of the learners provide the evidence that teachers need to inform and differentiate instruction.

Differentiating instruction is a critical way to meet the needs of all students and leads one to think about having high expectations for all students and about **all teachers being students of their students** (Parameter #1). The latter demands teachers investigate and evaluate the impact that their teaching has on each student's learning. It is knowing what students need, why they need it, and what strategies to use to meet those needs. Teachers who differentiate purposefully achieve CLARITY for students and precision in practice for themselves and their co-teachers.

> Many principals and system personnel [in the study] believe that when differentiated instruction is occurring, students experience more positive outcomes. Students are perceived as more engaged in their learning and are seen as performing better academically as well as developing more confidence and self-esteem as learners. (Ontario Ministry of Education, 2012a)

Differentiated instruction allows students to demonstrate their learning in ways that reflect their own learning needs. Only when tasks are robust and open-ended can all learners across abilities demonstrate their learning.

8. HIGHER-ORDER THINKING AND ROBUST PERFORMANCE TASKS

Tasks predict performance. The use of thick questions and thick answers centered on Bloom's Taxonomy make higher-order thinking tasks possible in every lesson and unit.

Teachers need to teach students how to craft thick questions and answers using the verbs from Bloom's Taxonomy, so that students become routine users of higher-order verbs. The six higher-order thinking verbs are: Creating, Evaluating, Analyzing, Applying, Understanding, and Remembering. Higher-order thinking verbs combine with the use of graphic organizers to make a powerful learning approach. Graphic organizers assist in marshalling students' thoughts in ways that support their use of higher-order thinking verbs and thought processes.

Graphic Organizers

A graphic organizer is a visual display that demonstrates relationships among facts, concepts, or ideas. Graphic organizers guide the learners' thinking as they build upon visual maps or diagrams. The term is also used informally to describe all visual learning strategies, such as concept mapping, webbing, mind mapping, and many more. The benefits to learners who use and create their own graphic organizers include the following:

- helping to structure writing projects

- encouraging decision making

- making it easy to classify ideas and communicate

- allowing examination of relationships and responsibilities

- guiding learners in demonstrating their thinking process

- helping learners improve reading comprehension

- making it easy to brainstorm

- organizing essential concepts and ideas

- making it clear how to break apart main ideas

Higher-order thinking, graphic organizers, and rich performance tasks are closely linked. In thinking classrooms, oral rehearsal, Accountable Talk, and the use of graphic organizers provide the framework in which learners have opportunities to discuss and think through the logic of meaningful tasks. Tasks must be relevant to students' lives.

Robust Performance Tasks

Assessment and instruction are inextricably linked in the planning for robust or rich performance tasks. I use *rich, robust,* or *rigorous* interchangeably to describe the subtasks along the way to and final performance tasks at the conclusion of a unit of study. Teachers use the self-assessment questions posed in Figure 5.12 when carefully planning for a rich performance task as the culminating product in a unit of study or an exploration. Cognitively demanding and engaging performance tasks use all eight components of high-impact literacy instruction and are most compelling when students have choice and voice in demonstrating their learning in the way that they learn best.

Figure 5.12 Self-Assessment of a Robust Performance Task

Key Questions to Ask When Planning a Robust Performance Task

- Is there a clear link between the Learning Intentions from the curriculum expectations and the task that students are expected to do to demonstrate their learning?
- Is there evidence of the big ideas and essential questions being asked?
- Are the students involved in the co-construction of the Success Criteria they will use to self-assess their performance task?
- Is there an opportunity to give Descriptive Feedback linked to the Success Criteria?
- Does the task demand Accountable Talk through partner and small group work?
- Is the text selection suitable to the age and ability of the learners?
- Are there different entry levels for different learners?
- Does the task require higher-order thinking, reading, and writing?
- Is there an opportunity to scaffold the learning for each student?
- Is the task relevant to students' lives?
- Will it allow the students to demonstrate the Success Criteria to achieve the highest level of performance—an "A," for example?

Source: Compiled by Michelle Sharratt, University of Toronto, 2015.

Figure 5.12 represents some of the questions that are forerunners of planning to create rigorous performance tasks. Interestingly, students were asked a key question on a high-stakes, national assessment. Below is the question and one student's answer. Determine whether it is a rich task and then read how the student responded.

Is This a Rich Task?

Question: If you were setting up an aquarium for your little brother or sister, in an effort to interest him or her in sea life, would you choose barnacles or seahorses?

Student Answer: Seahorses

Question: Why would you make this choice?

Student Answer: Seriously? You want me to choose between a seahorse, a very exotic beautiful sea animal, or a barnacle, a creature that just sits around and does nothing? You've got to be kidding me. What kind of an idiot would be, like, "oh, let's make a super fun aquarium and fill it full of barnacles"?

I wonder what mark the assessor gave this student? If you are unsure that your "rich" performance task is as clever as you think, just ask your students. They will tell you! (I hope she got an A+!). Are the rich tasks you assign worthy of students' time to complete them? Consider that if you ask students to answer low-level questions and to complete low-level tasks, that is exactly what you will get in return—low-level responses and results.

Sample of a Secondary-Level Rigorous Performance Task

Students in Grade 10 at Emmaus College, Diocese of Parramatta, gave very positive feedback about the performance task they were asked to complete together as the final demonstration of their learning from a unit of study on *Macbeth*. The teachers co-planning notes for the unit are shared here.

Learning Intention: We are learning to creatively explore and represent one or more key themes of Power, Manipulation, Appearance and Reality, Gender, and Emotional Turmoil by using visual or written language features and forms to engage our audience of fellow students in real-life dilemmas.

(Continued)

(Continued)

Co-Constructed Success Criteria

I can:

- Compose or create a highly original product, exploring an insightful idea with a clear **purpose**
- Engage, orient, and address the appropriate **audience**
- Use highly sophisticated, original, and appropriate **language**, relevant to the chosen form
- Manipulate the **structure** of the piece in a highly engaging and interesting way, in order to create, shape, and influence meaning

Rich Performance Task

Explore one or more of the key themes from Shakespeare's play *Macbeth* as reflected in the Success Criteria. It is up to you what you will explore and how you will present your ideas. Think of both visual and written language and what creative forms and features you can work with to visually appeal to your audience. You may work individually, in pairs, or in a group of three.

Figure 5.13 demonstrates the intent of the original products that the Grade 10 students created to demonstrate their learning. All of

Figure 5.13	Secondary Students' Rich Performance Task Descriptors
Title of Work:	**Explanation:**
"Stay, tell me more" **Composer(s):** **MADIE AND ROBERT**	The art of tarot: the gazing of the future through divine cards, letting the unexpected become expected. The perceptions of the Macbeth tale are told through tarot, allowing the cards to narrate the story in metaphor and symbolism. Starting off at the beginning of the end, the quote of his destined demise: The Tower. Macbeth's reading proceeds to his undying ambition and the moment of realization when he discovers the truth in the *false* hope given by the witches' words of twist: Five and Ten of Swords. The Lovers and Death reversed, two major cards flipped for their meaning by the hand destiny, each reflecting on the journey of the Thane of Cawdor, the journey of a man unsated by the throne.

Source: Students Madison McKenna and Robert Cardona. Veronica Schinella, leader of learning, Emmaus Catholic College.

their products not only appealed to their audience of engaged peers at their exhibition but also demonstrated their deep learning connecting Shakespeare's work to their real lives.

This Grade 10 final performance task for the unit of study on *Macbeth* reflects the report by Willms, Friesen, and Milton (2009), reiterating that impactful instruction is characterized by the thoughtful design of learning tasks that

- require and instill deep thinking,
- immerse the students in interdisciplinary inquiry,
- are connected to the world outside the classroom,
- have intellectual rigor,
- involve substantial conversation.

From their report (Willms et al., 2009) and my experiences, I have developed the following Success Criteria for rich performance tasks.

Success Criteria for Rich Performance Tasks

I can

- use various types of reasoning to think and reflect critically,
- solve the task in both conventional and innovative ways,
- find solutions in many places beyond the classroom,
- create and share my new knowledge with others,
- be creative, original, and reflective,
- use multi-modalities and multimedia,
- make my thinking visible in interesting ways,
- collaborate with my partners and my learning community.

These Success Criteria become a self-assessment tool for both students and teachers as teachers plan to craft robust performance tasks for and with students, keeping in mind that the goal is to challenge and create critically literate graduates. The SC can be fleshed out by students providing even greater CLARITY to the characteristics of potential response products created. The following case study demonstrates that we must always plan for cognitively demanding tasks with high expectations in mind (Parameter #1) both in elementary and secondary classrooms.

CASE STUDY: HIGH-IMPACT INSTRUCTION DEMANDS STRETCHING STUDENTS' THINKING

Instructional coach Tracey Petersen shared with me an observation during a Learning Walk and Talk (see Chapter 9) that I think illustrates the need for planning for instruction that stretches students' thinking and assumes that every student is capable of an "A," as illustrated in the above Grade 10 example, Figure 5.4. Sometimes it is not apparent to teachers that their expectations are too low.

The following are the typical evaluative descriptors of curriculum expectations for English in Grade 2.

Curriculum Expectation: Students can create an alternative description of a character drawing on their own experiences, imagination, and information learned.

Level A Descriptor: Uses evaluative vocabulary to present the character's nonstereotypical traits. Varies sentence structure, including simple and compound sentences.

Level B Descriptor: Uses adjectives and expanded noun groups to present the character's point of view.

Level C Descriptor (Expected Level): Creates an alternative description of a character based on own experiences, imagination, and information learned.

Level D Descriptor: Provides information about the character.

Level E Descriptor: Lists characteristics.

Performance Task: The students must look at a stereotypical representation of a fox in a picture book and reimagine the fox as the opposite (alternate) to the stereotype. They then must write an imaginative piece that shows the alternative character description.

Reflections: The "A" standard says, "evaluative vocabulary." As the teacher, if I am open to everyone achieving an "A," then I need to invite the students to think about what sort of a character the fox is in the book. How does the author tell you that? This instruction is about studying the evaluative vocabulary that the author uses so that the reader can place himself or herself into the position of the author. Then the questions become, "What sort of a character is fox in your story? How have you told the reader that?"

This is a cognitively demanding task in Grade 2. It's about being able to use the story to show that fox is kind—how would they describe him? What would he do that was kind? What would he say/think to show he's kind?

I believe that we should all be teaching to that "A" level. Our challenge is *leaving the space in the task for students to creatively solve that problem* using the above level "A" descriptor/Success Criteria for a rich performance task.

However, during the Learning Walk and Talk, Petersen observed that the students were given a picture of fox. The teacher wrote words around her picture to describe the fox. These were not taken from the text, the thinking wasn't linked to the text, and the teacher only used students' prior knowledge without showing how to do that. Then the teacher asked students to write words around their picture and—guess what?—they were the same as the teacher's. Then the teacher asked the students to write antonyms for those words. When I look at the achievement standards above, so far, the teacher has taught the students to be performing at level "E"!

Next, the teacher took the list of antonyms and showed the students how to turn them into sentences. The teacher then sent the students to write their own text. Again—guess what—they wrote cookie-cutter versions of the teacher's text. When I asked the students, "What sort of a character is fox in the story?" they could each say "kind." But, when I asked them what they had written that showed fox was kind, none of them could tell me. They hadn't done the thinking, so they just didn't know.

This is not a bad teacher. This is just representative of the culture of teaching and learning in which it is ok to aim for a "C." We think we must provide students with each of the small steps, small skills, and tiny

(Continued)

(Continued)

parts. In doing so we are locking them out of the big idea thinking and asking the essential questions that they want to know more about. By not routinely demanding the thinking about the essential questions, we are, inadvertently, being gate-keepers of students' progress.

If our mission is to support and challenge teachers to be able to identify the thinking that is required of the task, then we must put the text into the hands of students and let them do that thinking. I am constantly challenging leaders to stand in the classroom and determine who is doing the most thinking in this classroom. Who is doing the most work in this classroom?

Source: Tracey Petersen, personal communication, 2017.

Gallimore and Emerling (2012) discuss durable teaching changes that have been instructive in developing our thinking about the block that we have in creating cultures of high expectations for all students through teachers' changed practices. They suggest three considerations:

- develop and improve teachers' professional knowledge for teaching (assessment that informs instruction)

- develop the judgment capacity needed to deliver timely and effective instruction and [critically] re-instruction

- address some conditions probably needed at the local, district, and school levels to get teacher teams to challenge themselves rather than settle for improving how they already know how to teach

These three critical points, especially the last one, reflect where we have been in this chapter in the thinking about and illustrating high-impact instruction to empower all learners. In Chapter 6, I build on the specificity needed in assessment and instructional practices to consider student and teacher co-led Collaborative Inquiry (CI). Co-led CI is a promising practice in all classrooms, to move students from receivers of knowledge to active participants in building knowledge through structured, collaboratively planned inquiry processes that honor their voices and choices.

COMMITMENT

I commit to

● ensuring that my best teachers are teaching the most struggling students and coaching other teachers;

● understanding and using GRR to model moving from dependent to independent learners;

● insisting that a literacy skill is intentionally taught in each subject area lesson;

● ensuring that independent reading and writing occur every day, K–12, in every subject area;

● expecting struggling students come to flexible guided groups every day;

● not purchasing prepackaged solutions;

● ensuring that all teachers are prevention and intervention teachers;

● using daily assessment to inform and differentiate instruction.

A DELIBERATE PAUSE TO CREATE CLARITY

What are the components that need to be considered when teaching intentional literacy skills in the content areas? How do you do that? How does assessment inform instruction? Where are you and your colleagues in understanding the eight high-impact instructional strategies? Compare and contrast Bump-It-Up Walls and the co-constructed writing continuum and decide which approach you and your team will take in ensuring CLARITY for all your students—and why. What can you learn from the case study about the impact of having low expectations? How do you hold each other responsible to and accountable for having high expectations? What do teachers think about when planning for higher-order thinking tasks in their classrooms? How will you know if a task is rich/rigorous/robust?

Visit the companion website at
resources.corwin.com/CLARITY
for videos and downloadable resources

Processes That Support
Collaborative Inquiry
With Students

Wonderings...

If students are to engage in Collaborative Inquiry in classrooms,

1. What do students wonder about?
2. What do students love?
3. What will students learn?
4. What will students create?
5. What "wicked problems" will students solve?
6. What can students do to have an impact on their world?
7. How will we assess students who are engaged in Collaborative Inquiry?

What are you, the reader, wondering?

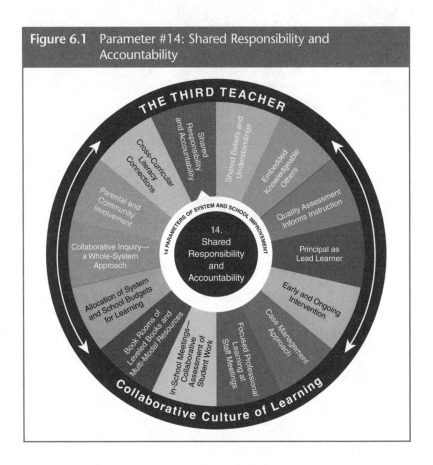

Figure 6.1 Parameter #14: Shared Responsibility and Accountability

PARAMETER #14: SHARED RESPONSIBILITY AND ACCOUNTABILITY

We are all responsible for every learner within and across our schools. The focus is that everyone knows and can articulate system, school, and classroom priorities that are clear, aligned, precise, and intentional.

"Where educational systems have developed their collective capacity and worked collaboratively, the achievement of students has increased more than in schools that have worked individually" (Sharratt & Fullan, 2009, 2012). In the same vein, "When teachers or students are working successfully on Collaborative Inquiry and achieving group goals, the Collective Efficacy created generates an effect size of 1.6" (Hattie, 2015).

Collaborative Inquiry (CI) in the classroom links directly to the discussion about instruction in the previous chapter. At its best, CI fosters students' and teachers' reflection and thinking while projecting a problem-solving disposition and embracing a commitment to further learning. Only then will students and teachers experience the Collective Efficacy to which Hattie refers.

COLLABORATIVE INQUIRY WITH STUDENTS

Mourshed, Chijioke, and Barber (2010) discussed that collaborative practice is the method by which a school system "hardwires" the values and beliefs implicit in its system into a form that manifests in day-to-day teaching practice. When system and school leaders model professional reflective practice through CI, as discussed in Chapter 3, teachers are able to support each other in modeling CI alongside students, as articulated in this chapter. System and school leaders need to think deeply about how CI will function in practice across the system, in all classrooms, and then take action to put structures and resources in place to make it possible for teachers to explore and emulate CI while teaching their students. The following case studies are examples of how teachers and students, from early years to secondary schools, develop a symbiotic inquiry capability.

CASE STUDY: COLLABORATIVE INQUIRY IN EARLY YEARS' CLASSROOMS

Katie Kniginyzky, Kindergarten teacher in Ontario, Canada, describes how to move from that top-down, teacher-directed model of teaching to a truly learner-centered approach using CI that enables teachers to listen to and build on the students' seeing, thinking, and wondering. It begins with listening to each child and noticing opportunities for implementing the curriculum expectations through rich literacy experiences and ongoing opportunities for collaboration and self-expression. For example, after a book introduction of *Stepping Stones: A Refugee Family's Journey* by Margriet Ruurs and Nizar Ali Badr (2016), Kniginyzky used purposeful questioning in order to differentiate instruction according to

(Continued)

(Continued)

each Kindergarten student's needs. Kniginyzky also provided a rich variety of resources that enabled her students to follow their wonderings while acquiring oral language, reading, and writing skills. This type of teaching demands a strong understanding of the curriculum standards and real adaptability in order to pull out those expectations through ongoing, in-the-moment questions and conversations with students.

Figure 6.2 shows one of the pieces of writing developed for the Kindergarten classroom during their work with the text. Kniginyzky invited Grade 5 students to create and write their stories about where they wanted to be in their stepping stones thinking. They modeled their writing, then read their illustrated stories to the Kindergarten students and engaged them in conversations from a writer's perspective.

Figure 6.2 Grade 5 Students Write for Kindergarten Students

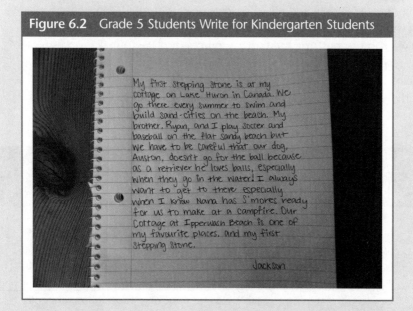

My first stepping stone is at my cottage on Lake Huron in Canada. We go there every summer to swim and build sand-cities on the beach. My brother, Ryan, and I play soccer and baseball on the flat sandy beach but we have to be careful that our dog, Auston, doesn't go for the ball because as a retriever he loves balls, especially when they go in the water! I always want to get to there especially when I know Nana has S'mores ready for us to make at a campfire. Our Cottage at Ipperwash Beach is one of my favourite places, and my first stepping stone.

Jackson

In another CI (Figure 6.3), Kniginyzky presented the children with a transparent painting easel and asked them what they could create together. They were instantly captured by the new perspective of seeing their fellow painters as they created together. At first, Kniginyzky and her co-teaching colleagues expected students would explore the materials, but they were surprised to see how the students collaborated from

Figure 6.3 Two-Sided Transparent Painting Project

Source: Katie Kniginyzky, Ontario, Canada.

the moment their paint brushes touched the canvas. The most insightful conversations developed as they created together. "I'm making the wind that's blowing the grass away" said S. J. "I'm making the clouds! One day I saw a lizard cloud," said A. G. "I'm making the sad rain and the big, happy grass. The grass is helping the rain be happy. That's what we have to do if someone is sad," said S. J. "I'm making a rainbow," said S. A. "I'm making the background of the sky," said A. G.

Kniginyzky noticed how the children listened carefully to each other and were inspired to add details together, creating a story through this captivating medium. As the teachers co-reflected on the conversations, they could

(Continued)

(Continued)

see the emotion and human characteristics that the children gave the elements of nature that they painted. This element of personification is often evident when students play outdoors together but seldom heard in classrooms.

Teachers as Researchers

Kniginyzky and her colleagues believe in the power of CI as it results in knowledge that forms from gaining multiple perspectives and points of view. They see that their critical role as educators has transformed to become "researchers of children and learning." They have formed a professional CI network where, as co-teachers, they are investigating the power of pedagogical documentation. This entails active listening, collaborative reflection, asking questions, and continuing to grow and learn together. A crucial aspect in the enhancement of their community of learners is the role of questioning their colleagues. Kniginyzky and her colleagues continue to ask themselves, "Why have we chosen this learning, for this child, and in this context?" as we plan, support, and learn alongside our students (Ontario Ministry of Education, 2016a).

An Early Years Assessment Protocol

These colleagues continue to use the Co-Teaching Cycle (see Chapter 8) to ask why and to support each other as they deconstruct the learning and reflect together. Just as it is the teachers' role to challenge and extend the children's learning, they have come to realize the importance of being risk takers when challenging each other as they grow together as teachers. Paramount in moving forward in their documentation is the "I see, I wonder, I think" protocol. These teachers are learning to support each other by sharing a sample of documentation, like a writing sample or a photograph of a learning experience, and following this protocol to unpack the learning in a small group. They have found that this protocol helps them to think carefully about

- the learning that is taking place,
- the role each child takes in the experience,
- appreciating different perspectives.

Questions and theories that arise using this protocol guide them to plan next steps as well as to create their analyses when writing their documentation panels.

Kniginyzky has come to realize the importance of creating an environment where fear is absent so that the potential for learning collaboratively is maximized. As colleagues in a constant state of inquiry, they are working together to rethink the learning environment (the Third Teacher—see Chapter 1) for their students as they support each other.

Source: Katie Kniginyzky, teacher, Ontario, Canada, personal communication, 2017.

Kniginyzky's narrative about CI is instructive as the lessons learned in Kindergarten apply to all grade levels, in every classroom, in every school. It's about inquiring into "good first teaching"—that is, the right of students to experience quality teaching in every classroom—and having clarifying discussions about "what works, why, and where do we go next?" How do teachers assess student learning in a CI?

ASSESSMENT IN ACTION

Assessment in action (Figure 4.4 in Chapter 4) is the ongoing process of gathering and interpreting information that accurately reflects the child's demonstration of learning relative to the knowledge and skills outlined in the overall curriculum expectations or standards. The primary purpose of assessment is to improve learning and to help children become self-regulating, autonomous learners (Ontario Ministry of Education, 2016a). Kniginyzky assessed each student using the expectations in *Growing Success: The Kindergarten Addendum: Assessment, Evaluation, and Reporting* (Ontario Ministry of Education, 2016a). Ongoing assessment of student-led CI focuses on observations, documentation, and reflecting on the learning, together, at the end of every lesson and school day. Kniginyzky followed the format of ongoing assessment of her students by documenting the following against the curriculum expectations (Success Criteria):

- Key learnings

- Growth in learning

- Next steps for learning

Through ongoing assessment in action, all of Kniginyzky's Kindergarten students could read and write at the expected levels by year's end in this joyful, investigative learning environment filled with wonder and curiosity.

The following secondary school CI example demonstrates again that CI is a powerful learning process for teachers and students, K–12, when assessment literacy—that is, owning your own learning—remains at its heart (see Figure 4.4).

CASE STUDY: COLLABORATIVE INQUIRY IN SECONDARY CLASSROOMS

How do you integrate technology in the classroom without "stapling new tools onto old ideas"?

That was the pivotal challenge Derrick Schellenberg says he and his team of high school English teachers faced when they began their Ontario Teacher Learning and Leadership Project with TVO, 2015.

Schellenberg, who is head of English at York Region District School Board's Sir William Mulock Secondary School in Ontario, Canada, worked with a team including three other teachers, all of whom were teaching Grade 11 University English.

Their investigation aimed to increase student engagement and deepen critical thinking, creativity, and innovation through the creation of authentic multimedia texts. Schellenberg defines these multimedia texts as "student-created, original, meaningful and relevant digital texts, which could include one or all of audio, video, and images." The teachers also wanted to align with the school's focus on CI.

The CI team began by teaching students how to use an array of digital tools, primarily the Google Apps for Education suite of tools, which includes Docs, Slides, Drive, Forms, and Drawings. Students were encouraged to experiment with the tools in order to expand their comfort level.

"We believe that by giving students tools for collaboration, both inside and outside the classroom, as well as providing the ability to see others' contributions in real time, we can create a more meaningful collaboration experience for our students," says Schellenberg. Their CI provocation was, "If we built a unit of study around inquiry questions and provided students with digital tools to access, analyze, synthesize and share information, then students would deepen their critical thinking skills."

"Ultimately, the idea was to move students from being users and consumers of digital tools to becoming producers and creators," Schellenberg says. That meant the teachers first had to know the tools well themselves, then explicitly teach the students how to use them—or be open to students extending the teachers' thinking. From there, the teachers connected the tools to the Ontario Secondary English curriculum.

Examples of Quality Student Work

So what did this look like in the classroom? "The teachers used the open-source learning management system Moodle as a central hub for the assignments," Schellenberg says, "along with the Google Apps for Education suite for collaboration and co-construction."

Below are some examples:

- A Grade 10 English performance task that used inquiry to engage students in learning about Shakespearean times. The students used Google Docs to develop their inquiry questions, collect research to discover answers, and create a final report on their findings. Teachers were able to leave Descriptive Feedback for each student right on the Doc.

- A Grade 11 English assessment asked students to develop a trailer (short video) and Google Form related to their independent study unit to ask their peers questions about their inquiry.

- Grade 11 and 12 English classes read an abridged version of Northrop Frye's essay "Archetypal Criticism: Theory of Myths" using Google Docs and in small groups analyzed specific sections using the "Comment" feature. Students then each created one slide and built a collaborative Google presentation slideshow about key ideas from the text.

- An independent study unit final rigorous performance task asked students to read a book, construct inquiry questions, watch a related film or documentary, conduct research, engage in a video blog discussion, make a film trailer to promote their independent study unit, and construct a final multimedia presentation (slideshow, video, etc.).

(Continued)

(Continued)

"Students created some impressive film trailers," he says. "Although students found the task to be challenging, teachers learned, through observations, conversations, and student reflections, that students found this performance task to be rewarding. For the most part, they became very engaged in their task and proud of and empowered by the work they accomplished."

Introducing classes to a variety of technological tools ultimately empowered the students. As they progressed through the units of study and the overall courses, there was a gradual release of responsibility, from teacher to student, so the students became more and more independent. They experienced this in terms of research, inquiry questions, and tech tools that students used. This led to greater self-management on the part of the students and more student-to-student collaboration, as opposed to individual dependence on the teacher.

Source: Used with permission from Derrick Schellenberg.

IMPACT!

Impact on Teachers

"This CI was extremely helpful and encouraged teachers to design their own Professional Learning and then share the learning with others in a variety of ways . . . The use of the apps in the ongoing assessments collected was a help in the teaching process," Schellenberg says. The team identified the following benefits of this CI:

- Management and access to student work was convenient and easy; for example,

  o It was easier to give feedback for formative work with the comment and chat features

  o Teachers could check in on student work in progress and conference as needed

- Students could view co-constructed Success Criteria (SC), which kept students focused on what was being assessed

- In administering online tests and exams, teachers could monitor progress, and students in other rooms could get clarification or help

- While assessing performance tasks, teachers could batch upload to Turnitin.com, leave comments and feedback, highlight SC, and ensure that students knew exactly when something had been assessed. (Note: Turnitin is an online writing tool. It is used for revision, feedback from student and teacher, checking originality and plagiarism, and assignment submission.)

- Designing our own investigation and job-embedded Professional Learning while working with like-minded peers was rewarding

Impact on Students

"We were especially pleased with the creativity and originality of the student work," says Schellenberg. "We also believe that what students learned about the use of technology will transfer beyond the secondary English classroom to other subject areas. Overall, we made better use of the technology students were bringing to class, and we challenged them to do higher quality and more complex work."

"What excites us as teachers," Schellenberg says, "is students' engagement during the learning and inquiry process, as well as the improved quality and complexity of students' products. As we introduced a variety of tools from which students select to demonstrate their learning, that empowered students by shifting control over key decisions involving texts, topics, inquiry questions, and types of products which synthesize their learning. As a result, we have been rewarded with differentiated, original, and authentic student work."

As Greg Whitby (personal communication, 2018) says, "Students now know this world so thoroughly that to them it is not technology; it is a lifestyle, or 'just the way we do things.' Students are continually learning through these networks of trust and sharing. Educators and education are, in many ways, catching up with real-life experience."

COLLABORATIVE INQUIRY IN THE CLASSROOM

CI not only occurs at a professional level, as in Chapter 3, but also with students as experienced in this chapter. The mixture of teachers and students inquiring together is exemplified in the above two Case Studies. Teachers and leaders have a moral obligation to move students to inquire beyond the four classroom walls in order to experience learning from and with others by being connected across the globe. The powerful nature of social media today as it redefines a new platform of connectivity, networking, and collaboration becomes the critical platform for learning.

Todd Wright (personal communication, 2018) states that giving teachers and students permission to inquire together is giving them permission to explore, create, fail fast, investigate, and discover new knowledge. They need collective permission to revel in the unveiling of new facts, opinions, and shifts in understanding that results when moving from individual prior knowledge to commonly understood new knowledge. As students continue to evolve in their use of social networking and other digital media tools, so must teachers find ways to enable students to communicate in these ways and to join them in a continued dialogue about the effective use of digital tools as enablers of learning in all learning spaces. Continuing changes in the nature and functionality of these tools must be part of every educator's understanding of modern learning.

COLLABORATIVE INQUIRY CREATES A CLASSROOM LEARNING COMMUNITY

CI in classrooms can take many forms: Project-Based Learning, problem-based learning, knowledge-building forums, and integrative thinking, to name just a few. All of them must involve processes and result in products of learning that require students' robust thinking. They all demand developing the life-long skills of working together: collaboration, real communication, and honest peer- and self-assessment through Descriptive Feedback. Each model of CI must have the six assessment "for" and "as" learning components (see Chapter 4, Figure 4.4), no matter what CI model is used:

1. deconstructed learning intention, co-created big ideas, and essential questions

2. co-constructed, accumulated SC

3. specific Descriptive Feedback

4. peer- and self-assessment

5. individual goal setting

6. robust learning tasks

Whitby (personal communication, 2018) continues,

Collaboration, if it is to work, must have a framework. This framework includes an implicit understanding and acceptance of some "standards" or structures in the way we do things. In much the same way that democracy and/or banking systems only work because of an acceptance of the rules to make it work. For example, you can bank anywhere, any time, and through any outlet you like because of these standards. The core of the interdependence is the recognition that it only works for the individual when this central agreement is reached. The necessary structures to which Whitby refers are discussed below.

SIX STAGES IN STUDENT-LED COLLABORATIVE INQUIRY

In my thinking, all CI processes have six definitive stages, as shown in Figure 6.4, and these stages must be taught. CI has to be seen to be, and must be treated as a "process," like a science experiment or writing an expository paragraph. In a class of several groups and several simultaneous inquiries, the stages will never be in lock step. The hard part for the teacher can be the messiness of inquiry. It is important to be a nimble leader or teacher who can gauge when to let students lead research, when to ask reflective questions without intruding, and when to jump in with a "just-in-time" lesson. This explains why CI is often represented diagrammatically by spirals or a helix, as in Figure 6.4, because, indeed, it is often two steps forward and three sideways. And that may be where different student inquiry pedagogies diverge with their tactical applications. Structure and routine within the CI process is important as teachers continue to embrace assessment for and as learning as their framework for classroom inquiries.

So, we called on teachers and leaders to embrace a collaboratively structured approach to learning for all students (Sharratt & Harild, 2015),

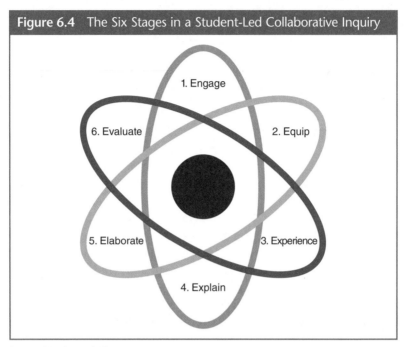

Figure 6.4 The Six Stages in a Student-Led Collaborative Inquiry

1. Engage
6. Evaluate
2. Equip
5. Elaborate
3. Experience
4. Explain

Source: iStock.com/AVIcons.

and they verified the six stages that are present in any CI, offering anecdotal explanations of each:

1. **Engage:** Use authentic, real-world, '"wicked problems"' that are age appropriate. Know the curriculum expectations thoroughly so you can hook students' curiosity onto them during the inquiry by knowing when to extend thinking and when not to intervene.

2. **Equip:** Ensure that students have the research skills, respectful operating norms, collaborative facilitation skills, and technology tools to do the exploration of their chosen topic.

3. **Experience:** Provide students with broad-based experiences that demand vocabulary enhancement in the discipline they have chosen to learn more about.

4. **Explain:** Give students time to articulate their learning to others by bringing them together frequently, always expecting them to bring evidence of their findings and big ideas and be able to support their claims through Accountable Talk.

5. **Elaborate:** Model questions that promote students' ongoing interest, demand their critical thinking, elicit students' defense of their discoveries, and expect that they can elaborate on what they have determined.

6. **Evaluate:** Teach students to evaluate their products against the co-constructed SC that are in an ongoing state of development through each inquiry. (Sharratt & Harild, 2015)

The essence of inquiry in the classroom requires more than simply answering questions or getting a right answer. It espouses investigation, exploration, search, quest, research, pursuit, and study. It is enhanced by involvement with a community of learners, each learning from the other in social interaction. (Kuhlthau, Maniotes, & Caspari, 2007, p. 2)

COLLABORATIVE INQUIRY DEMANDS NEW ROLES

Moving students beyond initial curiosity to a path of ongoing, deeper inquiry is one of the greatest challenges of inquiry-based learning. In this process, teachers play the all-important roles of curator, facilitator, guide, change agent, teacher, wise counsellor, and provocateur—whenever and whatever the situation demands (Ontario Ministry of Education, 2015b). An inquiry-focused classroom demands that students' thinking is in the center of the learning and that teachers

1. defer judgment,

2. encourage volume,

3. be visual [use graphics],

4. be succinct [summarize ideas],

5. listen to others,

6. build on others' ideas, and

7. encourage wild thinking. (Boss, 2012, p. 64)

Susie Boss (2012) says it is important for teachers to feel principals have their backs—to let them run with "out of the box" ideas in creating that culture of innovation. Melanie Greenan (personal communication, 2017) says that if teachers can let go of control, have trust in their students, and learn to get the right design for the curricular content through student-led inquiry and knowledge building, then CI will create huge learning gains for all students.

A common concern among educators new to inquiry is how to teach with an inquiry approach when there are so many curriculum expectations to address. By focusing on the big ideas (see Chapter 4) rather than on the specific expectations alone, students' questions often lead to, and often exceed, overall curriculum expectations (Ontario Ministry of Education, 2013b). In this way, learning through inquiry gives students reason to value, use, and develop skills, such as reading, writing, and critical thinking, and does so in ways that blur the conventional boundaries between discrete subject areas (Ontario Ministry of Education, 2015b).

Student inquiry is partly designed to produce "community of learner" behaviors. To create this within CI for students, the process needs to reflect operating norms discussed in earlier chapters and protocols for group processes and research procedures as developed in this chapter. The notions behind the six stages of inquiry in Figure 6.4 are not complex to write about or speak about, but executing them takes real planning, thinking, and reflecting. It is the work of teachers who want to develop persistently curious students who possess critical thinking, problem-finding, and problem-solving skills.

Figure 6.5 demonstrates how three approaches to learning—project-based learning, knowledge building, and integrative thinking—are each built on a foundation of a structured, collaboratively planned inquiry that is held together by Accountable Talk to achieve the desired and necessary outcome for all: improved student learning.

ACCOUNTABLE TALK SURROUNDS AND SUPPORTS COLLABORATIVE INQUIRY

In Chapter 1, I discussed that a key to enhanced learning is that teachers and students co-design the learning spaces in which all students and their inquiries can thrive. We called that learning environment the Third Teacher, after students' first teacher, the parent, and second teacher, the classroom teacher. Carefully co-designing the Third Teacher with students is foundational to creating an inquiry approach to propel students' growth and achievement forward. The social practice of Accountable Talk to promote critical thinking in these learning spaces

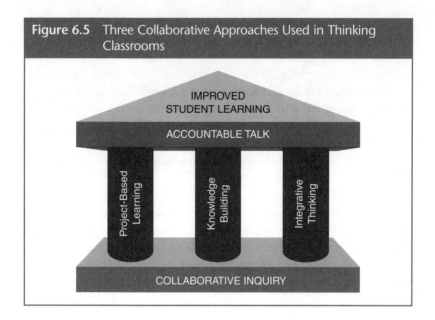

Figure 6.5 Three Collaborative Approaches Used in Thinking Classrooms

IMPROVED STUDENT LEARNING

ACCOUNTABLE TALK

Project-Based Learning

Knowledge Building

Integrative Thinking

COLLABORATIVE INQUIRY

is deepened through use of digital tools, including social networking tools, and supported by strong norms of acceptable behavior for every member of the class community. Figure 6.5 shows that Accountable Talk (see Chapter 5) is the driver of all CI.

THREE APPROACHES TO STUDENT-LED COLLABORATIVE INQUIRY

Each of the following three approaches is a powerful CI structure when supported by an archway of Accountable Talk (Figure 6.5). Lifelong thinking and group work skills result from each of these approaches when students' voices and choices are heard and valued. The three approaches differ in that they follow different guidelines or operating principles discussed in what follows; however, they are similar in that they each offer strong collaborative opportunities focused on building students' problem-solving skills. The choice of pedagogy belongs to the team of teachers in the school based on their skills and the digital or other tools available, their dialogue with students, their connectedness to community partners, and system support available for their choice or choices collaboratively made.

Students owning their own learning extends to the ways in which students can own their own learning tools. Gone are the days (or they should be gone) when the school or teacher determined the digital tools to be used by students. Locked-down desktops and devices that do not allow some elements of freedom and mobility in the choice of learning tools have always restricted the learning approaches of students and have framed the learning experience in a manner that is contrary to the spirit and reality of inquiry-based learning. (Wright, personal communication, 2017)

Each of the three CI approaches—Project-Based Learning, knowledge building, and integrative thinking—is discussed below. The goal in student-led CI is that students move through the above six stages, from engagement to evaluation and ending with empowerment, at which point they own their learning through questioning, reflecting, and applying new knowledge.

COLLABORATIVE INQUIRY WITH STUDENTS: PROJECT-BASED LEARNING

Gavin Hays, learning leader, Diocese of Parramatta, explains that Project-Based Learning is different from Problem-Based Learning. Both have an inquiry focus; however, Problem-Based Learning often has a shorter time frame (e.g., one or two lessons) and a stronger focus on content, rather than skills. For those reasons, I will investigate Project-Based Learning as CI with Hays (personal communication, 2018).

Hays definitely thinks all teachers can teach using the Project-Based Learning method as a powerful way for students to learn, by resolving "wicked problems," to become researchers, critical thinkers, and thought leaders. However, Hays cautions that the entire process of Project-Based Learning takes time to develop. Often teachers start with an authentic and engaging project, progress to a deeper understanding of the inquiry process, move to more effective use of collaborative structures, and finally develop a more comprehensive understanding using formative assessment processes. Sometimes, learning the entire repertoire of skills may take a number of years. Just like using the 14 Parameters as a reflective tool, using Project-Based Learning effectively is an ongoing process for teachers, hence the need for side-by-side instructional coaching. In Figure 6.6, Hays thoughtfully overlays and links my 14 Parameter Framework to the strengths of Project-Based Learning.

Figure 6.6 The Interconnectedness of Project-Based Learning and the 14 Parameters

Parameter	Links
Parameter 2: Embedded Knowledgeable Other	• Instructional coaches are important for schools implementing Project-Based Learning. They provide feedback on the nonnegotiables of Project-Based Learning. • Staff need support in project design to avoid common pitfalls like creating "dessert style" projects (learning is first then the project). Project-Based Learning should have the learning embedded through the entire project. • Staff need support in instructional practices. This is *in situ* support to implement appropriate collaborative discussion protocols, manage group work (specifically, accountability for all members), assessment for and as learning (Chapter 4), and fidelity to the inquiry process. • The gradual release and acceptance of responsibility is essential in scaffolding the learning of subject content and skills within the project. The co-teaching environment allows for the instructional coach to model effective protocols for both teachers and students. • Effective implementation of Project-Based Learning is often within a co-teaching environment. This affords one teacher the opportunity to facilitate guided workshops, while the other teacher facilitates collaborative and independent work on the project.
Parameter 3: Daily Sustained Focus on Assessment and Instruction	• It is very difficult to undertake Project-Based Learning without having a minimum 100 minutes of instructional time. • It is common practice for the teacher to start the lesson with the "need to know" list, and the class will identify a need to know in order for them to progress in a project. This is deconstructed as the Learning Intention and appropriate SC are co-constructed (the SC are used as an assessment measure to move a "need to know" to a "know"). This is paramount to the inquiry process. Without this process, you will not achieve deep inquiry with the opportunity for students to transfer knowledge and skills.

(Continued)

Figure 6.6 (Continued)

Parameter	Links
	• Assessment for and as learning (Chapter 4) is imperative in the inquiry process. Teachers need to be collecting data on individual students within small and whole class groups. This collected data will often inform the instructional workshops (mini lessons) that are provided to students throughout the lessons/unit of study. • Resources such as pacing charts, group portfolios, progress checks, etc., are used to support this process of using SC.
Parameter 4: Principal as Learning Leader	• This is key as many students don't enjoy working with other students, especially if accountability is maximized. The principal needs to have very strong understanding of the impact of the collaborative processes within a Project-Based Learning classroom to ensure fidelity to the model is maintained as all stakeholders (students, parents, and staff) learn new skill sets. • Furthermore, this could be a new instructional process for staff. They need time for project planning and *in situ* feedback on their implementation of student-centered practices.
Parameter 5: Early and Ongoing Intervention	• Teachers must observe and monitor the ongoing work, assessing as they do for opportunities to differentiate and bring assistance to those who require it, perhaps at a guided problem-solving table.
Parameter 6: Data Walls and Case Management Meetings	• Data Walls and Case Management Meetings are implemented in this whole-school approach to CI.
Parameter 7: Job-Embedded Professional Learning	• Teachers need ongoing, *in situ* Professional Learning that addresses how to ○ manage the collaborative environment to ensure all students are accountable (e.g., grouping strategies, group contracts)

Parameter	Links
	○ manage the inquiry process (e.g., need to know, instructional workshops, mini lessons, use of explicit instruction)
	○ use assessment for and as learning and final evaluation of learning in Project-Based Learning. Specifically, how to benchmark the learning with appropriate assessment for and as learning strategies, including Descriptive Feedback to ensure the projects are managed to achieve the identified subject curriculum expectations/outcomes
	○ manage student demonstrations of learning (e.g., gallery walks, group presentations, peer assessment, presenting student work in authentic way)
Parameter 8: Collaborative Assessment of Student Work	• No similar commentary
Parameter 9: Centralized Resource Rooms	
Parameter 10: Budget for "Just Right Resources"	
Parameter 12: Parent and Community Involvement in Supporting All Students' Achievement	• The authenticity of a project, from which "wicked questions" are drawn, is very important. Often parents and the local community members provide stimulating, authentic links. Some schools create a parent occupation database to link parent expertise with student team projects. This also allows parents to gain a greater understanding of the different learning processes.
	• Meaningful partnerships with the local community members provide students with relevance in what they are learning beyond the classroom.

(Continued)

Figure 6.6 (Continued)

Parameter	Links
Parameter 13: Appropriate Literacy Instruction in All Areas of the Curriculum	• Effective Project-Based Learning has a range of selected literacy strategies identified at the start of the project and are modeled and scaffolded to allow students/groups access to the curriculum content. • These are key factors in project design and ensure the learning experience is rigorous.
Parameter 14: Shared Responsibility & Accountability	• A network or Professional Learning Community (PLC) approach to Project-Based Learning is imperative as the opportunity to share resources (projects and protocols) ensures the ongoing sustainability of the change in instructional approach. • The PLC approach has been used in many successful implementations, where schools or systems share the responsibility of increasing student academic achievement and are mutually accountable to each other to ensure Project-Based Learning is feasible and sustainable. • Accelerated leadership capacity is gained by teachers who ascend to the roles of instructional leaders across a system. They have many opportunities to see a range of different implementation processes across different stages and key learning areas and share their learning across the system. • Collaborative dialogue across schools affords leaders the opportunity to share and to support each other in setting strategic directions and resourcing changes in instructional practices. This highlights the importance of Learning Walks and Talks, where there is a consistent focus and understanding of what the learning looks like in a Project-Based Learning classroom. As a result, all leaders are precise in what they are looking for in a student-centered learning environment and can provide Descriptive Feedback regarding the effectiveness of classroom instruction.

Source: Gavin Hays, learning leader, personal communication, 2017.

I appreciate that many of the 14 Parameters are embraced in the Project-Based Learning approach to leading, teaching, and thinking. Critical to the success of Project-Based Learning is that leaders are involved; assessment for and as learning is central; expertise from parents and the broader community is sought; and that the explorations demand an open-to-learning stance, collaboratively developed over time, by teachers, leaders, and students. The second CI process used in the classroom with students is *integrative thinking*.

COLLABORATIVE INQUIRY WITH STUDENTS: INTEGRATIVE THINKING

Integrative thinking is a pedagogy to develop metacognition and creative problem solving in K–12 classrooms used by teachers and leaders in education. This approach to problem solving leverages tension and opposing models to create innovative solutions. Too often, when students encounter models that are different from their own, they either compromise or believe that only one model can be right. Integrative thinking offers students tools to take the value of each model in an effort to generate a new model based on the benefits of both or the benefits of many models.

The integrative thinking process involves the following:

1. **Articulating opposing models:** In this step, students seek to understand what works about each of the opposing models by looking at the benefits of each model from different stakeholder perspectives. The Pro-Pro Chart (Figure 6.7), Causal Map (Figure 6.8), and Ladder of Inference (Figures 6.9 and 6.10) are the tools used here.

2. **Examining the models**: Students make sense of the benefits of each model and gain insights that can move them forward toward a solution. They ask questions and challenge assumptions as they purposefully experience the tension between the opposing models.

3. **Exploring the possibilities**: Students move from understanding the existing models to imagining several new, integrative possibilities to the challenge. They leverage the tools of design thinking, such as prototyping and ideation, to build out the solutions.

4. **Assessing the prototypes:** Students must understand the conditions that would have to exist for their prototypical solutions to thrive. They ask, "What would have to be true?" from the perspective of the multiple stakeholders. They also ask, "What do we understand from, and what can we further infer from, the pools of knowledge created in our Ladders of Inference re responses to the prototype we have created?"

Teachers and leaders have brought integrative thinking and its tools to schools and classrooms across all grades and subject areas. The following case study demonstrates how the power of integrative thinking shifts mindsets through real-world problem solving.

CASE STUDY: A POWERFUL EXAMPLE OF INTEGRATIVE THINKING

Middle-school teacher Rola Tibshirani faced a difficult task. At the beginning of the school year, in September, her students were competitive, egotistical, and self-centered. They lacked the thoughtfulness to appreciate ideas that were not their own—often speaking negatively about each other. More so than normal, students misbehaved to get attention.

Tibshirani quickly recognized that she needed to shift her classroom culture and mindset from one of searching, memorizing, and regurgitating the one "right" answer to one where collaborating, celebrating each other's learning, and striving to create better answers was the priority. She turned to integrative thinking as a pedagogy to leverage the tension between opposing ideas or models to shift her students' fixed mindsets and build cooperative communication and working skills.

Integrative thinking is an approach to problem solving that would have these students dive into their opposing options to develop new solutions rather than make trade-offs between opposing models. For Tibshirani, integrative thinking could push her students to believe that there is value in perspectives that are different from their own while solving problems that are important to their school.

Tibshirani's school, St. Gabriel, had a problem that was real and could be discussed from personal viewpoints: the school had recently changed its schedule based on feedback from staff. Last year's schedule was a balanced day: three 100-minute teaching blocks and two 40-minute nutrition breaks. This year, the new schedule was a more traditional one: four 75-minute teaching blocks with two 15-minute recess periods and a 60-minute lunch. Tibshirani's students were unhappy with this change. Going from 100- to 75-minute teaching blocks left them feeling that there was not enough time to reflect on their learning. Tibshirani recognized she had a perfect example of an either/or choice: her school could choose to stay the course or revert to a balanced-day schedule. Sensing the tension of opposing models in action, Tibshirani thought her students could explore this problem through the lens of integrative thinking.

The school schedule had a clearly identified tension—a balanced school day versus an unbalanced-day schedule. Students looked at the respective benefits of these two models from different stakeholder perspectives, a step in the process called the "Pro-Pro Chart" (see Figure 6.7).

By exploring the opposing models and developing a causal chart, like the one shown in Figure 6.8 using a different theme, students were able see the value of both, without necessarily having to choose or prioritize one over the other. Their thinking began to change.

Figure 6.7 A Student-Generated Pro-Pro Chart	
Balanced-Day Schedule Benefits for Teachers	**Unbalanced-Day Schedule Benefit for Students**
"With fewer transitions [teachers] can dig in more to do deep learning. We need time if we're going to go deep." ". . with the 100-minute blocks [teachers] can include time for reflection. In 75 minutes, you can do a task, but it doesn't give you the time to reflect, which [teachers] need if students are going to learn."—Avery and Danica	"Students need a break from the hard work of learning. By having three recesses instead of two in the balanced day, it gives students more opportunities to de-stress and come into class refreshed." –William and Chelsea

(Continued)

(Continued)

Figure 6.8 Students Intertwine Their Thinking Skills to Create a Causal Map

Source: Erin Quinn, Grade 8 teacher, Toronto, Canada.

Within the integrative thinking model, after completing the Pro-Pro Chart (Figure 6.7), the goal is to come to a new insight about the problem and open new possibilities for solutions. Note, these are not compromises but new possibilities. By using the Ladder of Inference, a model shown in Figures 6.12 and 6.13 below, Tibshirani's students came to realize that *both* models assumed that at *all* moments of the day, students have consistent needs and habits for learning. However, students recognized that this is not the case, and that their *capacity for focus and energy levels change throughout the day*. From this insight, students went on to develop their own schedule to better serve the needs of the stakeholders. Their solution integrated two 100-minute blocks and two 50-minute blocks. The 100-minute blocks happen at the start of the day and right after lunch, when students' energy is at its highest. Students hypothesized that this new schedule would allow for deeper learning, while minimizing misbehavior, and serve as a better model for all stakeholders.

This problem-solving experience was a tipping point for Tibshirani's classroom culture. Students now saw that no single person could have solved the schedule problem alone. Rather, real-world problem solving was best when made into a collaborative endeavor. They also learned that, in the same way, opposing models had value, so too did the opinions of other students, even when those opinions were vastly different from their own. Students came to believe that if they learned together, they would learn more. These exciting revelations drove Tibshirani to explore other integrative thinking tools with her students.

Source: Nogah Kornberg, associate director, I-Think, Rotman School of Management, University of Toronto; Josie Fung, director, I-Think, Rotman School of Management, University of Toronto; Rola Tibshirani, teacher, Ottawa Catholic District School Board, Canada, 2017.

IMPACT!

The most significant change Tibshirani saw in her students was an increase in their compassion. At the start of the school year, there was an individualistic mindset, where each student focused on creating his or her own product to get an "A+". Now, she found, "Students listen to each other, build on each other's ideas and thoughtfully question their respective thinking." Tibshirani captures this shift by saying that "They take each other's learning seriously." Sydney, a student in Tibshirani's class, describes it by saying, "We intertwine our skills. When we are collaborating, we are problem-solving together by taking the best of all of us. It's like putting a puzzle together."

Tibshirani is proud that her students are no longer complacent. Students know that the models they start with don't have to be the models they end with. As a community, their success comes from listening to models that are different than their own to increase their understanding. Shifting perspectives to create new solutions to real-world challenges is now their measure of success.

COLLABORATIVE INQUIRY WITH STUDENTS: KNOWLEDGE BUILDING

Knowledge building is complementary to the Integrative Thinking model discussed above. Essentially, the gathering of information phase in developing the Pro-Pro Chart (Figure 6.7) becomes a form of the knowledge-building circle, as you will note in the following commentary from Park Lawn Public School, Toronto, Canada.

I have learned a lot by conducting Learning Walks and Talks with leaders and teachers in classrooms across the globe (2008–2018). I have observed integrative thinking celebrations and witnessed that knowledge-building circles, as described by Scardamalia (2016), expand the notion of the power of CI. More than simple operating norms, the concept of knowledge-building circles includes the aspect of what I call "responsible belonger inputs." Students are part of the group and, as such, must contribute to the thinking or analysis, and other students will provide the safety within the group for students to do so (Scardamalia 2016).

Figures 6.9 and 6.10 are two anchor charts of knowledge-building prompts also from Park Lawn Junior Middle School. Anchor charts are

Figures 6.9 and 6.10 Sample Anchor Charts of Critical Thinking Prompts

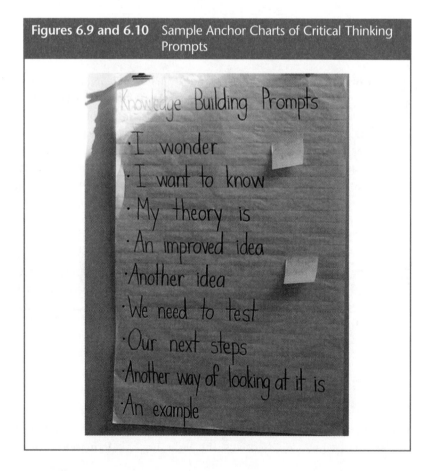

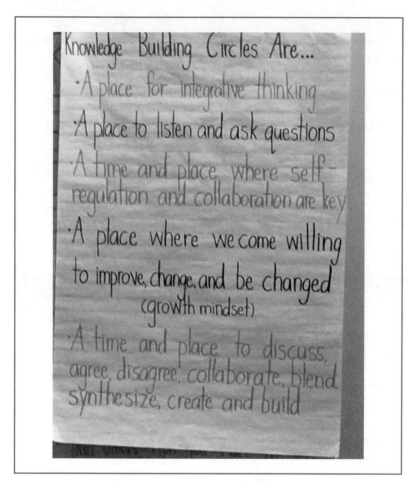

Knowledge Building Circles Are...
- A place for integrative thinking
- A place to listen and ask questions
- A time and place where self-regulation and collaboration are key
- A place where we come willing to improve, change, and be changed (growth mindset)
- A time and place to discuss, agree, disagree, collaborate, blend, synthesize, create and build

Source: Joel Allen, Grade 3/4 teacher, Park Lawn Public School, Toronto, Canada.

most effective in providing visual prompts so students can clearly articulate what they are learning and why they are learning it—especially if they are co-created and referred to often by both students and teachers. They also provide ongoing references for students when they are displayed in the classroom (Parameter #1).

Knowledge building is a theoretical model developed by Carl Bereiter and Marlene Scardamalia for describing what a community of learners needs to accomplish in order to create knowledge. The model is distinguished from similar activities such as Problem-Based Learning by an emphasis on collective cognitive responsibility (Zhang, Scardamalia, Reeve, & Messina, 2009).

Knowledge building provides an alternative that more directly addresses the need to educate people for a world in which knowledge creation and innovation are pervasive. Knowledge building may be defined as the production and continual improvement of ideas of value to a community, through means that increase the likelihood that what the community accomplishes will be greater than the sum of individual contributions and part of broader cultural efforts. (Scardamalia & Bereiter, 2003)

In the following case study, I talk with Grade 8 teacher Erin Quinn, supported by Principal Erin Altosaar, from Park Lawn Junior Middle School, about Quinn's work with Knowledge-Building Circles (KBC) to ensure that all students are learning with and from each other.

CASE STUDY: DEVELOPING GLOBAL CITIZENS

We have been experimenting with meeting in a KBC. Students bring their research or their ideas with them, and one by one they share. As the teacher, I stand outside the circle and they share with each other. I found the farther away I get, the better the conversation in the circle becomes. Students are sharing their ideas using the language of Accountable Talk (Chapter 5 and Figure 6.11), such as, "I'd like to add to your idea, or build on it, or yes, and, . . ." With that language, students are able to discuss each other's ideas so that individuals can add to their notes and their own ideas.

It's something new for me. We have conversations all the time in our class, and the first time that students attempt a KBC, they are always looking to me to ask, "Can I go next?" So, it is great to sit outside and listen to and observe their conversations.

We spent the first nine days of school working on collaboration activities in Grades 6, 7, and 8, so instead of having discrete language and math time, we did a series of integrated performance tasks that stretched across the subject areas, using our Accountable Talk phrases (see Figure 6.11). We looked at words they used and talked about the communication and how to be respectful with each other. These nine focused days culminated in a trip with assessment tasks that they had to do at High Park in Toronto. It's the first time we have seen Grades 6, 7, and 8 playing the same game without conflict.

Figure 6.11 Accountable Talk Discussion Starters

Sample Accountable Talk Phrases That Promote Thinking:

- Tell me more about . . .
- Is there another way to say that, Audrey?
- Can you build on Jackson's idea?
- Is there an example that explains what you are thinking, Ryan?
- What is your evidence to defend your thinking, Aeson?
- Why do you agree with that point of view, Clarke?
- I agree with Robbie, and I also think . . .
- That's a great idea, Penelope, and I would add . . .
- I disagree with Madeleine's point (not Madeleine) because . . .

For us, it was about developing learning skills, reflecting on how we learn and how we know how we learn, in order to help us to understand how other people learn. I have always done community circles, so students kind of understood that aspect, but our initial nine days of collaboration really helped to solidify how to engage with other people's thinking. The big learning in using Accountable Talk for our students was realizing that other people learn differently; it's not always that we all learn in the same way; and we must be respectful of the learning process of others, too. This gave my students collective agency. Students began to come up with their own ways of respectful talk.

So, we are now moving to another project—re-imagining another part of Toronto. We have looked at Evergreen Brickworks as an example of re-imagining spaces in Toronto. We also looked at the Christie Plant that has been shut down for a while to re-imagine it according to the community needs. Now their problem to solve will be to re-imagine a space within their own community. We have a parent coming in who is an urban planner and teaches at McMaster University, Hamilton, Canada. The students' jobs, using the Integrative Thinking tools (Ladder of Inference, Causal Model, Pro-Pro Chart), are to reimagine a space and how it would work.

(Continued)

(Continued)

Figure 6.12 is the teacher-created anchor chart as a reminder of the Ladder of Inference model, and Figure 6.13 is student-created Ladder of Inference model to solve their wicked problem in Grade 1.

Figures 6.12 and 6.13 The Ladder of Inference Used as a Tool for Thinking

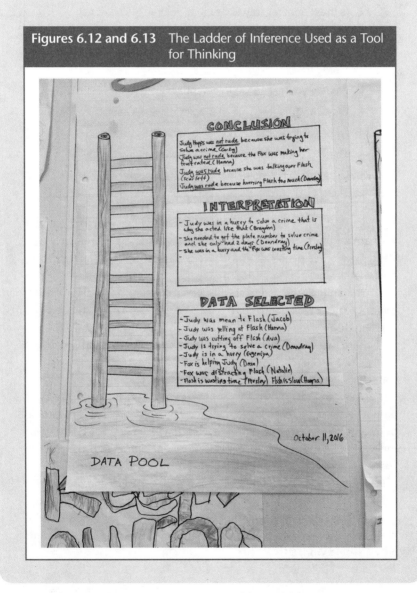

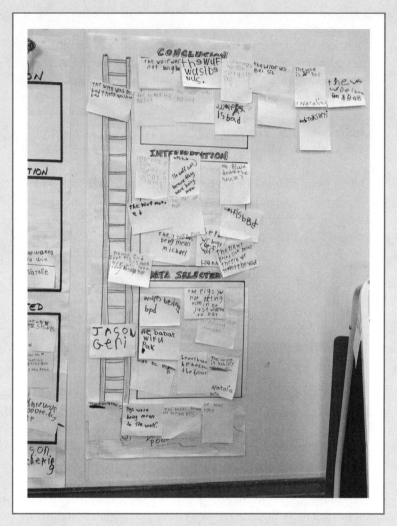

Source: Brian Charbonneau, Grade 1 teacher, Park Lawn PS, Toronto, Canada, 2017.

Integrative Thinking design for teachers and leaders moves up, down, and sideways. It moves up as we elevate our perspective to identify and articulate our vision of what type of learners and leaders we are hoping to help create. It moves sideways as we

(Continued)

(Continued)

seek commonalities in practice between disciplines and incorporate key research and evidence-based practices across the curriculum. It moves down as we use our diagnostic assessment data and pedagogical content knowledge to provide a clear zoom lens on each student as they display and work through misconceptions with quality prompting and Descriptive Feedback. (Melanie Greenan, personal communication, 2017)

Using integrative thinking, with the Ladder of Inference and Causal Model, provided organizational tools to demonstrate student thinking and illustrate their thought processes, as opposed to just writing questions and answers. Students had to show each step along the way and listen to someone else's thinking. Everyone in our classes contributes in some way; all voices are heard. Every single student shared in the knowledge-building circles.

Source: Erin Quinn, teacher, and Erin Altosaar, principal, Park Lawn Junior Middle School, Toronto, Canada, personal communication, 2017.

In KBCs and integrative thinking, the tools—Ladder of Inference (Figures 6.12 and 6.13), Pro-Pro Chart (Figure 6.7), and Causal Model (Figure 6.8)—are powerful ways to ensure the elements of differing models of thinking and decision making are made explicit. Then selection of the best elements of each of the options is possible. In this way, students can understand the logic and the limitations of the models. By thinking about their thinking, students develop a cognitive flexibility that allows them to solve problems in novel and unique ways. Making student thinking visual can help problem solvers annotate why the idea was stated in the first place and understand its relationship to our understanding of the world.

Lessons Learned: The Power of Collaborative Thinking With Students

Through my own teaching, discussions with valued colleagues, and watching great teachers in action using these three CI approaches, I have learned the power of teachers:

1. **CLARITY**. Teachers must be explicit in teaching students what metacognition or reflective thinking is. Students need to understand how learning deepens when they plan for it, analyze it, and monitor their progress. This becomes precision in teacher practice and the recording, reflection on findings, and subsequent presentation by students becomes precision in learning. I used to write about "The Reflective Practitioner" (Sharratt, 1992); now I think about "The Reflective Learner"—at every level.

2. **Skill.** The three models above are each forms of CI. A skillful teacher uses the components from her choice of model as they fit into her context to benefit students as they consider the problems they are solving. The models seem discrete but must be fluid and flexible. The important point is that skillful teachers give students access to and a practiced understanding of at least one, if not all, of these invaluable thinking tools.

3. **Observation.** As teachers become experienced with the models, they become really adept observers and thinkers themselves, continually making connections between the students' thinking and the curriculum expectations. Teachers ask each other as they become experienced, "How do you pull the curriculum expectations out of the students' work?" The answer lies in the intuitive part of teaching when everything aligns.

4. **Thinking and authentic assessment.** The ultimate accomplishment in every classroom is having all students able to articulate their ponderings and thinking, not regurgitate mindless facts. This is achieved when assessment practices are clear to teachers and used by students to self-assess their own learning and next steps. Teachers now empower students to own their learning by explicitly saying, "Pull out your best thinking, demonstrate it through your work, show us how you got there, and be able to share your knowledge with others" (see Chapter 4).

5. **Big ideas.** Teachers build on spontaneous questions that cause students to wonder and to ask further questions. Connecting student questions and ideas to big ideas overarching the curriculum expectations is the work of teachers and students together.

6. **Co-construction.** Teachers and students co-creating the learning environment (The Third Teacher, Chapter 1), the SC (assessment for and as learning, Chapter 4), and the demonstration

of learning in completing rich performance tasks (instruction, Chapter 5) are vital if students are to commit to the inquiry and own their own learning during it.

Web Resource 11: Knowledge Building From a Principal's Perspective complements the above approaches when Principal Erin Altosaar of Park Lawn Middle School, Toronto, Canada, reflects on how she brought the student-led CI processes together by engaging her whole staff in reflecting on and supporting each other to bring CI into classrooms at the school.

METACOGNITION: CREATING CRITICAL THINKERS

Students who engage in the thinking processes demanded by CI, such as Project-Based Learning, integrative thinking, and knowledge building, develop thinking skills, self-regulation capabilities, stamina, interdependence, and metacognitive skills that, over time, become intuitive—that is, a natural habit of mind (Figure 6.14). Metacognition is ensuring that students naturally develop deep cognitive insights and strong social-emotional connections not only to their own learning and thinking but also to that of others. Students know how they learn. As they become metacognitively aware, multiliterate, creative, and innovative thinkers, they achieve the prerequisites to thrive in our ever-changing world community.

As captured in the discussion of these three approaches, when students think beyond themselves to embrace and care for others, they create a better world community and become global citizens.

STUDENT VOICE AND CHOICE ARE NOT ENOUGH

Going beyond voice and choice is needed to consider how teachers and students become researchers and writers during ongoing CI processes. ***More powerful than ownership is authorship.*** Rachel Ryerson (2017) states that engaging students and teachers as researchers provides opportunities for them to negotiate who has the power to construct

Figure 6.14 Students Demonstrate Metacognition

SELF-REGULATION
- Being on task without being asked
- Using resources apropriately.
- Doing work on time and doing it good and neatly. Helping others without being asked
- Behaving appropriately without reminders

Initiative
- Participating In Class
- Willing to work hard
- Taking on leadership.
- Doing extra work in class.
- Coming in for extra help.

The best way to solve a problem is to not make it bigger

Bella
Kasey
Dayna
Jalen
Joel

(Continued)

Figure 6.14 (Continued)

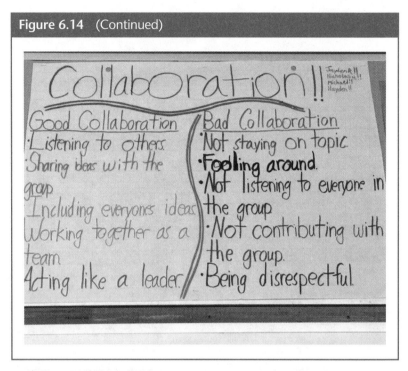

Source: Maria Siddiqui's Grade 6 students, Park Lawn Junior Middle School, Toronto, Canada.

knowledge. Teachers who considered themselves researchers emphasized the importance of taking a participatory approach: "It must be a collaborative process between teacher and students—the research is not <u>by</u> the researcher but <u>with</u> the researcher." Teachers who encourage students to become developers and writers of research acknowledge that "students are collaborators" and "have important things to say" to inform practices within classrooms, schools, and systems (Rachel Ryerson, Ontario Ministry of Education, Toronto, Canada, personal communication, 2017).

What tools do teachers have if their instructional approaches—like the eight high-impact strategies in Chapter 5 and the three CI processes presented in this chapter—are not working? Chapter 7 outlines ways that teachers and leaders can examine the data to prevent student failure and discover ways to intervene to teach even the most struggling learners. Low achievement is never the students' fault; teachers and leaders have just not found the most effective ways to teach them—yet.

COMMITMENT

I commit to

● modeling an open-to-learning, listening stance to move all students, leaders, teachers, parents, and community members forward;

● exercising "intelligent accountability";

● gathering a more developed base-knowledge that includes

○ corporate/system understandings,

○ change management skills,

○ capacity to build collaborative teams;

● making cross-curricular connections to the standards and aligning them with students' curiosity and critical thinking;

● adapting my thinking as I continue to learn, unlearn, and relearn about high-impact classroom practice;

● taking risks and failing fast as I try new approaches and take cues from my co-inquirers—students, colleagues, leaders;

● being patient and empathetic with myself and others in the learning as I keep student FACES central to the journey.

A DELIBERATE PAUSE TO CREATE CLARITY

What evidence do you have that students have moved from engagement to empowerment because they are involved in CI in each classroom? How might you explain how the three CI approaches fit together and support each other? How might you model the use of one or all of the CI approaches in your staff meetings or during PLC time?

Visit the companion website at
resources.corwin.com/CLARITY
for videos and downloadable resources

CHAPTER 7

CLARITY
Using Data for Prevention and Intervention

Wonderings...

1. Who are the students who are struggling, stuck, or needing extending?
2. How can we shift low achieving students into higher assessment bands?
3. How can we lift teachers' spirits and skills to be able to make the needed changes in student learning?
4. How can I get all teachers involved in owning all students' learning?
5. How do we get ownership of the data—urgently?
6. How do we get co-construction of a Data Wall?
7. Where do we build in the time to lead and participate in Case Management Meetings?

What are you, the reader, wondering about? What additional questions do you have?

Data comes in waves of indigestible, dehumanised information . . . we want teachers and leaders to be moved and inspired by data, and help pinpoint the action that will be effective. In short, *putting FACES on the data is* caring for students by helping them get better in their day-to-day learning. (Sharratt & Fullan, 2012, p. 2)

Generate data and use it in a way that makes the learner come alive in the minds and actions of leaders and teachers—on a large scale. (Sharratt & Fullan, 2012, p. 3)

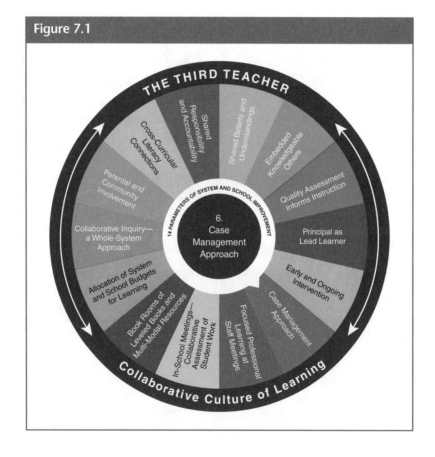

Figure 7.1

PARAMETER#6: CASE MANAGEMENT APPROACH

Do any of the following statements sound familiar to you?

> The students at this school will not become great achievers. They have too many disadvantages for us to overcome. We do our best just to get them through school.

> Yes, we believe all kids can learn, except maybe for Sally, Luis, or James—they'll never learn.

Our collective work is students' growth and achievement (Parameter #1). *Having a positive belief that all students can and will learn and that all teachers can learn to teach* is where we begin to move away from the negative mindsets that lead a few to believe that some students can't learn. The role of a teacher is to develop instructional expertise that will work best for each student. The role of a leader is to offer support, create the challenge, and facilitate the vision of shared beliefs and understandings so that whenever a teacher asks for assistance with a student that teacher will be supported.

In this chapter, I examine (1) Prevention using Data Walls to ensure that no students are falling between the cracks and their failure going unnoticed and (2) Intervention using the Case Management Meeting (CMM) to consider, "What avenues of support do teachers have if they experience difficulty teaching a student?" Teachers deserve a forum where they can discuss and get support from colleagues to face very real challenges and to live the vision of all students progressing at the expected rate.

THE CASE MANAGEMENT APPROACH TO MONITORING STUDENT PROGRESS

The Case Management Approach (CMA) is two-pronged: prevention and intervention.

1. Prevention: Co-Construction of Data Walls

A Data Wall is created by using wall space for the visual representation of student data. The purpose of Data Walls is to assist educators in identifying learning patterns at different levels and to plan instruction for each learner. Using co-constructed Data Walls, teachers and leaders assess trends that concern them, question each learner's progress, and begin work to prevent losing track of the progress (or lack thereof) of any learner. By doing the work collaboratively, staff quickly develop collective responsibility for all learners. Teachers and leaders work collaboratively on Data Walls at the school level to address the needs of every child in the school. Likewise, leaders work together at the system or district level to address patterns and trends from school to school to ensure that students at all schools are showing at least a year's growth every year.

2. **Intervention: Case Management Meetings to Monitor and Improve Student Progress**

   The CMM is an intervention process that uses data, including student work samples, to fully identify each FACE and hence each learner's needs. Planning for differentiated teaching response, and follow-up support are recommended at the CMM to ensure consistent and appropriate learner progression. The teacher is invited back to a scheduled CMM to report on progress. She knows she is not alone. Members of the CMM team collectively care for that teacher and student until progress is made. They regularly check in on the student's progress and offer ongoing support to the teacher.

   The CMA is an essential leadership tool in every school's and system's improvement toolbox. By physically putting FACES on the data, schools and systems can plan to take short-term actions, identify valuable Collaborative Inquiries, execute immediate triaging strategies, and action longer-term plans. As shown above, it is a two-pronged approach: (1) Data Walls for prevention: Who are our students who need help? and (2) CMMs for intervention: How can all teachers be supported to teach all students?

PREVENTION: DATA WALLS

No student should ever fall through the cracks and be forgotten. Preventing students from not demonstrating progress toward expected targets set by teachers and leaders is accomplished by "seeing" students' FACES on a Data Wall and taking intentional action before it is too late. The impact of Data Walls comes from the notion that, when co-constructed, they become Questioning Walls or Wondering Walls. When first created, they may present a stark reality, but very quickly they will begin to generate thinking and wondering. They are living evidence of students' growth and achievement—both are essential. They provide a visual reminder that teachers and leaders must be reflective practitioners and pose questions about student learning and about practice.

There is no one right way to visually display the data. What is important is that Data Walls are teacher and leader *co-constructed* because it is in that process that teachers and leaders begin to promote rich conversations about instruction to meet the needs of all students. The most effective Data Walls are in discreet locations away from students' and parents' eyes—in a place where teachers and leaders gather or pass by often and can stop to leave notes about their observations.

Capturing assessment data in a visual format marks an impressive leap of faith into uncharted territory for many educators. To see the assessment results of individual students displayed on a Data Wall, in a private space, leaves no question as to the achievement and growth of each FACE and the trend across all students in a class, cohort, school, and/or system. The Data Wall raises questions as to why, or how, or what can be done to bring each student to a higher level and how to ensure each grows "one year in one year of teaching" (Hattie, 2012). Data Walls also raise questions about what can be done to assist teachers to bring the obviously underperforming students to the expected level and beyond.

> When we began to co-construct our school Data Wall, we never thought the impact of the Data Wall would make such a difference to improving classroom practice and student outcomes. We have consistently used the 14 Parameters to reflect on our progress, so have refined our Data Wall and practice over the past three years. We are looking forward to sharing our journey with you. (Lee Scola, principal, Sydney Catholic Diocese, Australia)

Creating a Data Wall is a school and system affair. Each Data Wall will be unique, reflecting context and data that highlight needs. It is important that school staff members think through how they will show growth and achievement in co-constructing their Data Wall. It is important to get started and recognize that the new Data Wall won't be, nor should it be, perfect. The real strength in a school or system Data Wall is that with experience, those who co-construct it will continuously improve it, so the Data Wall constantly evolves.

Questions abound: What data and how will the data be displayed? How many grades will it cover? In how many subject areas, over how many intervals of assessment, might we want to track a trend? Do we track several subject areas simultaneously on individual student cards, or do we stay with a Data Wall of the most urgent triage work? Where will we keep the Data Wall to ensure privacy of student information and, at the same time, encourage spontaneous discourse about instruction among staff?

Whatever teachers and leaders decide is likely a good start; an insightful leader will focus staff members on what data are needed to give the complete picture of how each student of concern is progressing.

Brave or courageous conversations are necessary, and even braver commitments are needed to deal with many underlying issues in assessment that informs instruction. Sometimes getting to these conversations is a matter of putting the data on the wall; sometimes it takes courage to initiate intentional actions to mitigate the concerns. Consistent, insistent, and persistent courage is required to admit there are problems that need to be addressed and to raise these concerns intentionally. The very early introduction of operating norms around having and co-creating a Data Wall ensures that all staff members are intentional about mutual respect and about what will be produced and how users will know the Data Wall is valuable as a working tool.

MODELING OPERATING NORMS TO USE DATA WALLS EFFECTIVELY

The operating norms in Figure 7.2 can be shared with colleagues before the Data Wall co-construction begins and should be referenced whenever academic controversies arise during the development. These norms should sound somewhat familiar as they reflect the cultural tones of the Third Teacher.

GUIDING PRINCIPLES IN CO-CONSTRUCTION OF DATA WALLS

The guiding principles developed in Figure 7.3 are meant to deepen understandings of the big ideas in co-creating Data Walls.

Figure 7.2 Operating Norms to Support Co-Construction of Data Walls

- Everyone's voice is important. We listen respectfully.
- Being respectful in our engagement builds strong working relationships that lead to empowerment.
- We reflect on our work as we learn with and from each other.
- In collaborating, we empower our own learning and the learning of our colleagues; we build learning capacity together.
- Collaborating authentically builds confidence and success.
- We persevere. We believe all students can learn and all teachers can teach with impact given the right time and support.
- We believe in our interdependence to achieve students' learning goals.
- Having shared beliefs and understandings about student growth and achievement guides our work.
- We will establish clear Learning Intentions and Success Criteria for using Data Walls that we have co-constructed as a team; these will change over time as our needs change and evolve.

Figure 7.3 Guiding Principles in Co-Construction of Data Walls

- Data Walls are co-constructed and thus co-owned by all staff.
- Data Walls are used to promote reflection, questions, and rich conversations about instruction for every student.
- Data Walls are private and confidential for teachers and leaders only. They are located in discreet but easily accessible places. This should not be an obstacle to establishing a Data Wall; creativity is needed here.
- Data Walls are focused on conversations about changing instruction to meet students' needs.
- Data Walls are *not* electronic because the power is in students' FACES being continuously visible and "present." Data Walls need to be tangible, visible evidence of learning owned by everyone with the ability to physically "move" each FACE, avatar, or record card along the axis as evidence of growth is verbalized and agreed upon.
- Data Walls can be a small data set displaying students of concern drawn from school data or a large data set that includes all students. There is no one right way to display data. The power is in the conversation that takes place while co-constructing it and stepping back to discuss it.

(Continued)

Figure 7.3 (Continued)

- Data Walls display students who are struggling, stuck, or needing extending. These may be students in the lowest achievement bands, clustered in the middle, or in the highest bands.
- Student data need not only be assessment data. Informal notations made, for example on the number of personal associations ("caring connections") teachers have with students, can be powerful reminders that everyone owns all students.
- Data Wall conversations, respecting the operating norms, are robust and support Collaborative Inquiry processes.
- Data Walls show student growth over time as well as achievement.

HOW TO BEGIN DATA WALL BUILDING

Data Wall building begins with careful triangulation and scrutiny of more than one data source. In Figure 7.4, leaders and teachers in Seine River School Division have scrutinized three data sets and have discussed/recorded what is noteworthy, troublesome, surprising, and of concern about them. In addition, they have generated questions to uncover the meaning and relevance of the information. Beginning with data, generating and maintaining a Data Wall is a time-effective, high-impact strategy. Collective time is needed to ensure that Data Walls become meaningful pedagogical documentation shared by all staff.

Productive conversations do not just happen. When the principal and leadership team begin to analyze their school data and involve teachers in the process, they must provide ways for everyone participating to learn and be safe because there will be ragged edges in the data for everyone to see. The clarifying questions displayed in the sidebar (see page 233) can help focus the process and the conversations. As much as some may be keen to get into the data, others may be hesitant. As it is important to bring as many of a school team into the learning as possible, team members must genuinely believe that their thoughts are being acknowledged and appreciated by the group. The operating norms (Figure 7.2) must be in play and facilitated by the leader—so that that no one is ignoring, bullying, or demeaning others. Then, questions about the Data Wall will flow freely.

Figure 7.4 Data Analyses: What Is Noteworthy, Troublesome, Surprising, and a Question?

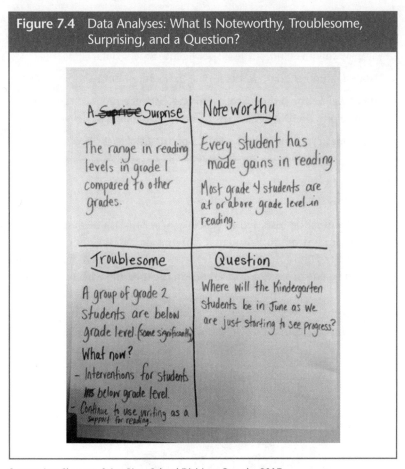

Source: Lyn Sharratt, Seine River School Division, Canada, 2017.

CLARIFYING QUESTIONS FOR LEADERS AND TEACHERS

- What are we doing here today and why?
- What will define success for us today?
- What will define success for us in the future?
- How can we display the key findings from our assessment data?
- How much data is enough to create the first Data Wall?
- Are there layers of data?

- What else do we need to know about each student?

- How can we bring other assessment data to the Data Wall that would amplify the meaning of these specific assessment data?

- How do interventions we determine to be important become realities?

- What will be the protocol followed and evidence brought to move students along the Data Wall axes to show growth and achievement?

- How does everyone own the FACES on the Data Wall?

PRIVATE!

Data Walls must be installed in places where only leaders and teachers can use them—away from students, parents, or the broader community and public. In Figure 7.5, the team leader is pulling a screen over the Data Wall as the data conversations that began the meeting with teachers and

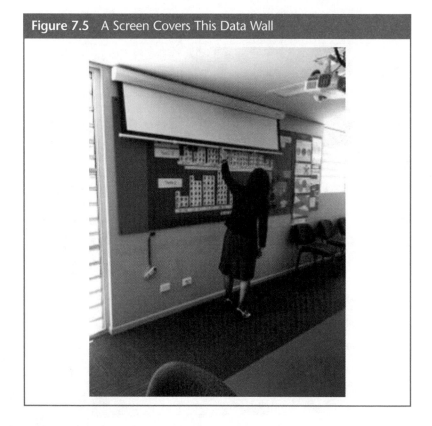

Figure 7.5 A Screen Covers This Data Wall

leaders are now finished and the privacy of the information is protected. I have experienced many ingenious ways to keep the Data Walls and conversations private.

In Figure 7.6, Master Teacher Penny Dewaele is leading Professional Learning in front of her school's co-constructed Data Wall. Dewaele begins every staff meeting with conversations at the Data Wall.

Figure 7.6 Using the Data Wall to Begin Every Meeting

Source: Principal Mona Anau, DDSWR, 2017.

DETAILED CO-CONSTRUCTION OF SYSTEM AND SCHOOL DATA WALLS

Let's look at detailed co-construction of Data Walls at the system and school levels and the benefits of each.

Schools do not operate in a vacuum. The system in which they operate has a responsibility to, and is ultimately accountable for, the schools' learning and learners. To understand trends within their schools and to be able to drill down into issues that become evident in specific schools or departments across schools, school systems or districts must create their own Data Walls. A key reason that system leaders would want to establish Data Walls is that the process of creating and maintaining them models commitment to the importance of personalizing data and taking immediate action. If every system meeting starts with a data discussion at the system Data Wall, there is no better modeling than to repeat that practice at the school level and in classrooms.

When schools and systems commit to using Data Walls and use them effectively, I have seen results that are nothing short of outstanding. This points to the importance of the following:

- a belief that all students can learn (Parameter #1)
- the involvement of the school principal and system leaders at every Professional Learning session (Parameters #4, #7, #8)
- high energy to get the work going and sustain it
- focus on data that informs nonnegotiable Data Walls and follow-up CMMs (Parameter #6)
- CLARITY of purpose and practice (Parameters #1 to #14)
- collaboration among staff and leaders to develop a systemwide culture of learning (Parameter #11)
- ongoing, differentiated system support to schools (Parameter #5)
- staying the course to get the results that leaders and teachers want (Parameter #14)

QUESTIONS TO ASK AT THE DATA WALL

- How was the Data Wall constructed?
- Who was involved in the creation of the Data Wall and what specific norms were helpful in pulling the team together?
- What are you proud of?
- What are you concerned about?
- Where are most of your struggling schools/students? Are your *best* leaders and teachers leading and teaching the most struggling schools and students?
- What additional supports are teachers able to access, such as consultants, resources, onsite Professional Learning time?
- How many students can read at the expected standard at the end of Kindergarten?

- How many students can read at the expected standard at the end of Grade 1?

- How do you know?

- How are your students doing in their transition year to high school?

- What is your graduation rate and number of graduates going to further education or to work?

- Where are your students who need extending—that is, who need to be consistently challenged to think more critically? How is this being achieved?

- Can school leaders and teachers articulate their improvement and students articulate their learning?

- Show me a teacher using high-impact strategies and one that is not. What actions are you undertaking to get the underperformer to a higher level?

- What are you wondering about? What isn't revealed in the Data Wall but is important for us to know and consider?

CASE STUDY: THE POWER OF CO-CONSTRUCTING SYSTEM DATA WALLS

Executive Director Greg Whitby and Deputy Executive Director Sue Walsh of the Catholic Education Diocese of Parramatta oversee 83 schools and 45,000 students. Sue and Greg believe that due to the implementation of a CMA at every level of their organization, their scores have dramatically increased, as outlined in the following case study.

For the last five years, our senior central office leaders have annually constructed a Data Wall to make the learning challenges visible in Parramatta. Toward the end of last year, a group of learning leaders took on the task of working out how, as a system, we were going to show on our Data Wall that there was equity across our schools in funding and human resources and that there was an agreed-upon identification of priority schools that we would focus on in 2018.

There was great satisfaction that we were ready to start the year with our newly constructed Data Wall so that when four new learning leaders arrived, we would be well-advanced in applying our thinking to ensure

(Continued)

(Continued)

that our funds and human resources were apportioned to support schools according to need.

Imagine my surprise when the new learning leaders, two weeks into the term, confided that they had no commitment to the Data Wall as they were not part of the construction and didn't necessarily agree with the decisions that had been made by the previous team members. It was one of those *ah ha* moments. **The power of the Data Wall lies in the co-construction.** It's the whole team working together to determine

- how best to represent the data on the Data Wall,
- what data should be included,
- how to consistently name and test assumptions that may be made about aspects of the schools' data.

Moving forward, several of the learning leaders have taken leadership of different aspects of the Data Wall and there has been vigorous and robust discussion about the data (see Figure 7.7). What started out as a project to construct a system Data Wall to establish priority schools in the

Figure 7.7 Deputy Executive Director Sue Walsh Leading Rich Discussion at a System Data Wall

Source: Sue Walsh, 2017.

categories of low, medium, and high has developed into a sophisticated Data Wall that includes multiple data sets: national assessments, student attendance, allocation of extra resources, identification of students with disabilities, and allocations of teaching educator support for *in situ* work in schools. The Data Wall co-construction has challenged us to articulate the focus of our action in working with our schools.

Frequently, when groups are discussing different aspects of our Learning Walks and Talks in schools, those groups will be seen in front of their Data Walls, checking out pieces of data. The Data Wall is a constant reminder to us of the power in having the data visible to challenge assumptions, test hypotheses, and align our collective and relentless focus on improving learning outcomes for every student.

Source: Sue Walsh, deputy director and director of system performance, teaching, and learning, Catholic Education Diocese of Parramatta, 2017.

Walsh's narrative highlights the power of collaborative co-construction of data in a safe environment where all voices are heard and considered. System Data Walls are revised often as more specific information is needed to understand context, content, and areas of urgent need in schools. In every region, the directors and system leaders are not only familiar with the students and schools represented on their Walls, but also actively monitor the personalization of their responses to ensure 100% of schools grow and achieve. This has now become a norm in the many districts in which I work, and it will also become a model for finding specific pockets of otherwise "hidden" schools or students who can be successful—through differentiated support, resourcing, and Professional Learning.

Figure 7.8 shows Gabrielle Doyle, director of teaching and learning, Catholic Education Western Australia (CEWA), examining the Data Wall that she and her team have co-constructed. It displays attainment and growth in schools using the NAPLAN standards-based assessment over two years. Each data sheet builds on the previous year's data (hence, two sheets shown per school). Differing graphs for each school depicted in Figure 7.8 show various ways the data can be displayed. The power of Data Walls is in the focused collective conversations that result in front of the wall, every day, about differentiated actions to take. Visual Data Walls provide CLARITY of focus that must result in a closer look at precision in practice.

Figure 7.8 System Data Wall in CEWA

Source: Lyn Sharratt, CEWA Office, 2018.

IMPACT!

My ongoing work alongside Doyle, consultants, and school leadership teams in CEWA involves implementing the 14 Parameters, a CMA, Learning Walks and Talks, and high-impact assessment and instructional strategies in selected secondary schools, K–10 schools, and primary schools, all in challenging circumstances. This intense work has more than paid off, as illustrated in Figure 7.9. These results are nothing short of outstanding and point to the importance of the following:

- a belief that all students' achievement is possible!
- the use of the 14 Parameters as a system and school self-assessment tool
- the participation of system and school principals with their teams at every Professional Learning session
- high energy needed to get the work going and sustain it
- data sources that inform living Data Walls and follow-up CMMs
- CLARITY of purpose that leads to change in practice

- collaboration among staff and leaders to develop cultures of learning
- ongoing, differentiated system support to schools
- setting high expectations and staying the course to achieve them

Figure 7.9 The Impact of CLARITY on Precision in Practice			
Cohort 1 Results in Work With Lyn Sharratt			
Secondary Schools Grades 7 and 9	Reading 2015 Grade 7 average mean achievement	Reading 2017 Grade 9 average mean achievement	Australian national mean achievement (+/−)
Australia	545.9	580.9	+35
Western Australia	542.7	582.6	+39.9
CEWA	**548.7**	**592.9**	**+44.2**

This powerful example of co-constructing and using system Data Walls applies at the school level as well.

SCHOOL DATA WALLS: ELEMENTARY AND SECONDARY EXAMPLES

The following two examples, one at the elementary level and one at secondary level, demonstrate the co-construction of a school Data Wall that informs leader and teacher decision making, Professional Learning needs, resource allocation and, most important, identifies the students of concern.

CASE STUDY: THE POWER OF CO-CONSTRUCTING AN ELEMENTARY SCHOOL DATA WALL

Principal Melissa Burke shares how the Data Wall at Bracken Ridge State School, Queensland evolved over the course of several staff meetings. Figure 7.10 represents the progression of thinking that occurred.

(Continued)

(Continued)

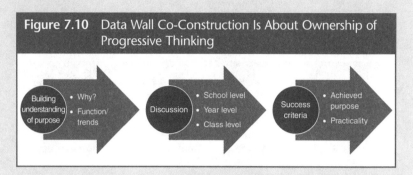

Figure 7.10 Data Wall Co-Construction Is About Ownership of Progressive Thinking

Success Criteria: A Result of Staff Collaboration

Burke and staff started with the focus questions arising from their data, which were displayed on butcher's paper. The checklist below shows the co-constructed Success Criteria by staff and leaders before the development of a co-constructed school Data Wall.

It was a three-part process:

1. Staff worked together on the design, function and technical aspects of the Data Wall, and to co-construct the Success Criteria for it.

   Co-Constructed Success Criteria for the Data Wall at Bracken Ridge School

   We will know our Data Wall is effective when

   - We know the students (personal; make our work about the real students)
   - We set goals for our students
   - We plan for our students—to extend and to support
   - We are moved and inspired because it is our moral imperative that every student can learn and has the right to learn
   - We understand whether the processes and strategies we have used are having an impact

- We measure "distance traveled"—which students have progressed? plateaued? regressed?

- We measure against school and state targets—who is at level? Above level? Below level?

- We house the Data Wall in a place that is easily accessible to all staff

- We ensure that the information is easily recorded, updated, managed, and private

- We organize the data by grade levels and not classes

- We update the data once per term

- We use the Data Wall regularly in our data talks and our reviews

2. Staff were provided with photo examples of Data Walls from neighboring schools. Staff worked together to create mock Data Walls and student cards, then voted to select the Data Wall that resonated the most.

3. Since co-constructing and establishing the Data Wall, staff have added two different types of tags to the Data Wall:

   A. A card describing the type of learning intervention the child is receiving that helps to identify students who are below target and are or are not receiving additional support (see Figure 7.11)

   B. A card that describes students who have been the focus of our CMMs and the next steps collaboratively determined for each student

It is very important for staff to develop a legend or key to assist others in understanding the categories shown on the Data Wall, as in Figure 7.12.

The work that Burke and her staff are doing in putting FACES on their data and actioning change in classroom practice is exemplary. They know and care about each student across this large school. It has worked

(Continued)

(Continued)

Figure 7.11 Data Wall Cards and Tags Depict Recommended Intervention Strategies

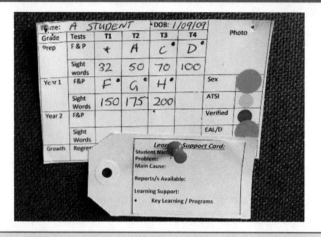

Source: Melissa Burke, principal, Bracken Ridge School, Metro Region, Australia, 2017.

Figure 7.12 Sample of a Data Wall Legend

DATA WALL STICKER GUIDE

● NO PROGRESS

● LIMITED PROGRESS

● ACHIEVING EXPECTED PROGRESS

B BELOW END OF YEAR TARGET

★ EXTENSION

★ CAP/IEP

★ READING RECOVERY

☆ SMALL GROUP INTERVENTION

★ ATTENDANCE BELOW 90%

Source: Luke Shaw, assistant principal, St. Joseph's School, Boulder, Western Australia.

well because the process has been informative as well as collaborative. As leaders, Burke and her team have been consistent, persistent, and insistent in using data to improve their school's growth and achievement (see Chapter 9).

Source: Melissa Burke, principal, Bracken Ridge School, Metro Region, Australia, 2017.

It's About FACES Not Subjects

Students' FACES on a Data Wall are not widgets on a tracking board. We ask, "who are the students of concern?" "What can we do to change practice and own all students' improvement?" Students may be of concern not because they are struggling but because they are stuck or need extending within a subject area. All students across any subject area can be placed on a Data Wall with specific flags on those whose profiles show assistance and collaboration among teachers are both required.

Lessons Learned: About Data Walls

1. **Location, Location, Location.** In more than one case, the initial Data Wall is located in the principal's office and established with no staff input. As a result, staff have little or no vested interest in the Data Wall, and when done, updating the data is predominately compliance driven. Being in the principal's office also means that parents and students are privy to the posted information. Three key considerations: (1) privacy; (2) co-constructed by all; (3) planned times when established and agreed-on data are used to move students along the wall of improvement.

2. **Tracking, Monitoring, and Celebrating Growth.** Leadership teams and teachers need to track students' progress over time, add relevant descriptive information on student cards to know each FACE, and develop collaborative professional inquiries about trends or patterns determined in the data.

3. **Growth and Achievement.** If you just capture achievement data then the Wall will quickly become wallpaper; if you capture both growth and achievement data, the Wall will become a living document of where students have been, where students are

now, and where you expect students to be in a defined period of time—using agreed-upon high-impact instruction.

4. **It's Not About the Size.** Data Walls can capture all the students or be limited to the students you are most concerned about at any place on the wall. The unanswered question by not showing all students is "*who* are we most concerned about, and *what evidence* causes that concern about only them?" Those students noted as being of concern, often by their teachers and others who know them, may have an additional stickie attached to their data card where teachers can record what they have collectively agreed to work on with these students.

5. **It's Not Written in Stone.** Just because staff make a decision to represent data in one way initially, doesn't mean it has to stay that way forever. They may decide within a term or a year to change the stickie format or even change the entire Data Wall format to more closely interrogate the data and answer the questions raised. In order to track growth and achievement, whatever the format, the student information cards should move with the class to the next grade level, so that no information or time is lost.

There is no one right way to display data—Data Walls are flexible and defined by student need. What is important is adhering to their integrity: purposeful, visual representations to uncover students' FACES and instruction needed for each. They are as applicable in secondary schools as in elementary schools, as the following example illustrates. This case study demonstrates how the co-construction of a Data Wall focused teachers' efforts to improve writing instruction.

CASE STUDY: THE POWER OF CO-CONSTRUCTING A SECONDARY SCHOOL DATA WALL

The 2016–17 schoolwide literacy focus at Parramatta Marist High, Catholic Education Diocese of Paramatta, Australia was to improve student outcomes in Grades 7 and 9, particularly in writing, as the national literacy assessment indicated that this was an area most in need of improvement.

In 2016, we decided to frame the population of the Data Wall around this writing focus and involve all teachers in the co-construction of the Data Wall. To scaffold this work, we focused on the "Aspects of Writing" component of the New South Wales *Literacy Continuum* (New South Wales Department of Education, 2014), which maps expected student achievement across 16 markers from Kindergarten to Grade 10.

The Process

Over the course of our first school term, our teachers examined a range of samples of student work and engaged in productive discussions in their teams around which marker best represented where each student was in relation to the *Literacy Continuum* concept "Aspects of Writing." The 16 clusters had an array of detailed indicators, including early stages such as scribbling, writing vocabulary, pencil grip, etc., to more sophisticated aspects such as sentence-level choices, range of punctuation techniques, and stages in developing the craft of quality writing.

At the end of each term throughout the 2016–17 school year, in our Professional Learning Teams we collected samples of student writing and tracked student progress as students' writing improved. The ongoing examination of student samples helped teachers identify and articulate student progress. Professional inquiry conversations enabled teachers to support each other in this learning journey.

The engagement with the data benefited everyone: teachers made students' achievement visible by putting FACES on the data, and students had teachers who were learning alternative instructional strategies needed to support their learning. The Data Wall is now alive with precise and endless possibilities for increased student performance; rich, focused conversations (see Figure 7.13) about practice; and teacher growth.

The Data Wall is located in a private space, the staff room, at the high school. All teachers revisit it frequently in their Professional Learning Teams. They developed a common assessment task; collaboratively assessed student writing samples from their classes across subject areas; and made judgments about any improvement in students' performance against the clusters of the *Literacy Continuum* (New South Wales Department of Education, 2014).

(Continued)

(Continued)

Figure 7.13 Rich Discussions at the Secondary Writing Data Wall

Source: Sister Mary Martinez and Sister Teresa Duch, teachers, Paramatta Marist Secondary College, 2017.

These adjustments were also tracked on the school's online tracking system (hence the presence of the laptops). The photos of those students who had demonstrated improvement (or not) against the clusters were then physically moved according to their progress (or not) on the Data Wall. Professional Learning Teams were also encouraged to discuss patterns that were emerging, note students of concern, and add tags for potential strategies to improve performance in aspects of the writing continuum clusters.

The process of handing ownership of our Data Wall over to the teachers was a powerful experience that fostered collective agency among staff, challenged them to know all students, and catered for support of students' diverse learning needs.

Source: Kurt Challinor and Gavin Hays, lead teachers, Parramatta Marist High School, 2017.

Lessons Learned: At the Data Wall

1. **Ownership.** Over the course of 2016 and 2017, leaders really saw that the use of the Data Wall had a significant impact on teachers and students. Having teachers completely engaged in the writing focus had a profound impact on them. Teachers owned the work as they saw it directly related to their own students and to the other students in the school. This shared commitment was a catalyst for further professional inquiry and learning.

2. **Differentiation.** The process challenged all teachers, first to improve their own understanding of literacy in all subject areas (Parameter #13) and also to understand specifically where each of their students was in relation to a common assessment continuum. From there, teachers were in a position to differentiate their ongoing literacy interventions (Parameter #5). This shift was most notable in the increasing number of informal conversations teachers were engaged with regarding the literacy needs of their students and strategies to support them.

3. **Growth and Achievement.** Over the year, a great number of students progressed by at least one marker. While some of this growth can be attributed to teachers gaining a better understanding of the *Literacy Continuum* and applying it more accurately, discussions with teachers also indicated that a majority of students demonstrated growth in their written compositions across subject areas.

4. **Focus.** Teachers commented that the Data Wall provided a point of continual focus to help them develop strategic literacy interventions specifically targeted to meet the needs of all learners. Many noted that being able to physically see where each of their students was placed on the Data Wall in relation to one another was beneficial in helping them plan differentiated and personalized learning strategies that met students at their points of need.

Often at the Data Wall, teachers' reflective conversations turned from prevention (knowing where students were achieving or needing extending) to intervention (knowing the students who were struggling and wondering what else would work for them). This leads to discussing case management meetings (CMMs).

INTERVENTION: CASE MANAGEMENT MEETINGS

At the school level, teachers most often make their own adjustments to instruction by gathering evidence of learning while they are teaching, or they gain helpful insights through informal conversations with colleagues. The need for some form of intervention for specific students becomes highly visible at the Data Wall; thus, the location and staff co-construction of the Data Wall are keys to promoting ongoing discussion about student need and discussion that may offer tips for sharpening CLARITY of instruction in classroom practice. Discussion relating to a specific student FACE on the Data Wall may resonate with other teachers who have students with similar learning needs.

As an element of the scaffolded teacher learning continuum, it is more than reasonable that leadership, too, "walk" the Data Wall on a regular basis, asking questions about student achievement where trends appear in a grade level depicted on the Data Wall. Experience counts. A timely comment to a teacher or group of teachers may result in useful insights and practices being exchanged or in a deeper conversation—sometimes even more courageous conversation—being held. The critical point is that having early and ongoing conversations at the Data Wall are the beginning steps of proactive leadership behavior alongside teachers.

SCHOOL CASE MANAGEMENT MEETINGS

Data Wall conversations lead to bringing one student of concern at a time to a regularly scheduled Case Management Meeting (CMM). CMMs offer forums where the expertise of teachers and leaders come together to collectively problem solve the most challenging issues in moving all students forward.

The CMM is a formal decision-making meeting for follow-up instructional strategy suggestions leading from Data Wall discussions. It is not a supervisory or evaluative forum; it is truly a grouping of Knowledgeable Others who provide support and instructional advice for teachers to try out in classrooms. A community of trust is built through nonjudgmentally sharing their concerns and feeling confident in seeking the expertise of colleagues. This is reciprocal as a teacher may struggle to meet the instructional needs of one of her own students and in another CMM may have exactly the right strategy to support a colleague's student. Teachers come to the CMM in two ways: (1) through a student concern raised at the Data Wall or (2) self-nomination to seek help with an issue of instruction.

Once a teacher has brought her or his student's work sample to the 20-minute CMM, has requested help with an issue of instruction, and shared what she or he has already tried, the group assembled recommends different strategies that haven't been tried previously. The teacher has time within which to honestly try one recommended strategy that she thinks will work in her classroom. This strategy is necessary for one student but may be good for many students in her class. In this way, teacher capacity for an expanded repertoire of instructional strategies is built. A few weeks later, the teacher will report back to the same team in a follow-up CMM, bringing evidence of success (or no success).

During the intervening time, members from the CMM team do regular Learning Walks and Talks that include this classroom, to support the teacher before the follow-up CMM. The teacher should never feel alone in this journey as the CMM outcome is for the team to "take on" responsibility for helping that teacher with that student. "We all now own that student."

Case Management Meeting Guidelines: 10 Steps to Success

1. Time (20 minutes) for CMMs is scheduled into the timetable so that all teachers have a dedicated time during which they can bring students of concern forward.

2. The chair is either the principal (who always attends) or the instructional coach, who follows the CMM template. For a template to use at a CMM, access **Web Resource 6: School Case Management Meeting Teacher and Participant Template**

   If this is a follow-up CMM, check out **Web Resource 7: Follow-Up Case Management Meeting Template**.

3. Attendance at the CMM is confirmed.

4. Time on task is critical. The recorder notes the actions decided on, using a template like the one suggested

Web Resource 6:
School Case Management Meeting Teacher and Participant Template

Web Resource 7:
Follow-Up Case Management Meeting Template

Web Resource 8:
System Case
Management
Meeting Facilitator's/
Chair's Script

above (Web Resource 6). The chair follows a focused, time-sensitive script as in **Web Resource 8: System Case Management Meeting Facilitator's/Chair's Script** to lend reassurance of the factual and objective nature of the ensuing conversation. This template can be adjusted to become the Chair's script for a school CMM.

5. The classroom teacher presents student work (e.g., on paper or video) as data/evidence of help being sought (everyone has received a copy of, or link to the student work sample to review before the meeting).

6. All voices around the table are heard. The teacher shares what has already been tried with the student and declares what help she or he is seeking.

7. A clear and specific recommendation is decided on by all and recorded. The classroom teacher agrees to practice the chosen strategy, deliberately, in his or her classroom for at least three weeks and with continued support of colleagues present on a "reach out/go to" basis until the next meeting. The next meeting date of the group to hear progress on this student is scheduled before the end of the meeting.

8. During regular, ongoing Learning Walks and Talks, leadership team members informally check in with the classroom teacher and the student, following the CMM, to check their progress and ask if any support is needed.

9. At the next scheduled meeting regarding that student, using the follow-up template (Web Resource 7), the classroom teacher reports back on the success or failure of the recommendation, with the student's work as evidence.

10. If successful, the school team examines another student work sample as presented by a classroom teacher. If unsuccessful, the group around the table repeats the meeting using a follow-up meeting template (Web Resource 7 above) and offers further strategies, repeating the CMM until the student shows progress or another form of intervention is put in place.

CMMs provide a supportive forum in which classroom teachers, one at a time, can present their instructional concerns and be supported. Figure 7.14 demonstrates how the school Data Wall and outcomes from the CMM can

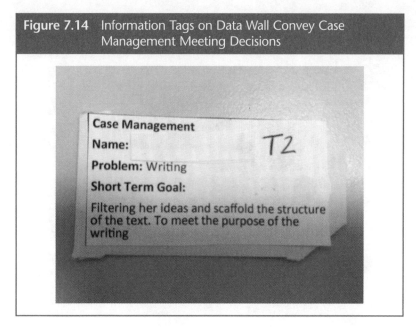

Figure 7.14 Information Tags on Data Wall Convey Case Management Meeting Decisions

> **Case Management**
>
> **Name:** *T2*
>
> **Problem:** Writing
>
> **Short Term Goal:**
>
> Filtering her ideas and scaffold the structure of the text. To meet the purpose of the writing

Source: Melissa Burke, principal, Bracken Ridge School, Metro Region, Australia, 2017.

be woven together. This is especially important when more than one teacher is involved with a specific student who has been taken to the CMM and all teachers who teach this student need to know the outcome. All teachers must have access to instructional decisions made at CMMs. Figure 7.14 shows one way of doing this, using student information tags on the Data Wall. Another way has been perfected by staff at McCarthy College.

Developing QR Codes to Store Case Management Meeting Information

McCarthy College, Parramatta Diocese, Australia, connects the student portfolio information collected at a CMM with the outcome of that support meeting by developing a QR code to place on a "sticky" for their Data Wall, shown in Figure 7.15, so that the student's teachers, using their smartphones, can instantly look at the student's portfolio of work and note decisions made at the CMM. How to develop a QR code to capture CMM information to put on a Data Wall is described in **Web Resource 9: Creating QR Codes for Your Data Wall**.

Web Resource 9: Creating QR Codes for Your Data Wall

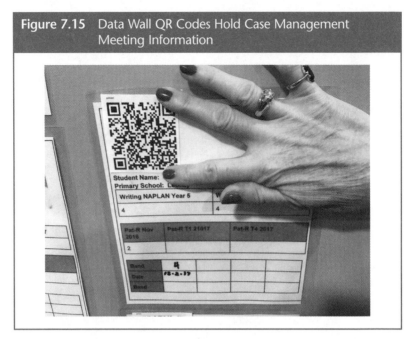

Figure 7.15 Data Wall QR Codes Hold Case Management Meeting Information

Source: Lyn Sharratt, McCarthy College, Australia, 2017.

Having the student information readily available can support all teachers who teach that student to ensure consistency of practice for him or her in the classroom.

At the end of each term, Principal Melissa Burke, her leadership team, and grade-level teachers at Bracken Ridge School review the CMM recommendations and subsequently develop a Collaborative Data Inquiry Action Plan. The critical part of this review is to identify and promote the highest-impact strategies that have had significant impact on student progress as a result of the accumulated CMM recommendations. These inform their next steps for Professional Learning and for refining their strategic direction setting, making impressive connections between research and practice that they use to ensure consistency of high-impact practice that leaves no students behind.

SYSTEM CASE MANAGEMENT MEETINGS

What has been learned at the school level has been translated easily into actions at the system level as leaders don't ask schools to do what they are not prepared to do. Now many system leaders begin their weekly leadership meetings at the system Data Wall with a discussion of the schools that appear to be causing concern and needing assistance in leading improvement in their achievement and growth, as evidenced by ongoing system data collection.

Similar to school-level CMMs, it is expected that senior system leaders will follow up with the school's superintendent or supervisor on progress in the school and will go with the superintendent into the school to see their Data Wall to continue to support the superintendent.

System Case Management Meeting Protocol

The system CMMs are chaired by the senior leader; the entire leadership team attends and participates to discuss "schools of concern." Case Management templates and scripts are found in **Web Resources 6, 7, and 8.** I have adapted the following system protocol for CMMs, first trialed by the senior team in Metro Region.

1. Chair clarifies operating norms, session recorder, timekeeper, and agreed duration of CMM.

2. Chair invites school supervisor to present the school data. (3 minutes)

   (a) What is the school socioeconomic status?

   (b) What is the school data, SMART goal, and Collaborative Inquiry question?

   (c) What is the specific issue needing support?

3. Chair invites clarifying questions from each group member around the table. No advice is given. (4 minutes)

4. School supervisor responds to questions and provides further information. (3 minutes)

5. Group provides advice—from each member around the table. (4 minutes)

6. School supervisor asks for any clarification about advice given.

7. School supervisor names one action that she or he has heard to implement this improvement work. (4 minutes)

Web Resource 9:
Creating QR Codes
for Your Data Wall

8. Group decides on what evidence of improvement the school supervisor will bring back to the table. (3 minutes)

9. Participants set date for same group to reconvene to continue the discussion about/review the evidence from this school. (1 minute)

(a) Put a QR Code on the system Data Wall that holds information recorded at the CMM (See **Web Resource 9: Creating QR Codes for Your Data Wall**).

10. Everyone owns the improvement of this school and acts as a critical friend to the school supervisor from this meeting onward.

11. Senior leader and the school supervisor will visit the school together and review its Data Wall and actions taken regarding the system CMM recommendation.

Lessons Learned: Case Management Meetings at School and System Levels

System leaders and I who have implemented system and school CMMs across contexts have been extremely successful in providing CLARITY of vision and practice and have learned the following lessons:

1. **Time.** System and school leaders must schedule the time for these critical CMMs and not cancel them. The number one reason for being there is to model the belief that all leaders can lead by ensuring that all students can learn and that all teachers can teach. The brilliant underlying foundation of the CMM is that strategies shared to assist leaders and teachers with one school and one student will inevitably help other schools and students.

2. **Commitment.** System and school leaders are to return and report on improvement. Dedication to the process is integral to the usefulness of the CMM.

3. **Collaboration.** Leaders and teachers are reminded that they are not alone. Providing ongoing support between the

meetings sends the important message that "we all own all of the students."

4. **Integration.** All 14 Parameters weave together. System and school leaders and others at CMMs must go into classrooms, during their regular Learning Walks and Talks, in the intervening weeks to look for evidence of the recommended strategy being employed. They ask students the 5 Questions (see Chapters 2 and 9), continuously gathering data to support learning, teaching, and leading by example.

5. **Instruction.** The CMM discussion is only about instruction. It is directed by evidence of school data and student work as data to consider support for school improvement practices and to help teachers with instruction. There is no attempt in this meeting to discuss responses to or referrals about behavioral issues, truancies, or family issues, for example. These are important issues that have other pathways for discussion and decision making.

6. **Descriptive Feedback.** What we have been discussing in CMMs above is a series of opportunities for Descriptive Feedback. Coaching the principal and teacher through new strategies and coaching a student through new learning can be influenced dramatically by enabling all learners to self-assess and adapt their work based on effective Descriptive Feedback. The CMM is an opportunity to provide constructive Descriptive Feedback at every level.

When intense intervention is needed, the planning for it begins at the CMM. Parameter #5 is a critical parameter, as intense interventions must be in place for the earliest, at-risk learners and be ongoing with continuous support for all struggling learners, K–12.

PARAMETER #5: EARLY AND ONGOING INTERVENTION

The case study below is a strong example of how a Knowledgeable Other and colleagues use ongoing CMMs to identify students of concern, beginning with their youngest learners (Parameter #5).

Figure 7.16

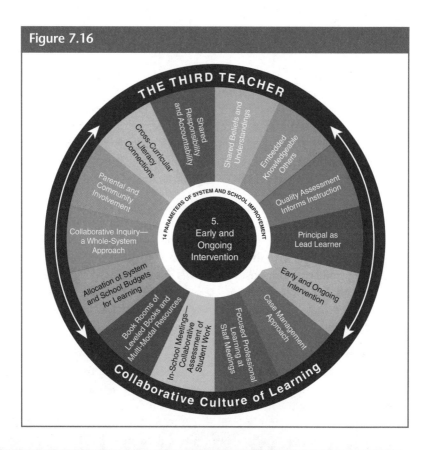

CASE STUDY: A CASE MANAGEMENT APPROACH TO EARLY INTERVENTION

Kari Lloyd, pedagogy coach, Hilder Road State School, and colleagues take a CMA to putting FACES on their data and taking immediate action to ensure prevention and intervention. Lloyd and the teachers use Differentiation Ladders (below), running record data collection, and a reading Data Wall to discuss focused strategies for each learner. Figure 7.17 is an example of records for CMMs focused on Grade 2 students. Every teacher, Kindergarten to Grade 2, is part of this Case Management process, using data scrutiny to differentiate instruction for all students—those who need extending, who are stuck, or who are struggling below expectation.

Figure 7.17 Hilder Road State School Differentiation Ladder

TEACHER/CLASS: Grade 2   SUBJECT: Reading—End Term 3 2017

Billy Blogs Level 30	• Significant Extension Required	**_Children operating within 12 months or more above expectation . . ._** • Extend literacy language • Focus on comprehension activities— Elle Cameron • Determine differentiated reading groups • Set individual reading goals • Focus on inference as comprehension skill needed • Word work—focuses on comprehension • Assess using _Words Their Way_ next term • Extend vocab knowledge and inferencing • Charlie: needs a wider range of text topics to read (always picks the same subject matter to read about)
Sarah Smith Level 27 Bob Down Level 26	• Some Extension Required	**_Children operating within 6 months above expectation . . ._** • Extend literacy language • Focus on several comprehension activities, such as retell, relate, reflect (Chapter 5) along with Sheena Crothers • Determine differentiated reading groups • Set individual reading goals • Wayne: stutters/anxiety, difficulty formulating answers. Working with school speech pathologist • More work on Level 26—work attack skills, reading strategies • Inferring comprehension skills for Levels 27 and 28

(Continued)

(Continued)

		Children operating at age-appropriate expectation ...
Tom Sayer Level 25 Tania Smith Level 24	• Achieving Year Level Expectations	<ul><li>Completing grade-level concepts</li><li>Focus on "fix-it-up" reading strategies</li><li>Differentiate reading groups daily</li><li>Set individual reading goals</li><li>Use more scaffolding and anchor charts as visual prompts</li><li>Tom: use *Leveled Literacy Intervention* Kit (Fountas & Pinnel) 4 times per week 1/2 hr—build confidence</li><li>Revision and repetition often</li><li>Oliver: needs to think more about what task is in front of him</li><li>Pat: needs to work on having a positive, resilient attitude—may need parent support</li><li>Bill and Tim: consolidate reading strategies—ask for home support</li></ul>
	• Some Support Needed	**Children operating within 6 months below expectation....** No children operating on this level
Fred Jones Level 3 Freda Jones Level 5	• Intensive Support Required	**Children operating within 12 months or more below expectation ...**<ul><li>Differentiate reading material at their instructional text level</li><li>Set individual reading goals</li><li>Provide explicit teaching in small groups</li><li>Teaching Assistant practices blends, sight words, daily writing</li><li>Both on *Leveled Literacy Intervention* Kit (Fountas & Pinnel) 4 times per week; provide visual prompts for fix-up reading strategies</li></ul>

		• Parent support to practice blends, sight words
		• Continue to offer learning activities that include physical movement and tactical experiences
		• Work on expanding vocabulary, alphabet consolidation

Notes

- Teachers use their ongoing assessment data sheets to fill in their ladders.

- The colors on both their Differentiation Ladders and their Data Wall correlate: green for progressing; yellow for stuck; red for below expectation.

- Teachers meet with Coach Lloyd at ongoing CMMs to discuss every student's progress in reading, writing, and math. Together they discuss the classroom adjustments that need to be made or the goals that need to be set for each child to continue to progress through the year.

- Lloyd and the teachers are focused on moving each child up the rungs of the Differentiation Ladders (Figure 7.17). Their goal is to have every child operating at an age-appropriate level or higher. To achieve this, they have to be very specific about what intervention strategies they put into place to match each learner's needs.

- During these CMMs, the teachers and Coach Lloyd are constantly asking themselves, "What specific skill or strategy do we need to focus on with this child to advance in his or her learning?"

This process is an impressive, ongoing, collaborative conversation about CLARITY and precision in practice with each early years teacher. Because of this intervention strategy impact, their Grades 3–6 colleagues are in the process of working with the head of teaching and learning (a new role) to hold CMMs to develop their own recording and tracking system to put FACES on the data.

Source: Kari Lloyd, personal communication, 2017.

AN EVIDENCE-PROVEN INTERVENTION IN EARLY READING

When students are struggling in reading and no intervention strategies recommended at CMMs are working, there is a third tier of intervention: one-on-one, early intervention for all students at risk of not learning to read.

Reading Recovery™ (Clay, 2001) is *my* intervention of choice because it is evidence proven to build teachers' capacity and students' strengths in becoming literate. Each component of the Reading Recovery (RR) lesson is intentional, staged or scaffolded, and critical in order to build the fluency and comprehension *processes* and lift the learning of each student daily (M. Sharratt, personal communication, 2018). The ultimate goal of this early intervention program is to enable young readers and writers to use literacy processing strategies effectively and independently so that they can participate successfully in excellent classroom literacy programs without the need for ongoing intervention or support.

In systems that successfully deploy RR teachers, these expert literacy teachers must become resources to the whole staff (see Sidebar). It is imperative to make the most of RR teachers and teacher-leaders as Knowledgeable Others and expert literacy resources in primary, middle, and secondary schools by having them

- work alongside other teachers to diagnose literacy needs,
- support resolving literacy difficulties,
- contribute as members of the school literacy leadership team,
- teach others about the implementation of the Gradual Release and Acceptance of Responsibility model in a balanced literacy approach (see Chapter 5).

Students in RR programs must return to classrooms where teachers mirror the RR approach, that is, quality literacy instruction that is tailor made and balanced, as in the Catholic Education Diocese of Parramatta.

Reading Recovery Professional Learning, using the teacher-leader model (see Chapter 8, the Knowledgeable Other), has always utilized a powerful learning community model that provides many opportunities for participants to marry theory with practice. Peurach and Glazer (2016, p. 1) recently described the Reading Recovery learning community as "an evolving, adaptive *epistemic* community in which teachers, leaders, coaches, and developers collaborate to produce, use, and refine the practical knowledge needed to support and sustain success among large numbers of struggling readers." Slavin (2016, p. 62) puts this idea more simply by saying "all members of the community are engaged in a process of learning and contributing intellectually to a whole that is bigger than themselves . . . it is enhanced by a focus on professionalism, and like professionalism, community contributes to both the effectiveness and sustainability" (Pru Smith, Reading Recovery trainer, personal communication, 2018).

Figure 7.18 depicts harsh conditions in which many students thrive when RR is the early intervention of choice.

Figure 7.18 Reading Recovery Makes a Difference Even in the Harshest Conditions

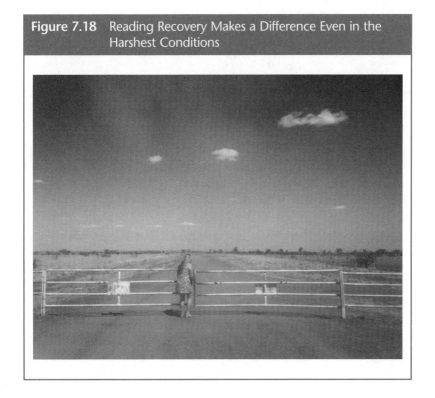

Source: Samantha Scholes, reading recovery teacher leader, Catholic Education, Broome, Western Australia, 2018.

IMPACT!

Sue Walsh, Catholic Education Diocese of Parramatta, reports that since 2011 a key system strategy to improve the literacy outcomes of all students has been the implementation of RR in all 55 primary schools to build classroom teachers' capacity because of the highly impactful training in literacy practices that they receive. While the focus of RR is to work with the most vulnerable students in Grade 1, leaders have ensured that teachers of RR are available to work with other vulnerable students throughout the school day, in small groups or with individuals as the needs demand. RR teachers are routinely selected as members of CMMs when support for presenting classroom teachers is needed in exploring and determining next steps to take with vulnerable students to improve their reading. In 2011, this system had 11 RR-trained teachers and at the end of 2017, they had more than 150 trained RR teachers working as RR teachers and also literacy coaches and class-room teachers. They now have many RR-trained principals and assistant principals. Once a RR teacher becomes experienced, he or she returns to the classroom with expert knowledge and another teacher trains from within the school. It's a never-ending loop of precise Professional Learning that has built a critical mass of expert reading teachers across the system. Did this implementation make a difference? In 2011, at the end of Kindergarten, there were 1,300 students who did not reach the "expected" benchmark, and at the end of 2016, only 245 students were below expectation at the end of Kindergarten. Walsh attributes this impressive result to the implementation of RR in every primary school. RR is evidence proven. The data show that RR-trained teachers are a key system strategy that improves reading for their earliest, most struggling Grade 1 learners. They continue to grow this strategy with outstanding results.

Source: Sue Walsh, deputy executive director and director of learning, Catholic Education Diocese of Parramatta, personal communication, 2018.

ALL EDUCATIONAL INTERVENTIONS MUST BE

1. **Early**—begin in Kindergarten and Grade 1

2. **Evidence Proven**—reflect increased, authentic results year after year

3. **Sustainable**—ensure all teachers become intervention teachers

4. **Customized**—match each student's needs

5. **Timely**—set and achieve targets in a reasonable time frame

RR meets all the above criteria.

All students must achieve—some against seemingly insurmount-able odds. Educators can provide for students only when they are with them—that time being often defined as "between the bells." There are many examples in this chapter of how to accomplish amazing things, between the bells and within the resources most schools and systems can provide, through precision in practice using co-constructed Data Walls as prevention and CMMs as intervention. Teachers and leaders need to use the information shared in Data Wall conversations and at CMMs to create inquiry questions to deepen understanding of effective, expected practices that will empower each learner. This leads me to think about the importance of formal and informal leaders who do the work described in this text, day in and day out. The final two chapters build on the learning and teaching sections of this book and focus on leading, by examining what it takes to lead the work of student improvement in all systems and schools.

COMMITMENT

I commit to:

- learning what trends the data in my system/school are showing me and taking action;

- creating a process of building a system/school Data Wall and taking underperforming student FACES from the wall into CMMs and following up with leader and teacher support through triage strategies recommended;

- ensuring every teacher is an intervention teacher;

- having a proven system strategy in place, like Reading Recovery, to ensure that every student can read by the end of Grade 1.

A DELIBERATE PAUSE TO CREATE CLARITY

What are you currently doing that aligns with the processes in this chapter? What must you adjust/review/fortify to increase CLARITY and a laser-like focus in your prevention and intervention practices?

Visit the companion website at
resources.corwin.com/CLARITY
for videos and downloadable resources

PART III
Leading

CLARITY
The Knowledgeable
Other—Leading Alongside

CHAPTER 8

1. How do I improve my teaching practice when I am so busy teaching?

2. Where do I go for help without fear of retribution?

3. Do I know how to teach every student to go beyond what I thought possible?

4. Do I believe that every student can learn given the right time and support? And what does that look like?

5. How can I have an open-to-learning stance to work alongside a Knowledgeable Other when, as leader, I should know all the answers?

What are you, the reader, wondering?

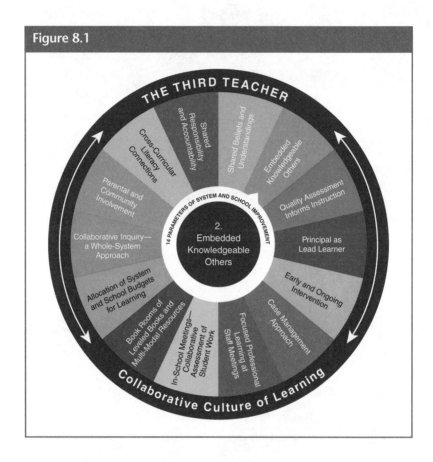

Figure 8.1

THE THIRD TEACHER

14 PARAMETERS OF SYSTEM AND SCHOOL IMPROVEMENT

2. Embedded Knowledgeable Others

- Shared Responsibility and Accountability
- Shared Beliefs and Understandings
- Embedded Knowledgeable Others
- Quality Assessment Informs Instruction
- Principal as Lead Learner
- Early and Ongoing Intervention
- Case Management Approach
- Focused Professional Learning at Staff Meetings
- In-School Meetings—Collaborative Assessment of Student Work
- Book Rooms of Leveled Books and Multi-Modal Resources
- Allocation of System and School Budgets for Learning
- Collaborative Inquiry—a Whole-System Approach
- Parental and Community Involvement
- Cross-Curricular Literacy Connections

Collaborative Culture of Learning

PARAMETER #2: THE EMBEDDED KNOWLEDGEABLE OTHER

My colleague, Martine Lewis, reinforces my notion that all teachers must be engaged in the process of improving the instructional program; principals cannot do this work alone or mandate this work. How does a principal inspire this process of learning from the best? Lewis believes this happens by really getting to know the individual teachers in the building. It involves having their best interests at heart and working toward finding and building connections that are relevant for each teacher. Lewis believes that working with people to develop varied pathways for their Professional Learning takes time but is incredibly rewarding. If the ultimate goal is improving student outcomes, then investing time working alongside each and every classroom teacher is the most effective way to build capacity. When teachers fully commit to their own learning, leaders know that they have built capacity on a deep and sustainable level. This requires school leaders to afford each teacher the opportunity to find and grow her or his learning passion, working alongside Knowledgeable Others (KOs) to do this work (Martine Lewis, principal, St. Augustine Catholic Secondary School, Toronto, Canada, personal communication, 2018).

The vision of a KO as described by Lewis is related to Parameter #2. A KO who works closely with principals, school leadership teams, and classroom teachers is an expert teacher who is embedded as a coach, mentor, or master teacher. The role is closely connected to the fourth dimension of Parameter #1: Educators must be able to clearly articulate why they do what they do every day.

Another way to look at the role is to place it on the competence-incompetence matrix (Figure 8.2) to determine the quadrant in which KOs operate. This learning stages model was developed by former Gordon Training Institute employee Noel Burch more than 30 years ago (Adams, 2018; Mind Tools, 2017). It is similar to the Gradual Release and Acceptance of Responsibility (GRR) model (Vygotsky, 1978). As in the GRR model where independent learning is the goal (see Chapter 9), "consciously skilled" is the most impactful quadrant in Burch's model. In my view, the ideal KO candidate must be in the fourth and most desirable quadrant, as shown in Figure 8.2. KOs must be consciously skilled to work alongside others in classrooms as master teachers with evidence-proven knowledge of teaching and learning and strong interpersonal skills.

BEING CONSCIOUSLY SKILLED

Why is being consciously skilled the desirable destination for all educators? I make the connection here between being consciously skilled and being a KO. According to the fourth dimension of Parameter #1,

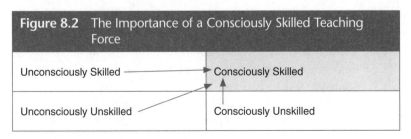

Figure 8.2 The Importance of a Consciously Skilled Teaching Force

| Unconsciously Skilled ——————→ Consciously Skilled |
| Unconsciously Unskilled | Consciously Unskilled |

Source: Adapted from Mind Tools (2017).

we must all be able to clearly articulate what we are teaching, why we are teaching it, and how we are teaching it. This only happens when we learn alongside others who have proven track records in teaching and learning. Those KOs who can articulate the difference that they have made for each student and teacher are consciously skilled and consciously competent.

Over the years, in many discussions with educators when I ask the question, "Who is the KO here?" it has been alarming to hear about the absence of knowledge of teaching and learning when system- and schoolwide decisions are being made. Unless every discussion, meeting, and Professional Learning Community forum has a KO, regardless of title or position, to guide the learning conversations (without participants fearing retribution), nothing of substance will be decided to improve students' achievement. Putting FACES on the data and taking action on the careful interpretation of the data demand that we include KOs in the conversations and at leadership decision-making tables. The KO must be a consciously skilled, highly competent teacher who can clearly articulate and model how to use assessment data to inform instruction and how to work alongside every teacher in every classroom.

In conversation with physics teacher Stuart Farmer, I discovered that many teachers' networks across the United Kingdom focus on these very capabilities. They celebrate, as I do, the concept of KOs who are needed in every school and system to move collaborative growth and precision in practice forward.

CASE STUDY: THE KNOWLEDGEABLE OTHER IN PROFESSIONAL LEARNING COMMUNITIES

It is important for school or school cluster Professional Learning Communities (PLCs) to have access to KOs to help progress learning and impact. Who these KOs may be, and what knowledge they may have, will depend on the nature and needs of the PLC, including the people involved and the type of Professional Learning and collegial working taking place. However, in almost all school-based PLCs, there is a need for a KO to help bridge the gap between school-based teachers, busy with day-to-day teaching, and educational research, which is often relatively difficult for teachers to access in relevant forms. This person can help feed in information as requested by the members of the PLC and also use her knowledge to support and challenge the thinking of the teachers in the PLC. In addition to bringing knowledge and challenge, there may well be a role for someone to help facilitate the smooth working of the PLC. Farmer believes that in his own subject area, physics, there is often a role for someone to help disseminate innovative and best practice in such areas as practical work or modeling approaches that work, using the GRR model. Farmer says KOs support improvement in both the teachers' subject matter knowledge and pedagogical content knowledge. In physics, for example, it is critical that KOs work alongside classroom teachers to explore and explain topics relatively new to the curriculum, like relativity, cosmology, and particle physics, which many teachers will not have experienced during their own education or initial teacher education.

Where these KOs might be found, or indeed "grown," is a major challenge facing education systems. There needs to be a relatively organic and flexible provision as PLCs across subject domains and stages will likely have quite diverse needs. One thing Farmer is sure about is that all KOs must be both passionate about their role and sympathetic and realistic about how they might interact with the members of the PLC as KOs are absolutely key to maximizing impact.

Source: Stuart Farmer, physics teacher and network coordinator, Scotland, personal communication, 2017.

As Farmer stated and I have learned, it is critical to have a role description as you begin to contemplate the implementation of the KO position. Careful selection of the KO from among candidates who can articulate evidence of their impact on building teachers' capacity, on increasing students' achievement, and can give examples of the following personal and professional attributes is critical!

My research and experience indicate that the ideal KO is a teacher and a learner who

- is respected and respectful;
- is trusted;
- is still teaching in the classroom part time;
- has strong interpersonal skills—reliable, responsible, resilient;

- is knowledgeable in content, process, environment and product in the classroom;

- is able to work alongside teachers;

- is not viewed by herself or himself as the expert;

- has facilitation skills;

- is flexible and humble;

- can demonstrate proven student success;

- has a wide repertoire and is curious about others' processes and practices;

- is well-versed in research-based practices and is able to adapt them to specific contexts and learning situations.

Colleague Tonya Ward Singer (2015) gives thoughtful tips on how KOs must proceed when working with a pair or a small group of teachers to shift teacher practice and personal professional expectations:*

- **Be sincere about fear.** Brainstorm together the worst possible outcomes of observing classroom impact together and notice the universal fears that emerge. Create norms together that honor those fears and create safety for team observations.

- **Choose a focus that matters.** Engage teachers in identifying a challenge in their practice that they especially want to solve and use that as the reason for their Collaborative Professional Inquiry (see Chapter 3).

- **Use a nonevaluative protocol.** Classroom observers watch to gather descriptive evidence of student learning, not to evaluate the teacher (see Learning Walks and Talks, Chapter 9). KOs use a protocol to keep conversations centered on impact and ask each other during the debrief, "What can we as a team do to refine our approach?"

- **Model risk taking.** The host teacher teaches the first lesson; the team plans and observes.

- **Honor imperfection.** When a lesson doesn't go as planned, teams have the richest conversations. Don't rob yourself of this experience by structuring or rehearsing lesson elements to the point of predictability. Invite imperfection so that together you can dare to push the edge of what is possible for students—and yourselves.

*Source: Tonya Ward Singer (2014, 2015), author and consultant, California.

Protected learning time in Professional Learning Communities (Chapter 3) must focus on building collective capacity for CLARITY in assessment (Chapter 4) and in instruction (Chapter 5), including Collaborative Inquiry with students (Chapter 6). Time in PLCs should include these six evidence-proven Professional Learning practices that KOs use in their coaching work alongside teachers and leaders:

1. Lesson study

2. Co-teaching cycle

3. Instructional coaching

4. Collaborative assessment of student work

5. Demonstration classrooms

6. Professional Collaborative Inquiry (discussed in Chapter 3)

These six high-impact approaches used by KOs are deconstructed as follows.

SIX EVIDENCE-PROVEN PROFESSIONAL LEARNING APPROACHES

1. LESSON STUDY

KOs find many ways to refine teachers' practice by being involved with them in Lesson Study. First practiced in Japan, Lesson Study adds pressure and support for guiding precise, specific, and targeted assessment that drives instruction with teachers keenly interested in improving their practice.

Lesson Study is Collaborative Inquiry when small groups of same-grade or same-course teachers come together with a KO to plan lessons working from curriculum expectations and achievement charts. Protocols are very helpful in staying focused and purposeful in the wise use of time during a small group Lesson Study of three to eight participants.

Lesson Study Protocol

1. Co-Construct Operating Norms

Co-construct group operating norms to maximize

- hearing all voices;
- investing in your own learning and the learning of others;
- creating a risk-free, safe, and fail fast environment;
- staying the course until a lesson is developed and taught twice;
- committing to revising practice to reflect the new learning.

2. Plan a Lesson Collectively

Brainstorm ideas and then focus on one big idea from the curriculum expectations. Collectively,

- plan a lesson, using all components of the Assessment Waterfall Chart (see Chapter 4),
- create a robust learning task for students that can be assessed against the Success Criteria (see Chapter 5),
- decide who will teach the planned lesson—do this last!

3. Observe Students' Thinking During the Lesson

Gather in the classroom in a small group, not to watch the teacher who offered to teach but to observe the students' thinking during the cooperatively designed lesson. Do not interfere with the lesson but, as observers, focus on students' learning and the thinking demanded in the lesson. Observe whether what was planned is reflected in the students' work.

4. Debrief

Debrief afterward, so that teacher-observers give feedback to each other and decide what worked, what didn't, and what they would do differently next time if they were teaching it to ensure students' higher order thinking. The group then revises the lesson based on the conversation about the collective observations and interpretations of the students' thinking.

5. Reteach

Another teacher from the group volunteers to teach the revised lesson with his or her class, with the same small group observing again, always with a focus on students' thinking.

6. Reflect and Record

As a group, reflect on the improvement in the lesson and record everyone's thinking. Commit to changing teaching practice using the most powerful new strategies learned as a result of this process. The same small group plans for the next opportunity to engage in this same Lesson Study process when two other teachers in the group will volunteer to teach a collaboratively planned lesson in their classrooms.

As one teacher said, "This is a fascinating process, going from brainstorming ideas that capture freely divergent thinking to firming up specific steps in a lesson. Establishing group norms to maximize participation was a valuable tool to frame this experience in a way that involves everybody." Another added his final impressions of being involved in Lesson Study by saying, "It was eye opening to follow a lesson from planning to providing the lesson. Watching without interfering gave me a chance to really understand how and what students were thinking and to determine if our tasks actually met the Learning Intention and gave all students an opportunity to achieve a high level, such as an 'A,' by assessing against the co-constructed Success Criteria." Another teacher commented that, "The debrief after the lesson was so valuable. As teacher, one cannot see everything going on; by having observers jotting notes, one learns a tremendous amount about each student's thinking and working during a group activity" (Kate Diakiw, former principal of Silver Stream PS and now superintendent of schools, York Region District School Board, Ontario, Canada, who continues to believe passionately in the Lesson Study approach. First published in Sharratt & Fullan, 2009)

> Lesson Study has been the most powerful job-embedded Professional Learning with which I have ever been associated. . . . When they retry the lesson, post revisions, they have been astounded, in many cases, to see the lowest level of achievement in the second class exceed the highest level of achievement in the first class. I have seen more teachers be "blown away" by the proof that what they do can change and increase the level of students' achievement. When teachers create the knowledge, themselves, it seems to be significantly more influential to changing their daily practice than any externally provided workshop or book. . . . It is awfully hard for participants to turn their backs on something they have

just proven to themselves works, through their own ideas and efforts. (Sharratt & Fullan, 2009; Kate Diakiw, personal communication, 2018)

Using the Lesson Study process in Ontario (Ontario Ministry of Education, 2012a), small groups of secondary teachers are exploring the notion of assessment that differentiates instruction in a safe and supportive environment by having the opportunity to

- be attentive to students' thinking,

- be alert to student voice,

- subsequently clarify points of view with Accountable Talk (Chapter 5),

- engage in developing a broad repertoire of instructional strategies upon which to draw when developing lessons collaboratively.

Lesson Study is one powerful example of how small groups of elementary or secondary teachers can develop their craft, guiding each other's practice by reviewing and refining instruction with a KO by their side.

2. THE CO-TEACHING CYCLE

The Co-Teaching Cycle is another key strategy that KOs use to bring coherence and precision to assessment that informs instruction (Sharratt & Fullan, 2012; Sharratt & Harild, 2015; Sharratt & Planche, 2016), as displayed in Figure 8.3. Co-teaching is an opportunity for two teachers to plan, teach, debrief, and reflect together on their practice and has very specific steps. I make three important observations here:

- **Critical**: planning is a mirror for each other's improvement

- **Imperative**: digitally recording the teaching so that the co-debrief and co-reflection processes focus on collecting the evidence of observable student thinking

- **Essential:** knowing that the process is messy and not lock step but ongoing, always striving for continuous refinement in practice

Figure 8.3 The Co-Teaching Cycle

Step 1: Co-Plan

- Find protected time with a trusted colleague or KO to plan, teach with video, debrief, and reflect

- Discuss what you each want to improve about your practice to give each other Descriptive Feedback during the process (your Collaborative Inquiry focus)

- Begin with the curriculum expectations, then plan the assessment to deconstruct the Learning Intentions, co-construct the Success Criteria, and provide a cognitively demanding performance task for students to be able to demonstrate their learning (Chapters 4 and 5)

- Plan the before, during, and after the lesson (Chapter 4), thinking about flow, timing, and pace

- Plan to use research-proven, high-impact instructional strategies differentiated based on student need (Chapter 5)

Step 2: Co-Teach

- Set up a digital recording device, like the swivel camera if possible, to follow the voice and images of the moving teachers

- Work side-by-side in a classroom

- Co-facilitate classroom Accountable Talk, hearing every student's voice

- Observe during teaching, "Who is doing the most talking and the most thinking in the classroom?"

- Monitor students' self-assessment by asking them, "What are you learning? Why? How are you doing? How do you know? How can you improve? Where do you go for help when stuck?" (See Chapters 2 and 9.)

- Change pace and flow if necessary

- Give ongoing Descriptive Feedback to students against the Success Criteria

- Check for students' understanding and learning against the Success Criteria

THE CO-TEACHING CYCLE

Step 4: Co-Reflect

- Discuss the co-teaching process: What worked? What didn't work? What would we do differently next time?

- Engage with partner in an open, honest dialogue about improving practice

- Identify and understand what changes in practice and beliefs need revision for you each to become consciously and competently skilled

- Plan next steps for students' and teachers' learning in this cycle of inquiry

Step 3: Co-Debrief

- Examine the video clip to look/listen for: more students' voices than teacher voice; higher-order questions and responses; creative critical thinking; students' use of the Success Criteria; students self-assessing and self-correcting

- Discuss teaching practices and prompts used

- Assess if the taught, learned, and assessed curriculum-based Learning Intentions were aligned using student work samples as evidence

- Give each other Descriptive Feedback about the Collaborative Inquiry question that each wanted to improve about his or her practice, looking closely at the video clip as a personal data source

- Use work samples to assess students' understanding and learning growth against the co-constructed Success Criteria. Ask, "Were they the correct Learning Intention and Success Criteria?"

- Decide what needs revision

Source: Adapted from Sharratt and Harild (2015).

Co-teaching (Sharratt & Fullan, 2009; Sharratt & Harild, 2015, Sharratt & Planche, 2016) is most powerful when a KO and a teacher have time during the school day to be engaged in the all steps of the process, as follows:

Step 1: Co-Plan

- Find protected time with a trusted colleague or KO to plan, teach with video, debrief, and reflect.

- Discuss what you each want to improve about your practice to give each other Descriptive Feedback during the process (your Collaborative Inquiry focus).

- Begin with the curriculum expectations, then plan the assessment to deconstruct the Learning Intentions, co-construct the Success Criteria, and provide a cognitively demanding performance task for students to be able to demonstrate their learning (Chapters 4 and 5).

- Plan the before, during, and after the lesson (Chapter 4), thinking about flow, timing, and pace.

- Plan to use research-proven, high-impact instructional strategies differentiated based on student need (Chapter 5).

Step 2: Co-Teach

- Set up a digital recording device, like the swivel camera if possible, to follow the voice and images of the moving teachers.

- Work side-by-side in a classroom.

- Co-facilitate classroom Accountable Talk, hearing every student's voice.

- Observe during teaching, "Who is doing the most talking and the most thinking in the classroom?"

- Monitor students' self-assessment by asking them, "What are you learning? Why? How are you doing? How do you know? How can you improve? Where do you go for help when stuck?"

- Change pace and flow if necessary.

- Give ongoing Descriptive Feedback to students against the Success Criteria.

- Check for students' understanding and learning against the Success Criteria.

Step 3: Co-Debrief

- Examine the video clip to look/listen for: more students' voices than teacher voice; higher-order questions and responses; creative critical thinking; students' use of the Success Criteria; students self-assessing and self-correcting.

- Discuss teaching practices and prompts used.

- Assess if the taught, learned, and assessed curriculum-based Learning Intentions were aligned using student work samples as evidence.

- Give each other Descriptive Feedback about the Collaborative Inquiry question that each wanted to improve about his or her practice, looking closely at the video clip as a personal data source.

- Use work samples to assess students' understanding and learning growth against the co-constructed Success Criteria. Ask, "Were they the correct Learning Intention and Success Criteria?"

- Decide what needs revision.

Step 4: Co-Reflect

- Discuss the co-teaching process: What worked? What didn't work? What would we do differently next time?

- Engage with partner in an open, honest dialogue about improving practice.

- Identify and understand what changes in practice and beliefs need revision for you each to become consciously and competently skilled.

- Plan next steps for students' and teachers' learning in this cycle of inquiry.

The best professional development time that I've ever spent is when I've been given release time by administrators to work with other teachers. . . . That's invaluable time. That's where we accomplish so much more because we are learning from each other and each other's experience. . . . Creating units and lessons for our classes—that's the time that we need. Together. It's the collaboration that is huge. (Ontario Ministry of Education, 2012, p. 54)

3. INSTRUCTIONAL COACHING

When planning to embed classroom improvement in assessment and instruction, a KO in an instructional coaching role is an invaluable asset. Collaborative Learning with a KO can have its advantages and its cautions as well. Jim Knight's insightful book, *Unmistakable Impact* (2011), clearly outlines the elements of impactful instructional coaching where effective coaches become partners with leaders and teachers to support change processes. Instructional coaches have expertise in quality teaching practices, such as assessment that improves instruction, and often in particular subject areas. They are highly sought after to share that knowledge. KOs as instructional coaches model practices in the classroom, work alongside teachers, and engage in supportive learning conversations. One of the important takeaways from reflecting on instructional coaching is that good coaches have learned to

- resist rushing in to solve the problems of others,

- help others to solve their own problems,

- listen actively,

- respond reflectively,

- support and partner (adapted from Knight, 2007, 2011).

When voice, choice, and respectful listening are evident while working with an instructional coach, teachers are more likely to feel a sense of partnership as professional equals, which helps to keep an important sense of efficacy intact (Knight, 2007, 2011). Effective coaches listen as much as speak or suggest. They focus on assessment that gives teachers information to differentiate instruction the very next day (see Chapters 4 and 5). Partners discuss learning, dialogue together to make sound decisions, and give each other feedback that increases learning for all involved—including learning for the instructional coaches. Instructional coaches, as KOs, use the GRR model to move from modeling *for* teachers to sharing and guiding practice *with* teachers to ensure that all teachers become consciously skilled, interdependent practitioners. Principals and coaches must realize the time commitment needed to do this work and what a partnership approach entails. They must balance that investment of time against the return in higher student achievement and the increased depth of teaching capacity created (Sharratt & Planche, 2016). KOs who approach colleagues with sensitivity and inviting dispositions are soon welcomed into teacher-leader learning conversations as valued instructional coaches.

4. COLLABORATIVE ASSESSMENT OF STUDENT WORK

Collaborative assessment of student work (CASW) occurs when educators examine and annotate student work with a partner or in small groups. Led by a KO, the process allows for students' thinking to be unpacked and students' understandings, strategies, and transitional conceptions to be discussed (Ontario Ministry of Education,

Web Resource 5:
A Professional
Learning Protocol
for Collaborative
Assessment of
Student Work

2007). CASW demands that operating norms are set and reviewed at the beginning of each session and that a definitive learning protocol to assess student work is in place in order to ensure objectivity. For sample norms and protocol, see **Web Resource 5: A Professional Learning Protocol for Collaborative Assessment of Student Work**.

Rather than simply working together to reach consensus on a grade or mark as in teacher moderation, CASW is meant to achieve a deep understanding about *how the assessment* of a student work sample:

- reflects the Success Criteria

- informs Descriptive Feedback

- drives the next level of instruction needed

The power of this process culminates when teachers around the table express feedback in two ways:

1. Descriptive Feedback for the classroom teacher on next steps for teaching the student

2. Descriptive Feedback that the classroom teacher will give to the student to deepen his or her understanding of the next steps needed in his or her growth and achievement

Given constructively, Descriptive Feedback can change not only learning conversations but also classroom practice. For collaboration to make a difference, it must focus on *the interpretation of the evidence* of student learning and on understanding what impact the instruction has or has not had. Ultimately, teachers and leaders need to understand how to best change classroom practice so that all students can achieve the expected levels of growth each school year (Sharratt & Planche, 2016).

Collaborative professionalism (Sharratt, 2016) begins to show in the work teachers and leaders accomplish together in CASW, especially when it involves the participation of teachers from varying grade levels across a division. Hearing the opinions of teachers in similar, previous, and subsequent grades to understand what they feel is required learning based on the curriculum expectations can stimulate learning about one's own teaching improvement needs—or can offer support to the view that the instruction is on target. If CASW takes place on a regular basis and several teachers share samples of student work at each session, program coherence is strengthened and consistency of practice across classrooms is more likely (Sharratt in Elliott-Johns, 2013). When embedded in PLC time, CASW accomplishes precision in practice when teachers learn and grow their practice together.

5. DEMONSTRATION CLASSROOMS OF EXEMPLARY PRACTICE

If teachers don't see what effective practice is, they will revert to the ways they have always taught, or worse yet, to the ways they were taught (Gallimore & Emerling, 2012). This is the rationale for ensuring that there are classrooms accessible to all leaders and teachers to observe, discuss, reflect, and act on exemplary practice.

To support the system goal of assessment-based instruction that is differentiated to meet the strengths, needs, and interests of all learners, it is important to move from informal visits with a few teachers to a strategic, systemwide implementation process of designating what I call Demonstration Classrooms. Some systems have systematic plans in place where strong teachers have been asked to open their classroom doors to visitors to share their exemplary practice. When this occurs, teachers and leaders begin to engage in conversations about what high-impact instruction looks, sounds, and feels like in engaging classrooms.

Demonstration Classrooms provide formalized opportunities for leaders and teachers to accompany their KOs to observe and review elements of classroom practice based on the concept that learning by experiencing successful practice will be an important support to changing teacher practice.

The selection and quality assurance of Demonstration Classrooms are key because Demonstration Classrooms must reflect the teaching and learning work of the system. They must be identified in consultation with superintendents, principals, and consultants who develop Success Criteria for the selection of the Demonstration Classroom teachers. School team visits to Demonstration Classrooms are coordinated by the system's Teaching and Learning Department. Visiting school teams always include the principal and plan to have time to observe and then dialogue with the Demonstration Classroom teacher. These visitations provide opportunities for KOs, teachers, and leaders to see high-impact practice in action and to discuss the implications for their own whole-school Professional Learning.

Each school with a Demonstration Classroom receives a wide variety of supports:

- technology for the Demonstration Classroom

- release time for ongoing monthly explicit Professional Learning sessions with principals, system consultants, and other Demonstration Classroom teachers to ensure that what they are sharing system-wide is truly best practice

- time for the Demonstration Classroom teachers to debrief with the visitors after each visit

Here is an example of a protocol for the visits:

1. Superintendent, school leader, and KO apply to a central administrator to book the Demonstration Classroom visit.

2. The central administrative assistant checks the shared calendar for availability of Demonstration Classroom teacher.

3. Date, time, and names of visitors are confirmed with visitors and Demonstration Classroom teacher.

4. Visitors fill out a planning template indicating preparation taken for the visit and questions developed to focus the time spent.

5. Template is shared with the Demonstration Classroom teacher.

6. After being in the classroom, visitors have time to meet with the Demonstration Classroom teacher and discuss their questions in order to further embed their understanding of the practices observed.

7. At a cluster meeting or area PLC meeting, Demonstration Classroom visitors report on actions taken, after the visit, to improve practice back at their schools, and how their learning will be mobilized with other regional leaders and teachers.

8. Others are encouraged to learn from these Demonstration Classroom experiences and to open further doors so that there is inclusive access to seeing high-impact practices and time to talk about changes needed.

In this way, exemplary practice becomes deprivatized and pervasive across a system in a systematic, shared approach to putting action around the three considerations previously suggested (on page 182) by Gallimore and Emerling (2012). System and school leaders design Demonstration Classrooms as one way to

- develop and improve teachers' professional knowledge for teaching (assessment that informs instruction),

- develop the judgment capacity needed to deliver timely and effective assessment and instruction and [critically] reinstruction,

- address some conditions probably needed at the system, district, and school levels to get teacher teams to challenge themselves rather than settle for improving how they already know how to teach (Gallimore & Emerling, 2012, pp. 41–50).

6. PROFESSIONAL COLLABORATIVE INQUIRY

KOs use the process of cyclical Collaborative Inquiry, as discussed in detail in Chapter 3. Employing a collaborative approach defuses the fear and focuses the conversations on what instructional practices are recommended to bring each student along (Knight, 2013). For those in fear of failing or of making changes to undifferentiated teaching practices, for example, the resulting discussions of specific pedagogical change are easier when they are perceived to be supportive by using one of these co-learning processes. KOs use an instructional coaching stance most successfully when the school culture authentically supports changing practice.

Tracey Petersen shared with me an instructional coaching experience in which, as a KO, she used the components of the Assessment Waterfall Chart (Chapter 4, Figure 4.4) and the Co-Teaching Cycle (Figure 8.3) to seize teachable moments in a small group Collaborative Inquiry opportunity.

CASE STUDY: A KNOWLEDGEABLE OTHER USES THE CO-TEACHING CYCLE TO WORK ALONGSIDE CLASSROOM TEACHERS

I was involved in a co-plan, co-teach, co-debrief, and co-reflect cycle (Figure 8.3) with a group of Grade 5 teachers. We first worked together to analyze the curriculum intent and assessment demands of a unit of work. The assessment task required students to discuss the way that the author of a novel created an emotional response in the reader. Students needed to be able to talk about the way the text was structured, the way

(Continued)

(Continued)

the sentences were structured, and the language features that the author used to create an emotional response in the reader.

We (coach and teachers) looked for a passage of text that would allow students to think about how the text made them feel and the features of the text that caused this reaction. We selected a passage that was about two pages long.

From there we started to plan the lesson. We considered it in two phases—curriculum input and curriculum output. That is, there would be some teaching (input) using the selected passage of text; then there would be an expected demonstration of learning (output) when students created text (orally) to represent their thinking. We planned that students would write a brief paragraph to describe their emotional response to the text and then describe how the author used text structure and language features to cause that response.

As instructional coach, I demonstrated to the teachers how to select and plan to deconstruct the Learning Intention (LI) and to co-construct the Success Criteria (SC) to provide their students with a clear picture of the expectations for the demonstration of their learning. Their LI and SC looked like this:

LI: We are learning to analyze how an author creates an emotional response in a reader.

SC: I can

- write a paragraph that describes how reading a passage made me feel,

- write a response that demonstrates how the author used text structure and language features to make me feel that way.

A Demonstration of the Co-Teaching Cycle

In the co-planning stage of the cycle, each of us could clearly articulate what it would look like if students could demonstrate this learning, and thus we had a clear, shared vision of what success looked like. We shared this specificity with the students.

The next step was to use the GRR model (Figure 8.4) to determine how we would scaffold students' thinking, first about the text they were

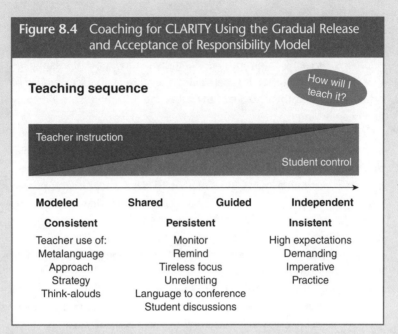

Figure 8.4 Coaching for CLARITY Using the Gradual Release and Acceptance of Responsibility Model

Teaching sequence

How will I teach it?

Teacher instruction

Student control

Modeled	Shared	Guided	Independent
Consistent	Persistent		Insistent
Teacher use of:	Monitor		High expectations
Metalanguage	Remind		Demanding
Approach	Tireless focus		Imperative
Strategy	Unrelenting		Practice
Think-alouds	Language to conference		
	Student discussions		

Source: Tracey Petersen, 2018.

reading and second about the text they were creating. In the modeled phase of GRR, we planned to use Think-Alouds to make clear to students how we think as we read the text.

As we co-taught, the teachers observed students' thinking while, as instructional coach, I unpacked the words in the LI and co-constructed the SC with the students; then I read the selected part of the text to the students. I provided them with a Think-Aloud that aligned with the intended learning. There were lots of things that we could have thought about in using this text, but it was very important that we kept our thinking sharply aligned with the learning that students needed to do. My Think-Aloud remained tightly aligned with the LI and modeled how to answer the questions "How is this part of the text making me feel?" and "How did the author make me feel that?"

As we moved into shared and guided phases of the lesson together, I invited the students to read the section of text with a partner and have a discussion about how the author had made them feel. I walked about the

(Continued)

(Continued)

room and joined conversations. I listened to students' thinking; I asked questions to clarify thinking; and I engaged students in the language that the learning required. I then called the students back to the larger group and asked them to share their thinking and the discussions they had been having.

One student reported to the group that the author had made him feel happy *and* sad. When I asked him to explain his thinking, he explained that when he had read the first paragraph he had thought that the main character was being made by his father to release two of the pelican chicks that he had been raising into the wild. He said that he felt happy about this because it meant that the character would be able to keep one pelican chick as his only friend. Then, when he read two paragraphs later, he realized that the character was actually being made to release all three pelican chicks and this would leave him with no friends. So the student felt that the author had structured the text to hide some information then reveal it later, and this had created an emotional response in the reader.

Our co-debrief between coach and teachers was enlightening. We all realized that this student had offered an interpretation that had not been provided by our modeling. The student's response demonstrated that he had met the Learning Intention and Success Criteria. In planning for this lesson, not one of us at the table had seen what this student described to us. None of us had seen that the author had held back some information then revealed it to heighten the emotional response in the reader. This student had brought his own enlightened thinking to the group and, in doing so, had developed and progressed the thinking of everyone, including the teachers!

In our co-reflection, we discussed the following:

- This is what it looks like to invite students to think.

- This is what it looks like when genuine collaborative learning happens.

- This is what it looks like when we are open to students surprising us by having an open-to-learning stance.

- This is what it looks like to use text to teach as a co-learner rather than insist students must adopt a certain point of view about the text.

> One teacher summed up, saying that his most powerful learning was, "*If* I reflect on the evidence of learning each day, *then* the students will be learning [LI] and know what to do to be successful [SC]."
>
> Reading is thinking so that you allow yourself to become part of the text and allow it to become part of you. When we show students *how* to think about text, rather than *what* to think about text, we invite them to achieve. When we invite students to contribute to the thinking of everyone, students and teachers become co-partners in the learning process.
>
> Source: Tracey Petersen, instructional coach, personal communication, 2018.

System and school leaders look to their cadre of specifically skilled collaborators or KOs (such as literacy coaches, curriculum consultants, master teachers, or subject specialists) when planning improvement actions. An instructional coach, such as Tracey Petersen, is a valuable asset who persuasively works alongside system leaders, school leaders, and teachers to make a difference—often one teacher at a time—which is affordable and scalable when we think about the number of students being impacted by each teacher over many years.

Systems and schools described in this book are exemplary learning organizations that focus on building leader and teacher capacity to increase all students' growth and achievement. Leader behaviors and skills needed to do this work are the focus of the final chapter, Chapter 9, as leadership is the culminating event that makes the 14 Parameter Framework come alive.

COMMITMENT

I commit to

- attaching myself to a KO to learn from and with each other,

- being part of a small group to change classroom practice using one of the six approaches in this chapter, such as the Lesson Study approach,

- being a KO who finds a partner to teach with using the Co-Teaching Cycle,

(Continued)

(Continued)

- having an open-to-learning stance to engage others in CASW,

- conducting Learning Walks and Talks in classrooms (see Chapter 9) to find teachers leading quality assessment and instructional practices who could become Demonstration Classroom teachers,

- developing Demonstration Classrooms across my system—starting first in my school by encouraging Co-Teaching and working with KOs.

A DELIBERATE PAUSE TO CREATE CLARITY

Consider your own level of comfort and skill with the strategies and concepts shared in this chapter. Identify where you are most "consciously skilled" and where you have room to grow. What steps might you take next in your own learning? In staff learning? How will you get buy-in from staff members to work alongside a KO to improve their practice? What processes might you use to engage staff in collaboratively examining promising practices? How will you protect time for staff learning? What are your criteria for selecting a KO to become a Demonstration Classroom teacher? What are the benefits of having Demonstration Classrooms in the system? How does instructional coach Tracey Petersen use assessment knowledge to move teachers' thinking forward? Compare and contrast the teachers' dispositions and learning in Petersen's instructional coaching examples at the end of Chapter 5 and Chapter 8. What can you apply to your context?

Visit the companion website at
resources.corwin.com/CLARITY
for videos and downloadable resources

CLARITY
Precision in
Leadership Practice

CHAPTER 9

Wonderings...

1. How can we build shared beliefs and understandings across our whole system and in my school?

2. How can we, as system leaders, keep our resolve and nerve to stay with the plan?

3. How can we drive the practice of collaborative leadership through the entire system?

4. How can we initiate and maintain system and school nonnegotiables? How can we foster ownership and active alignment of these nonnegotiables?

5. We have successful schools who don't know why and unsuccessful schools who don't why. How do we help each to know the "why"?

6. Where will I find the time and a circle of professionals with whom to broaden my circle of practice?

What are you, the reader, wondering?

Figure 9.1

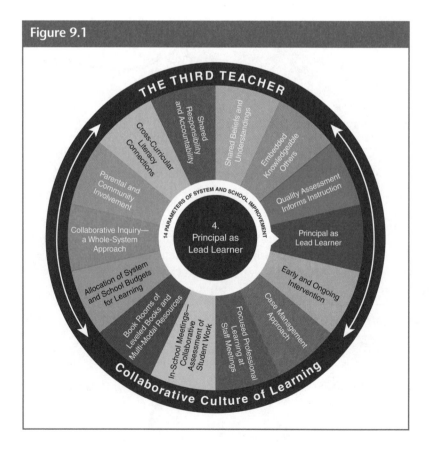

PARAMETER #4: PRINCIPALS AND SYSTEM LEADERS AS LEAD LEARNERS

Principals and system leaders are lead learners; what differs is only the context from which each leads. That belief and role attribution needs to be clearly embedded throughout the organization if it is to become a learning organization, that is, an organization continually at the top of its game and getting better, wanting every one of its students to continually grow and to succeed (Sharratt, 1996). To be valued as leaders, individual leaders must understand and exhibit the essential behaviors that research has determined to be associated with their roles.

> Educational leadership is a deeply social practice. Education professionals concentrate their efforts on promoting the advancement of their communities by fostering learning at all levels. They act as advocates for their communities' interests, as boundary spanners, brokers of knowledge and resources, and as facilitators of innovation and improvement. (Dr. Alvaro Gonzalez Torres, program coordinator, LIDERES EDUCATIVOS, Leadership Center for School Improvement, Pontificia Universidad Católica de Valparaíso, Chile)

Having CLARITY in all aspects of leadership behavior is key to making the entire enterprise of a school or system work best and become a learning organization (Sharratt, 1996). Leaders in learning organizations are *consistent*, *persistent*, and *insistent* in knowing, expecting, and seeing effective, high-impact practices that have a positive impact on all students in every classroom, as noted in the following narrative. Client and colleague Dr. Doug Ashleigh reflects on the leadership phases required to lead growth in achievement in a large educational system.

CASE STUDY: LEADING IN A TIME OF LEARNING GROWTH URGENCY

Leading in a time of learning growth urgency is a process peppered with paradox. However, the key Success Criteria should be reflected in leaders being easily replaced without the system or school losing momentum.

(Continued)

(Continued)

The success of any systemic learning growth strategy cannot be dependent on the personality and persuasion of the leader. To be impactful, system and school leader capability moves from

- leaders intentionally engaging in a dialogue of no excuses, focusing directly on the moral imperative of Parameter #1, to

- leaders being responsible in using evidence of learning that often requires input and shaping from Knowledgeable Others, stakeholder consultation, and a commitment to resourcing, to

- leaders who demand a systemwide focus on precision pedagogy, learning leadership, and intentional Professional Learning, to

- leaders who identify increasing numbers of remarkable leadership moments in which what previously seemed impossible learning growth becomes possible, to finally,

- leaders who are capable of establishing pervasive innovative and responsive cultures of growth characterized by relational trust

The leader is, therefore, called upon to create the conditions to allow learning growth and trust to flourish in every system and school. This is what "en-ables" momentum to be sustained when leaders leave.

Source: Dr. Doug Ashleigh, deputy executive director, Brisbane Catholic Education, personal communication, 2017.

IMPACT!

After reading Ashleigh's dynamic reflections, it is no surprise that Brisbane Catholic Education (BCE) has astoundingly increased their overall student performance using the 14 Parameters as their self-assessment tool. Leaders in BCE know how all students are growing and achieving. For example, BCE's growth in effect size in Grade 3 to Grade 5 for reading, writing, and numeracy is above the 2017 Australian effect size, including writing, which was below the Australian effect size in 2016. In comparing 2016 to 2017 data,

- 150 more Kindergarten (Prep) students are at the expected benchmark in reading,

- 250 more Grade 1 students are at the expected benchmark in reading,

- 550 more Grade 2 students are at the expected benchmark in reading,

- 1,050 more Grade 3 students are at the expected level in writing,

- 1,300 more Grade 4 students are at the expected level in writing,

- 1,250 more Grade 5 students are at the expected level in writing,

- 550 more Grade 9 students are at the expected level in writing.

To me, leaders who have powerful vision, like Ashleigh and the leaders highlighted throughout this text, are not only consistent, persistent, and insistent but they exhibit **adapt-ability.** They attain and maintain remarkable results through differentiated support and being "all over the detail." These leaders never give up, never quit, never accept excuses, and seemingly never get worn out.

As Ashleigh describes and Galdames reports, "educational leadership is distinct from other kinds of leadership because it is focused on the critical areas of teaching and learning. Great educational leaders prioritize learning above all other actions, actively supporting teachers to improve their capacities and working conditions in favor of students" (Sergio Galdames, educational researcher, Chile, personal communication, 2018).

I incorporate these views and those of my research colleagues (Sharratt & Fullan, 2012; Sharratt & Harild, 2015; Sharratt & Planche, 2016) in considering the dimensions of educational leadership and elaborate on the new sixth dimension, which was informed by the many practitioners who contributed to this book. Figure 9.2 depicts all six leadership dimensions that, when considered together, create systems and schools that are learning organizations:

1. Knowledge-ability

2. Mobilize-ability

3. Sustain-ability

4. Imagine-ability

5. Collabor-ability

and my most current research that indicates the need for

6. Adapt-ability

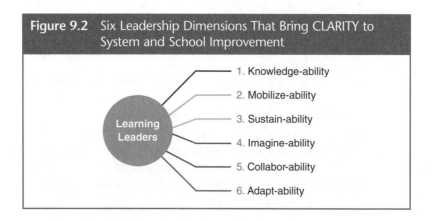

Figure 9.2 Six Leadership Dimensions That Bring CLARITY to System and School Improvement

Learning Leaders

1. Knowledge-ability
2. Mobilize-ability
3. Sustain-ability
4. Imagine-ability
5. Collabor-ability
6. Adapt-ability

FUNDAMENTAL CHALLENGE

Access the leadership self-assessment tool **Web Resource 10: Self-Assessing Against the Six Leadership Dimension Skills.** I suggest all leaders take this assessment before and after reading this chapter, then compare your contrasting responses. The assessment covers the six leadership dimensions and breaks down each one into several specific actions that *together* demonstrate full implementation of that skill.

The Self-Assessment Tool asks you as leaders to

1. Rate yourself on a (1) to (5) scale of awareness of the skill, where (5) is full implementation of the skill in your daily practice

2. Identify the next steps you will take to strengthen each skill toward (5)

3. Identify the Professional Learning you will need to improve on each skill

Web Resource 10:
Self-Assessing Against the Six Leadership Dimension Skills

Using this tool will assist in your reflection on what it takes to be an instructional leader at every level of a school system.

THE SIX DIMENSIONS OF LEADERSHIP

How does a district move from pockets of improvement in some schools to improvement in most schools and most classrooms, then importantly to improvement in *every school*, in *every classroom*? In other words, how does a system or district move to *all* students showing learning growth and achievement? This is the ongoing issue for us all, the issue for which we are responsible and accountable. This is our moral imperative. I am now convinced that the answer lies in the leadership it takes to become centered on learning—on our own learning, on that of our peers, and especially on the learning of *every* student.

The following six leadership dimensions and their component skills, displayed in Figure 9.2, must be considered as acting together—interwoven and inextricably linked—for any leader to be considered an **impactful** instructional leader.

1. STRONG LEADERS ARE KNOWLEDGEABLE

Leaders need to be Knowledgeable Others (Sharratt, Ostinelli, & Cattaneo, 2010) when leading sustainable change in classroom practice. As one research respondent said, "leaders need to know how to teach and how to think like teachers" (Sharratt & Fullan, 2012). There is a specific skill set required here: knowing how teaching causes learning and vice versa. To me, being a Knowledgeable Other is more about listening hard to "hear" the questions to ask rather than "telling" everyone the answers. Knowledgeable leaders use questions to bring CLARITY to data concerns and to bring transparency to niggling problems. They confidently work alongside staff to interrogate the data, asking, "How will we teach to stretch this student's thinking?" and "What will we do if this student isn't learning?" As all meetings move to become inclusive problem-solving tables focused on learning, knowledgeable leaders explore the processes of assessment and instruction necessary for each student to accomplish cognitively demanding and engaging tasks.

Leaders who are unsure about their own level of competence in thinking like a teacher must find Knowledgeable Others in order to learn alongside them. In sum, leaders need to know the right questions to ask of themselves and their colleagues and strive to find a multiplicity of answers gleaned from implementing collaborative sharing processes.

Leaders with **Knowledge-ability** ask,

- Do I model a belief that all students can and will learn and all teachers can learn to teach?

- Do I use relevant data to make decisions to improve learning for all and measure impact of teaching on learning?

- Do I use improvement data to track my effectiveness as a leader?

- Do I provide for and participate with teachers in ongoing Professional Learning to ensure wise and timely use of relevant assessment data to differentiate instruction every day?

- Do I conduct Learning Walks and Talks every day to collect evidence of the impact of Professional Learning sessions and of classroom instructional practices?

- Do I have open-to-learning conversations by talking with teachers about their practice after many Learning Walks and Talks? (Sharratt, 2008–2018)

2. STRONG LEADERS MOBILIZE SELF AND OTHERS

Leaders need to clearly articulate a shared vision. Guskey's (1986) finding that changes in teacher beliefs and motivation come after changes in practice suggests that to achieve deeper conceptual change, beliefs will change only after each teacher sees the effects of new strategies on student learning and not as the result of prolonged discussions about theory. Successful practice changes beliefs only when the vision articulated by leaders aligns with the shared beliefs and successful practices. Leaders know how to mobilize teams to refine the improvement work together in ways that allow team members to **hear each other's thinking to build collective capabilities.** Mobilize-ability involves formal leaders, principals, vice-principals, headteachers, superintendents, and consultants listening and thinking alongside teachers in an atmosphere of mutual respect. Together, they must "leave their titles at the door" and embrace ego-free leadership. Leadership through an equity lens enables and drives authentic, student-centered learning—together.

Leaders who mobilize themselves and others determine the evidence of learning in classrooms by rolling up their sleeves and learning alongside others *how to do the work*. Strong leaders learn what is working and what is not working with the help of a master teacher or Knowledgeable Other at their side. Collaborative Professionalism (Sharratt, 2016) truly means everyone must be brought along and mobilized to put FACES on the data, so that the system and school vision is *realized*.

Leaders with **Mobilize-ability** ask,

- Do I create a sense of collective urgency to put FACES on the data and convey the vision of a shared moral imperative?

- Do I provide encouragement and support for teachers to take the lead by distributing leadership, sharing responsibility, and modeling accountability?

- Do I have and communicate high expectations for every student and teacher?

- Do I create and participate in rich conversations about every FACE by co-constructing Data Walls and providing timetabled problem-solving forums called Case Management Meetings?

- Do I create a learning environment in my school or system which permits, enables, and fosters an absolute belief that I care and that my colleagues care about every thoughtful opinion expressed?

- Do I give and get feedback?

- Do I use information to inform and guide my own practice as a leader?

3. STRONG LEADERS SUSTAIN THE WORK

As a colleague and friend Dr. Avis Glaze (2017) writes,

> One can only hope that one's professional imperative has been to bring about meaningful change, where needed—changes that have an enduring impact on people and their organizational culture by reaching the heart of leadership. This means, among other things, cultures that are healthy, people- and results-oriented, focused on capacity building and responsive to change. It also means becoming instruments of change and reflective stewards, constantly honing their skills and cogitating on the reasons they chose leadership in the first place.

The process of scaling up improvement strategies needs to be considered carefully—think big and start small. While every new strategy must be scalable to include all schools in a system, start small, get it right, assess again, and add more schools in Professional Learning forums. The positive momentum generated from small wins along the way can be more powerful than launching a well-tested, grandiose change effort. Small wins, one student and one teacher at a time, lead to high energy and sustainable synergy within a system. Maintaining integrity to the changes being advocated on behalf of all students demands nimble leadership that includes continuous evaluation of what has been achieved in order to move forward swiftly where action is required.

Sustain-ability is not only related to the leader. We think that if the leader leaves, the improvement will dissipate or disappear. Not at all. Sustain-ability should have the characteristic of "simplexity" (Sharratt & Fullan, 2012), in other words, be both simple and complex. Sustain-ability doesn't just come from the leader in charge, although it helps if she is mindful of her important role in developing other leaders. Sustain-ability comes from those who do the work and mobilize new knowledge. Sustain-ability of improvement efforts is in distributing leadership to all and in achieving collective understanding by all (Harris, 2014). Simplexity is empowering all to deliver precision in practice in every classroom.

Leaders must be able to see the process unfold from their position of being both "in the balcony" and "on the dance floor." A continual review process causes leaders to self-reflect and self-evaluate often and demands that they differentiate their leadership support to followers through modeled, shared, guided, interdependent, and applications stages (see Chapter 9) in every classroom.

Sustaining the work is about breaking the mindset that, "I am the expert and I need to know all the answers" and moving humbly to an inquiry stance, "How do we, together, accomplish success for all?"

As a leader, it takes confidence to risk and be wrong—to be a strong example and a weak example in the same week. The Sustain-ability test must be, "Can I be replaced without anyone noticing?" Strong leaders leave many behind to lead so that when they are gone, no one falters.

Leaders with **Sustain-ability** ask,

- Do I open classroom doors to make teaching and learning public?

- Do I build a caring community of learners which includes parents and the broader community as partners?

- Do I create a "we-we" culture of learning where there is responsibility and accountability for all students' within and across schools?

- Do I create a trusting and respectful learning environment where students and teachers feel safe to take risks, make mistakes—and where mistakes are seen as learning opportunities?

- Do I develop and leave many leaders behind to continue the achievement work when I am gone?

- Do I ensure transparency, accountability and ownership by all for achieving the desired results?

- Can I be easily and seamlessly replaced? (Sharratt, 2016)

4. STRONG LEADERS POSSESS IMAGINE-ABILITY

Tracy Petersen (personal communication, 2018) defines Imagine-ability as

the willingness to undertake a true Collaborative Inquiry. In a true Collaborative Inquiry, you don't know *before* you begin the answers you may find *during* the inquiry. It is a leap of faith to investigate something that may or may not impact learning. Without the mindset to do this we see leaders who want to try new stuff, but who are too afraid to fail. Therefore, they wait and watch and hope someone else will tell them what to do.

A leader who progresses to Imagine-ability has an open-to-learning stance and models the belief that all students can participate in the workplace and in society and achieve their own personal best.

This leader challenges every student to be confident enough to feel that she or he can change the world. These leaders achieve high levels of system and school performance and share this leadership knowledge with others. They take calculated risks informed by research and lead where no one has gone before; in addition, they try alternative approaches to achieving increased student success for all when no one else believes there is a problem that requires a solution.

The leader with Imagine-ability identifies opportunities for all students and teachers and acts on them thoughtfully. She or he sets the collaborative conditions to enable students and teachers to develop a sense of "what is possible" from the perspective of multiple collaborators, including business and industry community partners, and advocates for change in the status quo to influence policy decisions that will result in equity and excellence in student outcomes.

Leaders with **Imagine-ability** ask,

- Do I bring everyone together with a clear sense of purpose for the improvement work?

- Do I communicate high expectations?

- Do I model the beliefs that students come first in every decision made together?

- Do I invite parent and community stakeholders to be part of our decision-making and problem-solving tables?

- Do I have a clear definition of equity and excellence to convey to others?

- Do I provide a sufficiently clear safety net to protect those who risk to offer new ideas and are willing to try innovative projects to benefit our students?

- Have I considered the alignment of our work at the system, school and classroom levels?

- Have I provided opportunities for team members to consider how all the pieces fit together?

- Am I willing to test and try out new ideas that encourage relentless curiosity? (Sharratt & Harild, 2015)

5. STRONG LEADERS HAVE COLLABOR-ABILITY

Leaders who use collaboration to move educators toward the vision articulate a clear purpose for collaborative work; organize time periods and schedules for collaborative work; reinforce shared beliefs and understandings about all student and staff success; build consensus on what specific areas for collaborative learning stand out through the analysis of student data; research and implement high-impact practices; deconstruct clear Learning Intentions and co-construct Success Criteria for learning through collaborative discourse and analysis; solidify a commitment to embedding an inquiry approach to collaborative work; establish and implement norms and protocols for collaborative engagement; support goals with ongoing scheduled time, resources, and reflection; project a growth mindset by modeling a belief in the capacity of others to learn; model responsibility and accountability for individual and collective learning; facilitate the work by using agreed-upon operating norms and learning protocols; and include and empower many voices in the work.

Leaders with **Collabor-ability** ask,

- Do I leave my title and ego at the door when working with others?

- Do I create learning spaces, during the school day, for open-to-learning collaboration for all staff, focused on student growth and achievement?

- Do I ensure and protect time of team members, formal and informal, to collaborate authentically?

- Have I attached a Knowledgeable Other to my side to ensure that accurate knowledge of practice is evaluated, utilized, and mobilized?

- Do I seek to use thoughtful facilitation skills in leading collaborative learning?

- Am I inclusive not exclusive in inviting staff to learn alongside me?

- Do I provide time to debrief learning processes and meetings to reflect on process and progress? (Sharratt & Planche, 2016)

These are the leading and learning skills that all leaders must possess wherever they are in an organization. Learning organizations, considered nimble and successful, have leaders who provide a compelling vision, select "just in time, just right" resources, recognize and alter barriers to learning, understand and promote high-impact classroom practices, and strengthen culture to focus all decisions on leading through learning (Sharratt, 1996).

Educational leadership today requires skills to be applied in a wide variety of ways through transformational leadership, instructional leadership, and evidence-proven leadership. Research participants for this text contributed to the addition of a sixth leadership dimension. They said that the complexity of system and school leadership roles is growing with a huge multiplier effect, meaning that the ability to be *nimble and agile is a highly rated, urgently needed skill for all leaders.*

THE NEW SIXTH LEADERSHIP DIMENSION

Leaders learn and lead at the same time. They use the process of *co-construction of thinking*, at every opportunity, to promote teacher and leader collaborative decision-making that creates collective efficacy. Inspired by their own sense of efficacy, which is contagious, leaders empower others to do great work, all the while seeing the forest and the trees, providing the calm and stability, even in turbulent cultures of constant change. I call that ability to work through change and adversity to build collective efficacy **Adapt-ability**. Leadership for today and tomorrow demands adaptability.

6. STRONG LEADERS HAVE ADAPT-ABILITY

Leaders who are agile and adept have adapt–ability! They confront, explore the meaning of, and consider others' perspectives in adapting to and embracing change. They know how to manage change, are comfortable with ambiguity, and hear others' points of view. Leaders with adapt-ability recharge, reenergize, and renew to experience the elegance of success. They fail fast, know where to go for help, and are not too proud to ask. Leaders with adapt-ability are culturally responsive, recruit energetic, passionate people who possess a sense of urgency for the vision, and are part of the solution by creating space to solve problems collaboratively. These leaders deal directly to resolve conflict and implicitly trust their teams with noble intent. Importantly, they stay the course, tweaking along the way, and they hold their nerve until they get the results they want and students deserve.

Leaders with **Adapt-ability** ask,

- Do I embrace the ambiguity of chaos in these turbulent, changing times?

- Do I run device-free meetings so all are "present"?

- Do I see technology seamlessly integrated into the school day to be more effective and efficient?

- Do I use technology to advantage as a tool and as a teacher—often learning from the students?

- Do I manage little and lead often? Do I model and monitor, flexibly changing course if needed?

- Do I reflect on who is doing most of the talking in my conversations and meetings?

- Am I the ambassador for the team and for the organization?

- Do I really model the belief that all students and all teachers can learn, given time and support?

- Can I navigate tensions between collaborators and/or innovators?

- Do I ask the right, tough questions?

- Do I empower myself and others?

- Do I know how to excite, initiate, and pull things together?

- Do I allow myself and colleagues to fail fast and keep going?

- Do I keep distracters away?

- Am I able to stay calm amid chaos?

- Do I leave no room for hierarchy or bureaucracy?

- Do I give and get feedback by paying attention to feedback loops?

- Am I aware that I build collective efficacy? How do I measure it?

FUNDAMENTAL CHALLENGE

Take a few moments to reflect upon your own learning journey as a leader by selecting one or two of the above questions from each of the dimensions to explore. Taking time to consider your own evidence of recent learning is a valuable exercise and helps leaders to understand the complexity of the task and the importance of identifying the next right step in your own growth.

I have talked about the sequence and integration of system leadership and school leadership and how understanding the thinking behind system-ness permeates strong systems. Collaborative Professionalism (Sharratt, 2016) is a style, a process, and a product that is a value-add in every system and school. Reflections that follow by Dianne Hawkins, Racquel Gibbons, Tracey Petersen, Jill Maar, and Brian Harrison are not just personal; they are exemplars of leaders who understand system-ness, systems thinking, the power of networked learning communities, and authentic school leadership capabilities. Their narratives demonstrate that they embrace and display all six leadership dimensions. It is in leaders' Adapt-ability to move between macro and micro work, and from first-order to second-order work, that change for improved student achievement happens.

SYSTEM LEADERSHIP IN ACTION

System leaders relentlessly model, guide, coach, and monitor school performance, moving from walking alongside school leaders to declaring urgent nonnegotiables, always with the FACES of student improvement in view. There is no time to waste in beginning the process of improving all students' achievement.

Dianne Hawkins leads in a large, successful school district where she oversees and works directly with 24 big, busy elementary, middle, and secondary schools. Hawkins has positive classroom experiences that form her foundation, has learned the "system-ness" of the successful district, and is sustaining those practices across her schools. Hawkins explains in the narrative below that a system leader needs to understand what she calls the "macrocosm" and the "microcosm" and have the agility that comes from experience to move back and forth between these realities carrying information from each to the other and impacting positively on both.

CASE STUDY: SYSTEM-NESS IS MAKING CONNECTIONS

The leader carries the big picture of the curriculum expectations that come from the Ministry of Education, has been part of setting them into the System Improvement Plan and helps to make connections between what the Ministry wants the system to do, and what contextually is understood that the schools can and will be able to do. That is the macrocosm—the big picture.

A system leader also must have a very good sense of the microcosm. The system leader must know that each school's Improvement Plan is based on the macro elements being brought into its individual context. The system leaders must know, from personal observation, a school's ongoing record of student achievement and its pedagogical practice, as pedagogy will have the greatest impact on student achievement and well-being. So leaders move from the macrocosm to microcosm, from the big system picture to knowing the detail of student achievement in every classroom.

The role of system leader is to assist and insist that principals

- ensure teachers know the components of critical thinking,

- work with teachers to show how to build a culture of critical thinking in classrooms,

- embed the expectation of challenging tasks to stretch students' thinking.

Finally, Hawkins thinks about the tremendous loss of system-ness, at every level of the organization, when specific pedagogical knowledge leaves through staff turnover. System leaders must have processes and structures in place to "catch up newcomers" and review what is foundational practice; what is expected practice in every classroom; and who among staff and the school leadership team is missing this information. By having clear expectations about what she must see in classrooms and across schools, Hawkins is building sustainability into her work as a system's thinker.

Source: Dianne Hawkins, superintendent of schools, York Region District School Board, Ontario, Canada, personal communication, 2017.

The system-ness erosion Hawkins writes about is even more dramatic when systems are "serial adopters" of new pedagogies or technologies or any other form of emphasis. In highly autonomous systems or where system leaders do not have the macro to micro view that Hawkins discusses, rogue leaders choose their own adventures, destroying system-ness and in-school coherence of practice, so essential to sustaining school and system equity and excellence. What is nonnegotiable?

What is the constant? A focus on *learning, teaching, and leading* as defined by the 14 Parameters is nonnegotiable, no matter who the new leader is or what the new pedagogy is.

Lessons Learned: System Leadership Is Consistent, Persistent, and Insistent

Successful leadership is not an end-of-year review of results but a continuous review with pressure and support, ensuring there is ongoing, tangible evidence that demonstrates a positive trajectory toward a vision of measurable, expected improvement. The following are characteristics of strong system and school leaders:

1. **CLARITY**. Recognize the importance of being consistent, persistent, and insistent.

2. **Vision**. Have a clear vision (understood by and with all) and measure movement toward it.

3. **No Excuses**. Operate between the bells—and accept no excuses for lack of student learning.

4. **High Expectations**. Have high expectations for all students and staff.

5. **Quality Practices**. Know and demand effective, expected practices at the system, school, and classroom levels.

6. **Assessment Literacy**. Know the specificity of strong assessment practices that differentiate instruction.

7. **Partner.** Make connections with parents and the broader community.

8. **Long-Term View.** Build sustainability loops into their consciousness.

System leadership attributes meld into school leadership attributes. Parameter #4—Principals as Lead Learners and Leaders of Learning—specifically refers to the importance of all school leaders attending and participating in Professional Learning alongside teachers and support staff. System leaders must recognize that without system and school leaders showing up and doing the work together, nothing will happen to improve schools' effectiveness and students' learning and achieving.

SCHOOL LEADERSHIP IN ACTION

My definition of principals as leaders of learning is quite explicit. The principal's role is to observe and monitor student progress, to offer direction, to support teachers to deliver student success against high expectations, and to ensure teachers have the resources they require to do the work.

In *Realization* (Sharratt & Fullan, 2009), Michael Fullan and I introduced what principal Jill Maar was able to accomplish in a short period of time in a very large multicultural school in Ontario. She impressively led her staff to significantly improve student performance and to sustain the gains made. Recently, Maar was asked by her system to tackle another school in challenging circumstances. Her narrative defines for me how the 14 Parameters of system and school improvement continue to define her laser-like focus on students' progress as an outstanding principal who makes a difference.

CASE STUDY: USING THE 14 PARAMETERS TO LEAD SCHOOL IMPROVEMENT

I can see many of the Parameters in action, in each of the five schools I have been asked to turn around. The one fundamental building block underlying every decision that I have made has been, and continues to be, the strong belief that all children can learn and that all teachers can teach (Parameter #1).

This is a suburban K–8 school with 430 students and 38 teachers, most of whom have worked together for a long time. It has had a few years of "not so nice" history. In times of change, the one thing that I have noticed that we can all hold onto—across all the schools—is a common set of beliefs and understandings. When we structure decisions around common beliefs and common understandings, we can hold difficult discussions, such as, how we will make the work come together collaboratively, or how we will work to be more effective and efficient with our time? Staff really value that difficult decisions are based on an agreed-upon foundation, a touchstone, like Parameter #1.

When I start in a new school, I know I need to start with first-order changes to provide the structure for second-order changes like creating a

(Continued)

(Continued)

culture of learning. Building relationships with staff takes time, but at the same time, our students can't wait until we come to the point of all being on the same page and using the same language. There is an ever-present urgency, so working together, focused on students, becomes the work of both building relationships and creating a culture of learning.

For me as principal leader, first-order changes enable collective second-order changes to occur. Thus I look for some really quickly achieved, first-order changes I can make by asking myself,

- What types of resources are there?

- Are there centralized materials that all teachers can access to improve students' achievement?

- What kind of data collection are teachers currently using?

- How have teachers been analyzing data to know that they are on the right track?

- Where can I best support teachers?

These physical changes draw attention to the mood of "change" I want to create; however, these aren't changes for the sake of changes—they are structural, first-order changes to facilitate longer-term second-order changes. I have cleaned out cupboards of out-of-date resources, and yes, I have hired dumpsters to take away old, often stashed-away, unused materials. These actions signal to the school community that our daily decisions have a powerful impact on student learning and that, as a collective, we are invested in providing a high-quality learning experience for students and teachers. These actions are moving our thinking toward second-order change.

Changing the face of the Third Teacher [see Chapter 1], the learning environment, is also what I think about as I craft the new school feeling to be able to put FACES on the data. The footprint of the classroom belongs to the students, and we are merely operating within it to facilitate their thinking and learning, particularly as we move toward notions of inquiry-based learning. There is one key difference in the leadership situation between what I had to do in my first principalship and what I need to do in this school, my fifth principalship. In this school, there are many more managerial and operational demands placed on my time. I can't lose sight that it is critically important that I not move away from my key role as instructional leader. So, any time each day that I can fit in even one conversation with one student in a classroom to ask the 5 Questions, I do [see Chapter 2].

In terms of assessment "for" and "as" learning, I regularly meet with teachers to discuss their students' data through Case Management Meetings—one student at a time. In staff meetings, I talk about the frequency of the data collection, where student voice is within that assessment process, and whether students are setting their own learning goals. In my daily Learning Walks and Talks, I am looking for

- the explicit intentionality of the lesson;

- the CLARITY of the Learning Intentions and evidence of co-construction of the Success Criteria;

- strong and weak examples to guide students in their decision making;

- the gist of the Descriptive Feedback—is it merely motivational in terms of comments such as "great work," or is it really digging deeply in terms of the steps that students need to take to move forward?;

- evidence of students' ability to peer- and self-assess.

What I've learned through experience is that data come from many sources and that it's really important to provide some formal opportunities for the voices and the choices of students and staff to be heard. So, we regularly have students come to the formal staff data conferences to talk about their learning, what matters to them about some things that they feel particularly proud of, and some things that, as a school, we need to work on.

Input from families is also an important leadership consideration. For example, our parents have helped us with chronic issues of late arrival at school and chronic absenteeism. We have collectively resolved some

(Continued)

of the issues by clearly articulating our newly co-developed mottos of "learning happens here" and "every day counts." We are making sure that there is CLARITY around being here on time and being ready to learn. We have had to make some first-order, structural adjustments. For example, students are now permitted to come into the school at an earlier time to prepare themselves and get ready for the day instead of having to wait outside. Elements of self-regulation have been brought into the classrooms in order to establish the growth mindset needed—that place of calm where students are ready to learn or can learn how to get a mental reset during the day when that is required.

Students have been giving teachers feedback about these changes. Making the change and getting student and parent feedback is important. Another way we listen to the voices in our school is that both the vice-principal and I take guided reading groups on a regular basis with some of our most vulnerable learners. In that way, we assist both teachers and students and pick up a lot of informal data about who the students are academically, socially, and emotionally.

While we have really struggled to decide what our clearly articulated school plan will be, we're all very clear now about our vision: "Every child will succeed to the best of his or her ability while in our care"—in line with Parameter #1. Providing opportunities for input into formal meetings is a structural change that I made at this school. It has physically and organizationally opened communication without formally changing the meeting structure. Literally opening the classroom doors and having CLARITY of communication but retaining the security of the existing structures, for now, are conditions that have offered us a chance to work toward Parameter #14, Shared Responsibility and Accountability.

We have started to look at overall school trends and are beginning to bring the macro view to the staff, moving from "me to we." To that end, we have begun to collaboratively assess work samples across classes, grade levels, and divisions so we can see where our students are starting and where they need to be, on a continuum, not just in relation to the school but to the system and to the province of Ontario. Teachers are gradually gaining the opportunity to see beyond their own classrooms.

When we notice that we have a weakness in instruction, need help with any students' work, or need support in teaching a concept, we find the system supports available to us. We have strengths on staff in terms of our knowledge, expertise, and experience, but the staff is beginning to accept that it's also important to reach beyond our school building to seek input from Knowledgeable Others around some key issues with which we might be grappling. Staff are beginning to be comfortable with inviting those support teams in to work alongside us because it is in the best interests of our students. This to me is the essence of Parameter #1 and the 14 Parameter framework to which we refer often.

Source: Jill Maar, principal, Ontario, Canada, personal communication.

IMPACT!

Maar's widely recognized leadership capabilities have led to astounding results in just one year at her new school (see Figure 9.3). It is possible! These annual, standards-based provincial assessment results were above the district and provincial results, and the school continues to flourish well beyond expectation, Why? I believe Jill reflects the six leadership dimensions and is consistent, insistent, and persistent in her pursuit of equity and excellent for all students. She seeks and celebrates the remarkable moments.

Hawkins, her system leader, has commented that Principal Maar's presence in classrooms during her daily Learning Walks and Talks has made a visible difference in developing consistent, high-quality classroom

Figure 9.3 Results of Precision and CLARITY in School Leadership

Percentage of Students in Top Two Bands (% Increase)

	Grade 3	Grade 6
Reading	79 (+17)	94 (+35)
Writing	88 (+20)	86 (+51)
Mathematics	79 (+13)	47 (+17)

(Continued)

practice. Further, by going into classrooms and following up with positive, sometimes courageous, conversations with teachers, her plan for broader change in student behavior in the school itself (initially a serious issue) has taken a new, faster, positive trajectory.

Lessons Learned: School Leadership Demands Precision in Practice

This case study reflects Maar's thinking through the questions that she has each day: "Where do I start?" and "How do I get teacher buy-in to inquire about changing assessment and instructional practices?" Here are the lessons I've learned from watching and walking alongside Jill Maar:

1. **Parameter #1**. Begin by developing and circling back to shared beliefs and understandings at every opportunity.

2. **Consensus.** Establish a sense of purpose and vision that is built by consensus and can be articulated by all.

3. **Implement.** Move from first-order changes (structural changes) to intentional second-order changes that positively impact students' increased achievement.

4. **Data-Based Decisions**. Use data, including student work samples, to have rich conversations about practice with teachers.

5. **Do the Work**. Build relationships by doing the work together and by being worthy of being trusted.

6. **Learn in Classrooms**. Walk and Talk in classrooms every day as a critical part of your data collection and of living your commitment to openness, listening, and learning.

7. **Hear.** Invite the voices of students and teachers to inform your next leadership steps.

Maar and Hawkins work in a collaborative Professional Learning Community that is networked across Hawkins's schools. Networks are burgeoning everywhere as the way to reach out to many in order to learn, to inquire, and to share together. Similarly, another large school district in which I work is trialing an effective way to learn together across their schools. Leaders like Racquel Gibbons, highlighted in the narrative below, understand the power of networks to bring learning across schools in this system. Evidence of successful learning is now tangible and validated for her.

CASE STUDY: SYSTEM AND SCHOOL LEADERS KNOW THE POWER OF NETWORKED COMMUNITIES OF PRACTICE

The senior leadership team in Metropolitan Region, Queensland models the use of high-impact strategies by establishing and continuously updating their regional Data Wall and conducting weekly Case Management Meetings, at the system level, to review school performance and identify areas or sites needing a sharper and narrower focus.

A group of eight schools were identified from the region's Data Wall to participate in a collaborative cluster—a Networked Community of Practice—focused on the inquiry question: "How can we improve the number of students in the upper two bands of NAPLAN in underperforming schools?"

The eight schools were large primary schools (900–1,250 students each) with a similar mid-range socioeconomic index; each had shown improvement for at-risk students to achieve above the national minimum standard; however, school data was well below national standards for the proportion of students in the upper two bands of reading results. All schools were working with the same senior leader, Assistant Regional Director (ARD) Racquel Gibbons, which ensured consistency, alignment, and regular, ongoing opportunities to observe and to give feedback on progress.

Gibbons invited the eight school leadership teams to be part of a collaborative cohort known as the Networked Community of Practice to share responsibility and accountability for the upper two band improvements by working together and supporting each other. Gibbons allocated additional support to the schools for two semesters by assigning time with two key regional project officers to work with schools to implement their

(Continued)

(Continued)

action plans and provide a feedback loop. Funds were also allocated to the schools to assist with the following:

- releasing classroom teachers for the collaborative cluster meetings
- planning time with regional project officers and colleagues
- providing relevant Professional Learning

Gibbons immersed the group of schools in a collaborative approach by meeting to work together:

- clarifying the purpose and expectations of the network
- reviewing a menu of support
- establishing Success Criteria for their work together

As part of this initial session, the schools interrogated their data profiles, mapped their needs against a proposed support menu and developed action plans. Gibbons and school leaders negotiated an ongoing Professional Learning program that included opportunities to share and compare data, classroom practice and insights. Each school hosted a half-day program per semester to articulate what work had been progressed in the school and sought feedback from colleagues to assist with their next steps. During each session, Gibbons and the regional support team provided relevant and timely Professional Learning to build team and individual capacity in both data analyses and high-quality instruction in the context of the curriculum standards.

Schools undertook an intensive review of their multiple sources of data to identify which students would be targeted for intervention. Schools put FACES on the data by identifying those students in Grade 2 and Grade 4 who would be in the upper two bands in national testing in 2017 in order for the schools to meet their reading targets. The identified students continue to be monitored through common leveled assessments and classroom work samples to check their progress toward expected performance.

During the first 20 weeks in this network, there were four full-day Professional Learning sessions with a half-day Learning Walk and Talk in two schools on each day. Those experiences saw schools share their data and action plans as well as open their classrooms to their colleagues to share both the confident and tentative steps taken to reach their goals and targets as a result of this intensive collaborative networking.

Learning Walks and Talks at each school revealed the use of the following:

- enhanced and targeted high-impact strategies in classrooms
- Data Walls
- a sharper data analysis
- setting higher expectations for students
- rich and more complex texts
- more precise reading instruction
- increased collaborative teams within schools, focused on learning from each other about teaching approaches
- students' answers to the 5 Questions to gauge how explicit the teaching was
- more evident instructional strategies for higher-order thinking

All schools in Gibbon's network have been able to model and celebrate stories of growth and success but also have been open to seeking feedback from colleagues on other ideas and perspectives. The impact of the Learning Walks and Talks has been obvious as teachers have identified effective strategies from others and implemented those in their own classrooms immediately.

Feedback from teachers has indicated the value of the collaborative approach. A teacher from School C says,

I thoroughly enjoyed observing and listening to how other schools are working toward maximizing student achievement. I felt very proud to be a part of our school team and the journey

(Continued)

(Continued)

we are on to maximize student achievement in reading. I no longer feel a sense of panic about the possibility of being observed by other schools. Instead I feel a little excited to show off the excellent pedagogy and rigor in our reading program. Being a part of today's Learning Walks and Talks highlighted for me what we do exceptionally well in the teaching of Reading, and, also made the feedback regarding reading goals a lot clearer and more helpful to me.

The second 20 weeks of the network's collaborative sessions saw a greater emphasis on increasing the rigor. Each school identified which expected practices would be the focus of Descriptive Feedback from the classroom observations and conducted Case Management Meetings of identified Grade 3 and Grade 5 students with the cross-school group. This led to a sharper and narrower focus for the network's collaborative meetings and for the work of teachers and school leaders.

All resources used in the network are stored in an online community site, providing schools with access to Professional Learning materials, templates, school stories, and resources. Schools have developed innovative approaches including an online literature circle (Rocket Readers) that has encouraged a learning community of students across classrooms and beyond school hours, including over vacation periods.

Source: Racquel Gibbons, assistant regional director, Metro Region, Queensland.

Leadership is Walking and Talking in the direction you wish to move while taking others with you. (Research Participant)

IMPACT!

Results in Figures 9.4 and 9.5 show impressive progress over time in Gibbon's Networked Community of Practice.

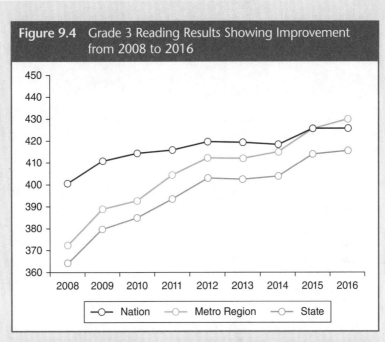

Figure 9.4 Grade 3 Reading Results Showing Improvement from 2008 to 2016

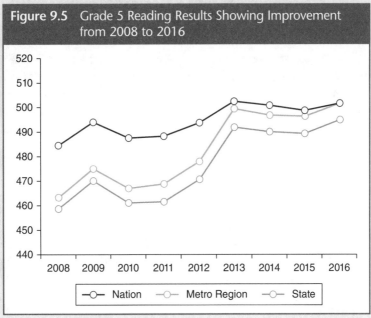

Figure 9.5 Grade 5 Reading Results Showing Improvement from 2008 to 2016

(Continued)

(Continued)

The changes in practice for the leadership teams and classroom teachers in this network are evident in several ways:

- the increased precision of planning
- the prevalent use of data to inform teaching and effective monitoring
- the honest evaluation of the impact of strategies and actions taken

Student performance on reading measures has generally shown improvement though not all students have reached their targets at this point.

What has been heartening in this narrative has been the expansion of cross-school networks with

- a common, clear focus,
- expectations and targets,
- increased purposeful interaction between schools,
- the strengthening of leadership and learning teams as a result.

Teams are not just meeting and collaborating on the scheduled days but are seeking ongoing opportunities to do the work together. As one principal commented, "Being part of this broader team with a common pursuit has given us the courage to be innovative and creative. It has afforded change in a much shorter timeframe than otherwise anticipated."

Lessons Learned: Networked Learning Communities

It is clear from this Networked Learning Community work that the CLARITY and focus of the senior leader, Gibbons, caused the improvement to happen at lightning speed. Improvement is possible everywhere if leaders reflect and act on the lessons learned from this narrative.

1. **Change Practice**. When school staffs work across a community of learners, brought together by a leader who can clearly

articulate the common purpose, and use the 14 Parameters as the learning framework, teachers commit to changing practice and improving student outcomes.

2. **Set Targets.** When data are used to develop improvement targets, focused Learning Intentions and Success Criteria are easily developed.

3. **FACES.** When Data Walls reveal which student FACES need to improve, differentiated strategies are undertaken collaboratively.

4. **Relationships.** When Networks are seen to be supportive, teachers are willing to take risks to change practice together.

5. **High Impact.** When teachers and leaders conduct Learning Walks and Talks in each other's schools to identify high-impact strategies together, they SEE what is possible and return to their own schools and classrooms to implement them in their own contexts.

6. **No Ego.** When senior leaders work alongside school leaders, teacher-leaders, and teachers, improvement is tangible and validated.

The strength of this networking trial lies in the fact that it can be replicated anywhere, anytime. However, it takes the will and perseverance of the leader (Parameter #4) and the commitment of differentiated district resources (Parameter #9) to see it through to successful completion.

When leaders from across schools Walk and Talk in each other's schools, as Gibbons and her leaders do, learning energy is sparked and conversations continue beyond the Walk. This is my very positive experience with Principal Learning Teams (PLTs) in Ontario, Canada, where principals conduct a Learning Walk and Talk before each PLT session.

PRINCIPAL LEARNING TEAMS

Principals describe learning experiences as "energizing" when they are engaged in learning that takes them beyond the operations of the school and beyond classroom management (first-order change) into the true realms of learning and achieving (second-order change). Leaders who are making a difference are master learners within their environments, modeling and monitoring processes that will change learning environments to increase students' and teachers' learning. The understanding of learning processes is an essential ingredient in the tool-box of the instructional leader who deeply understands and evaluates classroom practices that have impact (Todd Wright and Jim Forbes, personal communication, 2017).

As Sharratt, Hine, and Maika report (2015), PLTs offer a space and place where ideas can be tested and developed. Each member of the PLT builds his or her inquiry. Their inquiries are always connected to system and school improvement plans; however, powerful and meaningful principal inquiries are very specific and center on what principals need to understand and do in order to move their thinking forward to support teaching and learning. These are very personal and deep wonderings, often coming from a place of vulnerability.

An example may be a principal wondering about assessment practices within a curriculum area. Other *inquiries* might be built around the following questions:

- What do I need to understand in order to support staff and students?

- What can I develop as a theory around this work that makes sense?

- Where is my curiosity taking me?

- What is a focused Collaborative Inquiry question?

- How can I build and test my theory?

- How might I give and get feedback?

- As I revise and build my thinking, can I begin to see what my Collaborative Inquiry might account for and what it might not explain?

- Is my Collaborative Inquiry supported by a major author or by research?

- Can I identify my deepest thinking?

- Have I come to a place where I begin to identify ideas and actions?

Principal Brian Harrison in Ontario, Canada, notes that there is no linear sequence for an inquiry. We both believe that when we move more deeply into inquiry, a number of scaffold prompts may be activated simultaneously by different members of the PLT. Harrison participates in a PLT that involves five colleague principals, each with his or her own inquiry. Support comes from others "adding to" and identifying "significant" or "new" learning to his and others' inquiry questions. Agreed-upon operating norms for the PLT are as follows:

- It is not a space for argument or criticism.

- It is a nonevaluative space for participants to appreciate the thinking and vulnerability of a colleague doing similar work.

- It is a space to understand, reflect, add to, and help the presenting principal to refine his or her thinking.

- It is a space where misconceptions can be voiced and worked out and new concepts can be formed.

SAMPLE PRINCIPAL LEARNING TEAM PROTOCOL

1. Self-select a small group of colleagues to come together.

2. Commit to attending monthly meetings.

3. Include a Knowledgeable Other/pedagogical coach.

4. Place value on time spent.

5. Conduct a Learning Walk and Talk at the beginning of each meeting—taking turns to host in each other's schools.

6. Use data to construct each individual Collaborative Inquiry question.

7. Take turns in presenting and discussing each Collaborative Inquiry question and grapple with questions that arise.

8. Construct conversations to understand pedagogical leadership.

9. Commit to trying recommended actions and return with evidence of improvement (or not) at the following meeting.

10. Commit to authentically helping each other; cheer for each other's small wins.

11. Plan to each form a new collective of five principals in new PLTs in the next school year.

Participants in PLTs acknowledge the pitfalls, such as

1. **Finding Time**—carving out the time to meet regularly and complete the learning and reflection tasks

2. **Accessing Expertise**—most areas (for example, math) require the support of a Knowledgeable Other who has sufficient pedagogical content knowledge to appropriately facilitate the learning of the PLT

The benefits outweigh the barriers in that participants in Harrison's math-focused PLT reported that the math knowledge they gained from their participation in the PLT gave them greater confidence in embracing and guiding teachers' learning of mathematics within their own schools. They also reported that they were more transparent and open with the teachers they were leading about the learning they were engaged in by modeling a lead learner stance.

I asked Harrison to comment on what the impact/evidence of student achievement and well-being was, and he replied that, based on their ongoing monitoring, his colleague participants reported increased confidence in using research-based models, evidence-proven strategies, and common terminology by teachers and students as a result of the knowledge principals had gained and applied in their ongoing math inservice work at their schools.

In addition, as a result of their work within the PLT focused on math learning, principal participants were able to guide teachers to have a greater awareness of the importance of having a positive mindset and disposition in creating math learning communities for students.

Lessons Learned: Principal Learning Teams

The members of this PLT believe that an autonomous, small, self-selected and self-directed PLT is highly impactful *if* the work is defined by school and student data, district improvement goals, and connected to high-impact practices (Harrison, personal communication, 2017).

Educational leaders improve learning experiences for all students when they believe and trust that day-to-day quality teaching promotes

- high expectations of all students,
- teachers working collaboratively,

- coherence between the vision of the future and daily practice,

- being across all classrooms, inquiring and sharing about the learning done.

These concrete actions fill schools with life, energy and successful achievement of high expectations. (Isidora Recart, chief executive officer, Arauco Foundation, Chile and Simón Rodriguez Espinoza, senior consultant of development area, Arauco Foundation)

LEARNING WALKS AND TALKS: LEADING TO ENSURE THE GROWTH OF ALL STUDENTS

There are two ways of authentically monitoring student progress and teacher collective capacity building:

1. Developing and maintaining working Data Walls leading to Case Management Meetings

2. Engaging in a daily Learning Walk and Talk

Successful systems I work with have embedded both these ways to answer the question, "How do we know all students are learning?" Answer #1, Data Walls and Case Management Meetings were both discussed in Chapter 7. I discuss answer #2, Learning Walks and Talks, here.

Possibly one of the most powerful leadership and teacher "learnership" tools I have found is implementing Learning Walks and Talks. When the rationale is deeply understood by all staff members and the protocol followed, Learning Walks and Talks are a practical way of

- observing alignment of school and system improvement plans,

- seeing if Professional Learning has been transferred to classroom practice,

- noting school trends and patterns over time,

- hearing student and teacher voices,

- determining if students know what they are learning and how to improve.

Once the rationale, protocol, and culture of trust are established, Learning Walks and Talks become a data collection tool so that system and school leaders become even more effective instructional leaders. A key aspect of the protocol is knowing that the Learning Walks and Talks process is positive, not punitive nor evaluative, and is designed to offer insights into potential improvements in classroom instruction.

A critical shared understanding is that after many Learning Walks and Talks in classrooms, a school leader, who will often walk with another instructional leader, will take a planned opportunity to provide Descriptive Feedback to the teacher. It is only after many walks that the principal will have a true sense of consistent observations to share, as comments after only one Walk would be very misleading.

Learning Walks and Talks always begin at the Data Wall. Walkers identify a FACE from the wall and walk to find that student. What is she doing? How is she doing? Can she answer the 5 Questions? Has the teacher differentiated instruction as recommended during the Case Management Meeting?

Conducting Learning Walks and Talks in either secondary or elementary schools is an opportunity to observe expected, effective assessment and instructional practices. Leaders ask themselves, "Am I observing any practices in this classroom that this teacher can share and guide a small group of other teachers who are not quite there yet?" Observations made during many Learning Walks and Talks in classrooms offer concrete visual evidence of how the learning is progressing in the school. What can and should be observed during the time in classrooms has been discussed in Chapter 4 (Assessment) and Chapter 5 (Instruction).

THE FOUR TYPES OF LEARNING WALKS AND TALKS

1. **System Learning Walks and Talks**: At a selected school, the Walk begins at the Data Wall. System leaders and central office staff walk through schools to look for evidence of the system priority, to gather evidence about strengths and areas of growth, to determine the impact of system Professional Learning sessions, to access and differentiate system resources, and to design and implement next steps needed in planning for system Professional Learning.

2. **Network Learning Walks and Talks:** Network and Professional Learning Community members walk in the school chosen for their meeting. They all begin at the Data Wall and

walk into classrooms to look for evidence of Network and school goals and determine next steps for the work being carried out together in their Network.

3. **Professional Growth Learning Walks and Talks**: A leader walks with a critical/supportive friend, starting at the Data Wall, to gather information and identify areas of strength and growth to design and implement individual leader Professional Learning plans.

4. **Home School Walks and Talks:** School leaders Walk and Talk in their own schools daily, beginning at the Data Wall, to gather evidence of school goals and students' learning progress, to build relationships, and to create opportunities for conversations with students and teachers about their learning.

THE 5 QUESTIONS CONNECT TO THE ASSESSMENT WATERFALL CHART

Learning Walks and Talks are an opportunity to see high-impact assessment and instructional approaches in action. If they are not seen, then that is data for leaders to change up their Professional Learning sessions and conversations with staff to be very explicit about expectations. During a Learning Walk and Talk, walkers select one or two students in each class, when they are not involved in direct instruction, to answer the following 5 Questions (also discussed in Chapter 2):

5 Questions Educators Ask Students During Learning Walks and Talks

1. What are you learning? **Why?**

2. How are you doing?

3. How do you know?

4. How can you improve?

5. Where do you go for help?

Notice I have added *why* to the first question as I've been thinking that students may know what they are learning but not why they are learning it! How does this learning connect to their worldview? Has the teacher made it clear *why* this learning will be important to students in their everyday lives?

Questions 2 and 3 require that students can find evidence of success or "not successful yet" in their own learning. This means, therefore, that the questioner must also understand and see the Success Criteria in the classroom in order to make any valid determination about the student's progress.

Figure 9.6 makes the connection between the 5 Questions to ask students and the Assessment Waterfall Chart (Chapter 4, Figure 4.4). Answers to the 5 Questions illuminate the CLARITY and precision of assessment "for" and "as" learning practices that differentiate instruction in classrooms. They will also add to the documentation that is being captured through walkers' precise observations to determine next steps in differentiating Professional Learning for staff.

When walkers see that the components of assessment "for" and "as" learning are explicitly in place in every classroom and students can articulate each component of the Assessment Waterfall Chart by accurately answering the 5 Questions to self-assess their efforts, then walkers know that students are empowered to own their learning and excel beyond what they may have initially thought was possible.

Reflective Questions After Learning Walks and Talks

Typically, walkers debrief by asking each other reflective questions, such as

- Do students know what has been taught? What did they say that gives you that impression?

- Do students know why they are learning what they are learning?

- Can you identify that the Learning Intentions and Success Criteria are the right ones? (from the appropriate grade-level curriculum expectations)

- Do students know how they are being assessed?

- Do students know what they are being assessed on?

(Reflective questions continue on page 334.)

Figure 9.6 Linking the 5 Questions for Students to the Assessment Waterfall Chart (Figure 4.4)

5 Questions for Students	Teachers Do . . .	Students Say . . .	Leaders Observe . . .
1. What are you learning? **WHY?**	• Deconstruct curriculum expectations to develop Learning Intentions (LI). • Work with students to develop LIs in student-friendly language. • Ensure students know why they are learning what they are learning. • Post LI's in classrooms for students' reference. • **Discuss and record the big ideas and essential questions (Chapter 4) for a unit of study.**	• "I am learning to discuss and use more descriptive words in my narrative writing." • "I am adding more descriptive words to my writing so the reader knows what I am thinking as an author." • **"I am learning about _____ because I will need to use it when I _____."** • **"Learning _____ will help me understand how to _____ in the future."**	• Purposeful talk among students in classrooms. • More student than teacher talk. • Whole group/small group—individual work in classrooms. • Students clearly articulate LIs and why they are learning them. Leaders identify that Learning Intentions are grade level appropriate, directly from the Curriculum Expectations • No students are saying "I don't know." • The five questions are posted and have obvious signs of being discussed and worked on in all classrooms to serve as a reminder of intentional teaching. • **Displayed anchor charts of big ideas and essential questions are annotated by students and teacher to unpack the vocabulary necessary to understand and articulate the concepts being studied.**

(Continued)

Figure 9.6 (Continued)

5 Questions for Students	Teachers Do . . .	Students Say . . .	Leaders Observe . . .
2. How are you doing?	• Co-construct with students how to be successful. Anchor charts are displayed in classrooms to make the learning evident. • Ensure that students use Success Criteria (SC) language and they understand what they look like. • Develop SC that are not checklists. • Add to SC as lessons progress.	• "I am able to do the first SC at a Level 4." • "I am working on the second and third SC." • "Here's my work that shows how I can do the first SC."	• Anchor charts/prompts/scaffolds are clearly visible in classrooms. • These charts are marked up (not laminated) indicating frequent use by students—who can answer "How are you doing?"
3. How do you know?	• Give timely, relevant feedback based on LIs and SC. • Work with students to identify success in student work and to fix up work that is not quite successful. • Teach students how to peer and self-assess accurately based on LIs and SC.	• "My teacher and I have talked about my writing, and we decided . . ." • "I got feedback on my narrative from my friends, and they said . . ."	• Written comments on students' work are explicit and do not include "well done" or "good work" or other such platitudes. • Teachers are giving explicit oral feedback and recording it for follow-up. • Documenting evidence of learning through pictures, work samples, postings, anchor charts, use of strong and weak examples in the classroom

5 Questions for Students	Teachers Do ...	Students Say ...	Leaders Observe ...
4. How can you improve?	• Model to students how to use Success Criteria to fix up work • Make anecdotal notes of written and oral feedback to give ongoing feedback. • Track and monitor feedback given to know students' progress and plan next steps.	• "I am working on being better at . . . " • "The teacher gave me this writing feedback sheet to put in my binder as my goals for this work."	• Students can clearly articulate their next steps to improvement of their work using the strong and weak exemplars or writing continuum posted in the room to discuss where student needs to go next.
5. Where do you go for help?	• Work with students on becoming independent, self-regulatory learners by teaching them where they can go for help beyond the teacher.	• "I go to [name of classmate] as s/he is very good at . . . " • "I look at the chart we made in class to remember where I can go for help." • "I go to our class website to look again at the lesson." • "I go to my parents or to a homework help online site when I'm stuck."	• Scaffolds in classrooms show discussions of where supports are for students' learning. • Students can articulate several places where they can go for help in addition to the teacher.

Source: Adapted from Sharratt and Harild (2015).

(Continued from page 330)

- Are the Success Criteria the right ones to successfully meet the Learning Intentions and therefore the curriculum expectations? Can students achieve an "A" using the Success Criteria?

- Do students know what they need to do to be successful? How? Could students refer to anything to show you how they would be successful? Are the Success Criteria evident in the classroom? Do students refer to them and use them to self-assess? Is there evidence that they have been co-constructed with students?

- Do students get feedback that helps them to reduce the gap between where they are and where they need to be? How do they get it? Did you see examples of feedback?

- Do students know where and how to get help?

- Do students know what they need to do to complete their task? How do they know? Could they show you?

- Do students know where they are now with the task? How? Was there a progressive set of exemplars for reference—like a writing continuum or a Bump-It-Up Wall?

- Do students have a Learning Goal that they are working on? Do they know this goal? Is it visible or written out in a journal or on a tablet?

The answers are revealing. When walkers can answer these questions confidently and accurately, with direct evidence from the classrooms, then they know that student self-assessment (the ultimate!) is in place—because teachers have been explicit in making their expectations for successful learning transparent to their students.

After being in a classroom many times, walkers have a very good sense of what the teacher is teaching, starting with the curriculum expectations, how it is being taught, hearing student voice and choice, and what evidence is there that the learning is being co-constructed with the students.

While some educators advocate and train teams to use clipboards and tablets and to "wear" an evaluative demeanor in their clinical-style invasions of classroom spaces, in Learning Walks and Talks there are no notebooks, no paper, and no conversation with teachers in the moment.

After each Learning Walk and Talk there is to be an opportunity to record reflections away from the classrooms so that the Learning Walk and Talk process is not seen as evaluative but as growth-promoting in strengthening practice together.

RECORDING THE DATA COLLECTION

Leaders become even better instructional leaders by becoming keen observers. They collect and record data after Learning Walks and Talks that will better inform conversations with teachers about what practices are or are not working in classrooms and why. The purpose is also to be unobtrusive, to observe and interact with students during a very limited 5- to 8-minute time frame (but replicated many times in different classrooms during each week to get a complete data collection picture). After leaving the classroom, the small group of walkers briefly make their notes, quietly (and privately) discuss their individual data collected, and reflect on what they each heard from students and what they noticed in the learning space to answer the above questions. The data collected when Walking and Talking are reflections on the impact of the leading. They shape leaders' ongoing conversations and Professional Learning sessions with teachers. This leads me to conclude that leaders who conduct Learning Walks and Talks and observe classroom practice daily, have the stamina and consistency to persist, resist, and insist—which is needed to manage complex change.

ADAPT-ABILITY TO
MANAGE COMPLEX CHANGE

Leaders showcased in this text manage complex change with agility that illustrates Leadership Dimension #6: Adapt-ability. System, region, and school leaders need to consider what it takes to change performance through careful consideration of vision, skills, a focus on FACES—of all learners—to achieve beyond potential, resources, and an action plan. We also need to keep in front of us what happens when each of these elements is missing. Change has a personality that often reflects the leaders' values, shared beliefs, and understandings—and biases if not curbed. It is critical to model and monitor Parameters #1 and #14 in taking action to achieve equity and excellence for all.

COMMITMENT

I commit to

- understanding what and how learning is occurring in each school and classroom using the Learning Walks and Talks protocol with consistency;

- sharing the 5 Questions for students/teachers/leaders and discussing how those questions influence our work with schools by retelling, relating, reflecting, and receiving feedback;

- having no more school *visits* but engaging in regular Walks and Talks;

- digitally recording my Learning Walk and Talk and asking students the 5 Questions to collect data on the CLARITY of learning in classrooms;

- determining how to schedule teachers' time in order to see each other's craft.

A DELIBERATE PAUSE TO CREATE CLARITY

What aspect of leadership identified in this chapter is most likely to enhance your current performance and improve outcomes for your students? What steps are you prepared to take in moving forward? In reviewing your Leadership Self-Assessment profile (Web Resource 10), what are your areas of strength and what is an area of need? How do you know? Where can you go for assistance for PL in your area of need? Where can you find leaders who model and monitor expected, effective practices? How can you begin a PLT in your jurisdiction?

Visit the companion website at
resources.corwin.com/CLARITY
for videos and downloadable resources

CONCLUSION

CLARITY: LEADERSHIP FOR THE FUTURE

In conclusion, my friends and colleagues, Barbara and Jim Watterston, discuss the CLARITY needed today and the urgency of "the now," to lead our students, teachers, and leaders confidently into an unknown future.

People are our most precious resource, and education is a way forward to build and enable nations to flourish. No matter where you sit within an education system, whatever your role, leaders in education require a line of sight to how their actions and decisions are made in the best interests of all students in order to impact classrooms and answer two core questions:

- How is this student, classroom, school, or system better because I teach, lead, empower, and support it?

- How do I know? What is my evidence?

So, what is the future of leadership? While we already have evidence-informed research, standards, and processes to support learning for leadership, we do need to utilize these more precisely so that all leaders continually seek to improve their practice by

- ensuring students have access to rich progress data to inform their learning journey with any teacher, anywhere, any time;

- valuing, sharing, and celebrating teaching as a high-status, deprivatized, collaborative profession;

- clarifying then articulating a common understanding of what good teaching and learning looks like to ensure more teachers are "teaching like the best";

(Continued)

(Continued)

- ensuring that decision making is diagnostic and learning is differentiated and personalized by recognizing the varied stages of development of individual schools, staff members, and students. This is the "system-ness" factor in education.

Leadership in education cannot be viewed in isolation as the success of any leader lies in recognizing the interconnectedness and interdependency of mindsets, policies, and processes that contribute to and inform career-long, high quality leadership development and practice. This includes placing a high value on leadership and talent and achieving success through people by providing them with the right conditions to thrive, from transitioning to renewal.

Ongoing leadership development requires

- engaging aspirant leaders in relevant and meaningful learning opportunities,

- planning for succession in a disciplined and strategic way, and

- responding with programs to meet the needs of experienced principals to support them in remaining current and challenged in this exciting and ever-changing environment.

The picture that emerges from talking with school leaders is that they want to make a difference in the lives of children, their staff members, and in their communities. To become authentic leaders of learning, time is needed to reflect and refine practice together with training and development tailored to enhance their professional growth. When leaders work alongside staff to improve teaching and learning, and work practices in general, they are role models of best practice and enable shared leadership and strategic capacities to grow and flourish.

The challenge is how to bring together the capacities leaders need to develop with the actions they need to take. This requires attention to the diagnosis, prescription, investment, and impact of Professional Learning. The "system-ness" factor is represented in the 4 Ps below that emphasize the inextricability of Professional Learning and practices of system and school leaders who continually reflect on and build leadership capacity aligned to roles, expectations, and strategic directions.

Pipeline: Identification, Preparation and Ongoing Development

A strategic, coherent approach to leadership development requires funding, for which governments/employers need to take the lead. This process also requires a framework, performance criteria to guide the process, and a proactive emphasis on talent identification by developing leaders early on and throughout their careers.

Personalization: Diagnosis and Precision Learning

To become true leaders of learning, time is needed to

- reflect and refine leadership practice,

- align ongoing training and development to improvement practices, and

- provide greater CLARITY around leadership pathways and opportunities.

Future school leaders are more likely to make themselves available if they can see that Professional Learning meets their needs and provides a support structure from the center, district, and school perspective for both development and practice.

Partnerships: The Power of the Profession

The profession plays a critical role in building leadership capability from talent identification and development and from personalized strategies through coaching, mentoring, and shadowing to contributing to policy and strategy as authentic partners in this process. Engaging aspirants in learning with and through others is the key to personal, team, school, and system effectiveness.

(Continued)

So, What Gets in the Way?

A fourth P is **politics.** Ultimately, to enhance this emphasis on system-ness to empower leadership in education and create the enabling conditions for classrooms, schools, and systems to thrive, a bipartisan approach to the development and implementation of education policy would remove the distraction of politics and use the valuable professional capital and resources available to all of us with precision, confidence, agility, and speed. Every student's education must be empowered by systems and governments who embrace a shared vision and a collaborative bipartisan approach to equity and excellence—that is CLARITY in practice, which is necessary at all levels.

Source: Dr. Barbara Watterston, director, Watterston Consulting; Dr. Jim Watterston, dean of education, Melbourne University, personal communication, 2017.

THE FACES OF CLARITY

As the Watterstons demonstrate, strategic leaders **stay the course of CLARITY,** shown in Figure C.1, to create the stability needed. They aren't persuaded to get off-track by the next new thing. There is no next new thing. Figure C.1 finalizes my thoughts that all students will achieve when surrounded by professionals at every level who

- build trusting relationships;

- use the 14 Parameters as data to assess their impact;

- focus on developing an open-to-learning culture as co-learners among parents, community, system and school leaders, and students;

- celebrate small wins every day.

Staying the course with relentless consistency is the golden key to Parameter #14: Shared Responsibility and Accountability to increasing all students' growth and achievement—our core business. Students deserve our commitment to implementing all 14 Parameters.

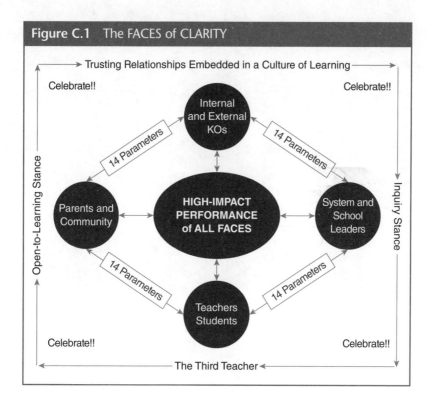

Figure C.1 The FACES of CLARITY

Learning, teaching, and leading with consistent, persistent, and insistent effort results in CLARITY of purpose and practice and a developed sense of shared responsibility and accountability, which matters MOST to raising the bar and closing the gaps for *all* students.

AFTERWORD

As I mentioned in the "In Memoriam" at the front of this book, I have been influenced by my student, colleague, and valued friend, Melanie Greenan, who passed in August 2017—far too soon. Here are some of our collective thoughts, in our last discussion, to bring this book to closure.

When students are able to control three key assessment strategies: (1) deconstructing Learning Intentions and co-constructing Success Criteria, (2) using Descriptive Feedback through peer- and self-assessment, and (3) integrating the process of metacognition, they become owners of their own learning.

We call that state *Transformative Assessment*: when students become owners of their own learning. As students become independent learners, educators' time availability increases so they can provide more quality Descriptive Feedback and individual coaching. It is then that teachers and leaders can engage in self-generative change, where they are inspired through their awe of student thinking and learning to engage in new learning themselves (Franke et al., 2001).

We must transform teacher thinking in order to transform teacher practices. We need classroom practices that enable students to be creative, critical, empowered thinkers. As one Grade 6 boy verbalized, "I can think for myself; I don't need my teacher to think for me." Teachers need to hear that voice, be open to listen, and value student thinking to ensure that real change in practice happens.

As a result of implementing *Transformative Assessment* and student-led inquiry, we are reculturing our classrooms into spaces for critical democratic engagement. Students are involved in dialogue, debate, innovation, knowledge building, and knowledge mobilization connected to social and global issues that affect us all.

As global citizens, students who are leading inquiries are sharing their thinking across the world through the use of technology. Collaboratively, they take local action to implement solutions to global issues. Students are becoming engaged with curriculum in ways that are locally relevant and culturally appropriate through their empowerment. They use their voices, make good choices, and experience metacognition. Students are engaged in and empowered by *what matters MOST!*

—Melanie Greenan, student, colleague, and valued friend
Personal communication, 2017

GLOSSARY OF TERMS

Accountable Talk: purposeful talk in every classroom and in system and school meetings

Anchor Charts: visually displayed scaffolds or prompts co-created by teachers and students

Bump-It-Up Walls: an approach to peer- and self-assessment that provides visual CLARITY of expectations

CLARITY: not an acronym, but capitalized for emphasis to ensure that explicit expectations are clear for all students and teachers

Co-Construction: *Co* means *with*. When we add the prefix *co* onto educational practices, it implies that educators are working together to achieve learning that would not be possible in isolation (Greenan, 2012). The co-learning processes outlined in this book are powerful Professional Learning tools

Effect Size: John Hattie's research (2016b & 2016c), into what works best rather than what works, ranks various influences in different meta-analyses related to learning and achievement according to their effect sizes. An effect size greater than .4 has a direct impact on increasing students' achievement

FACES: not an acronym, but capitalized for emphasis to put a focus on the importance of knowing every learner, not just as a statistic or number but as a real person who will learn, given time, support, and quality instruction

Fail Fast: trying, getting fast feedback, determining success or not, and feeling sufficiently safe to risk getting right back up to give it "another go" in a new direction

Good First Teaching: the right of all students to experience quality teaching in every classroom before being labeled "special needs"

Gradual Release and Acceptance of Responsibility: an approach that embraces modeled, shared, guided, and independent stages that move all learners from dependence to independence

Learning Intentions: directly derived from the curriculum expectations and unpacked with students so that students can answer the questions "What are you learning?" and "Why?"

Scaffolding: incremental learning and teaching that takes students from where they are to where they need to be

Success Criteria: teachers and students co-construct statements so students are clear about how to be successful (How are you doing? Where do you go for help?). Teachers assess only against the Success Criteria

The Third Teacher: the culture of learning established when attending to thoughtfully co-created learning spaces at every level of an educational system

Watermark: the indelible word underpinning an improvement plan that demonstrates what a system or school stands for

REFERENCES AND FURTHER READING

Abrams, J. (2009). *Having hard conversations*. Thousand Oaks, CA: Corwin.

Adams, L. (2018). *Learning a new skill is easier said than done*. Retrieved from http://www.gordontraining.com/free-workplace-articles/learning-a-new-skill-is-easier-said-than-done/#

Australia Curriculum and Assessment Reporting Agency. (2016). *National assessment program literacy and numeracy (NAPLAN)*. Retrieved from http://www.acara.edu.au/assessment

Australian Bureau of Statistics. (2013). *Programme for the international assessment of adult competencies, Australia, 2011–12*. Retrieved from http://www.abs.gov.au/ausstats/abs@.nsf/Lookup/4228.0Main+Features202011-12

Bandura, A. (1977). *Social learning theory*. New York: General Learning Press.

Bandura, A. (1997). *Self-efficacy: The exercise of control*. New York: W. H. Freeman and Company.

Barron, B., & Darling-Hammond, L. (2008). How can we teach for meaningful learning? In L. Darling-Hammond et al. (Eds.), *Powerful learning: What we know about teaching for understanding* (pp. 11–70). San Francisco, CA: John Wiley & Sons.

Barth, R. (1990). *Improving schools from within*. San Francisco, CA: Jossey-Bass.

Barth, R. (2006). Improving relationships within the schoolhouse. *Educational Leadership: Improving Professional Practice, 63*(6), 8–13.

Beverly, B. (2017). *Processes toward partnerships: How universities and K–12 schools make sense of partnering*. East Lansing: Michigan State University.

Boss, S. (2012). *Bringing innovation to school: Empowering students to thrive in a changing world*. Bloomington, IN: Solution Tree.

Campbell, C., Osmond-Johnson, P., Faubert, B., Zeichner, K., & Hobbs-Johnson, A., with Brown, S., . . . Steffensen, K. (2016). *The state of educators' professional learning in Canada*. Oxford, OH: Learning Forward.

Chiarotto, L. (2011). *Natural curiosity: A resource for teachers: Building children's understanding of the world through environmental inquiry*. Toronto: Ontario Institute for Studies in Education, University of Toronto.

City, E. A., Elmore, R. F., Fiarman, S. E., & Teitel, L. (2009). *Instructional rounds in education: A network approach to improving teaching and learning*. Cambridge, MA: Harvard Education Press.

Clay, M. M. (2001). *Change over time in children's literacy development*. Portsmouth, NH: Heinemann.

Commonwealth of Australia. (2013). *Budget 2013–14: National plan for school improvement*. Retrieved from https://www.budget.gov.au/2013-14/content/glossy/gonski_policy/download/NPSI.pdf

Dana, N. F., Tomas, C., & Boynton, S. (2011). *Inquiry: A districtwide approach to staff and student leadership*. Thousand Oaks, CA: Corwin.

Darling-Hammond, L., Barron, B., Pearson, P. D., Schoenfeld, A. H., Stage, E. K., Zimmerman, T. D., . . . Tilson, J. L. (2008). *Powerful learning: What we know about teaching for understanding*. San Francisco, CA: Jossey-Bass.

DeWitt, P. M. (2015). *Lack of collaboration? Maybe it's you*. Retrieved from http://blogs.edweek.org/edweek/finding_common_ground/2015/10/hatties_10th_mindframe_for_learning.html

Donohoo, J. (2013). *Collaborative inquiry for educators: A facilitator's guide to school improvement*. Thousand Oaks, CA: Corwin.

Drucker, P. (1999). Managing oneself. *Best of 1999: Harvard Business Review* (pp. 1–11). Boston: Harvard Business Press.

Dufour, R., & Eaker, R. (1998). *Professional learning communities at work: Best practices for enhancing student achievement*. Alexandria, VA: ASCD.

Dweck, C. (2006). *Mindset: The new psychology of success*. New York, NY: Random House.

Eddy, P. L., Amey, M. J., & Bragg, D. D. (2014). *Creating strategic partnerships: A guide for educational institutions and their partners*. Sterling, VA: Stylus.

Edugains. (2016). *Adolescent literacy guide revised 2016*. Retrieved from http://www.edugains.ca/resourcesLIT/AdolescentLiteracy/Vision/AdolescentLiteracyGuide_Interactive.pdf

Elliott-Johns, S. E. (2013). Transitions in instructional practice: Teachers' voices on classroom reading instruction. In S. E. Elliott-Johns & D. H. Jarvis (Eds.), *Perspectives on transitions in schooling and instructional practice*. Toronto, ON: University of Toronto Press.

Evers, J., & Kneyber, R. (Eds.). (2015). *Flip the system: Changing education from the ground up*. London: Routledge.

Fendick, F. (1990). *The correlation between teacher clarity of communication and student achievement gain: A meta-analysis* (Unpublished doctoral dissertation). University of Florida.

Franke, M. L., Carpenter, T. P., Levi, L., Fennema, E. (2012, January). *Capturing teachers' generative change: A follow-up study of professional development in Mathematics*. American Educational Research Journal, Vol. 38, Issue 3, pp. 653–689. First published January 2001. Retrieved from http://journals.sagepub/doi/10.3102/00028312038003653.

Fullan, M. (2014). *The principal: Three keys to maximizing impact*. San Francisco, CA: Jossey-Bass.

Fullan, M., & Quinn, J. (2015). *Coherence: Putting the right drivers in action*. Thousand Oaks, CA: Corwin.

Fullan, M., Quinn, J., & McEachen, J. (2017). *Deep learning: Engage the world change the world*. Thousand Oaks, CA: Corwin.

Fullan, M., & Sharratt, L. (2007). Sustaining leadership in complex times: An individual and system solution. In B. Davies (Ed.), *Developing sustainable leadership*. London: Sage.

Gallimore, R., & Emerling, B. A. (2012, Fall). Why durable teaching changes are elusive and what might we do about it? *Journal of Reading Recovery*, 42–53.

Glaze, A. (2017). *Reaching the heart of leadership: Lessons learned, insights gained, actions taken*. Thousand Oaks, CA: Corwin.

Glaze, A., Mattingley, R., & Andrews, R. (2013). *High school graduation: K–12 strategies that work*. Thousand Oaks, CA: Corwin.

Greenan, M. (2012). Mapping the right drivers for third order educational change. *Principal Connections*, *16*(2), 7–15.

Greenan, M. (2015). *Cross panel perspectives on student learning reinforce integrative school improvement design*. Toronto, ON: CPCO.

Greenan, M., & Fornasier-Reilly, A. (2013). Better together: Supporting places and spaces for innovative pedagogy. *Principal Connections*, *17*(1), 38–41.

Greenan, M., Wild, P., & Galvao, A. (2015). Up, down and sideways: Integrative school improvement design leverages commonalities. *Principal Connections*, *18*(3), 8–11.

Guskey, T. R. (1986). Staff development and the process of teacher change. *Educational Researcher*, *15*(5), 5–12.

Hallinger, P., & Murphy, J. (1985). Assessing the instructional management behavior of principals. *The Elementary School Journal*, *86*(2), 217–247.

Hargreaves, A., Boyle, A., & Harris, A. (2015). *Uplifting leadership: How organizations, teams and communities raise performance*. San Francisco, CA: Jossey-Bass.

Hargreaves, A., & Fullan, M. (2012). *Professional capital: Transforming teaching in every school*. New York, NY: Teachers College Press.

Hargreaves, A., & Fullan, M. (2013, June). The power of professional capital. *Journal of Staff Development*, *34*(3), 36–39.

Hargreaves, A., & O'Connor, T. (2017). *Collaborative professionalism*. World Innovation Summit for Education Report #12. Qatar: WISE.

Hargreaves, A., & Shirley, D. (2012). *The fourth way: The inspiring future for educational change*. Thousand Oaks, CA: Corwin.

Harris, A. (2014). *Distributed leadership matters: Principles, practicalities and potential*. Thousand Oaks, CA: Corwin.

Harris, A., & Jones, M. (2010). *Professional Learning Communities*. London: Leannta Press.

Harris, A., & Jones, M. (2015). *Leading futures: Global perspectives on educational leadership*. New Delhi, India: Sage.

Harris, A., Jones, M., & Huffman, J. B. (Eds.). (2017). *Teachers leading educational reform: The power of professional learning communities*. London: Routledge.

Hart, M. (2015). Research: Collaboration is key for teacher quality. *The Journal*. Retrieved from http://thejournal.com/articles/2015/07/06/research-collaboration-is-key-for-teacher-quality.aspx?m=2

Hattie, J. (2009). *Visible learning: A synthesis of over 800 meta-analyses relating to achievement*. London: Routledge, Taylor & Francis Group.

Hattie, J. (2012). *Visible learning for teachers: Maximizing impact on learning*. New York: Routledge.

Hattie, J. (2015). The applicability of visible learning to higher education. *Scholarship of Teaching and Learning in Psychology, 1*(1), 79–91.

Hattie, J. (2016a). *Hattie ranking: Interactive visualization.* Retrieved from https://visible-learning.org/nvd3/visualize/hattie-ranking-interactive-2009-2011-2015.html

Hattie, J. (2016b). *Hattie ranking: 252 influences and effect sizes related to student achievement.* Retrieved from https://visible-learning.org/hattie-ranking-influences-effect-sizes-learning-achievement/

Hattie, J. (2016c). *Shifting away from distractions to improve Australia's schools.* Jack Keating memorial lecture. Retrieved from http://education.unimelb.edu.au/news_and_activities/events/upcoming-events/past/2016/dean_lecture_series/professor-john-hattie

Hattie: Less focus on standards, more focus on growth. (2011, December 7). *The Melbourne Newsroom.* Retrieved from http://newsroom.melbourne.edu/news/n-715

Herbst, S., & Davies, A. (2013). Co-constructing success criteria: Assessment in the service of learning. *Education Canada.* Retrieved from https://www.edcan.ca/articles/co-constructing-success-criteria/

Hill, P. W., & Crévola, C. A. (1999). The role of standards in educational reform for the 21st century. In D. D. Marsh (Ed.), *ASCD yearbook 1999: Preparing our schools for the 21st century* (pp. 117–142). Alexandria, VA: Association for Supervision and Curriculum Development.

Institute of Education Effectiveness. (2013). Reading Recovery. *What Works Clearinghouse.* Retrieved from https://ies.ed.gov/ncee/wwc/Docs/Intervention Reports/wwc_readrecovery_071613.pdf

International Literacy Association. (2018). *Why literacy?* Retrieved from https://literacyworldwide.org/why-literacy

International Reading Association. (2009). *New literacies and 21st century technologies.* Retrieved from http://www.reading.org/Libraries/position-statements-and-resolutions/ps1067_NewLiteracies21stCentury.pdf

Joyce, B., & Showers, B. (2002). *Student achievement through staff development* (3rd ed.). Alexandria, VA: ASCD.

Knight, J. (2007). *Instructional coaching: A partnership approach to improving instruction.* Thousand Oaks, CA: Corwin.

Knight, J. (2011). *Unmistakable impact: A partnership approach for dramatically improving instruction.* Thousand Oaks, CA: Corwin.

Knight, J. (2013). *High-impact instruction: A framework for great teaching.* Thousand Oaks, CA: Corwin.

Knight, J. (2015). *Better conversations: Coaching ourselves and each other to be more credible, caring, and connected.* Thousand Oaks, CA: Corwin.

Knoster, T., Villa R., & Thousand, J. (2000). A framework for thinking about systems change. In R. Villa & J. Thousands (Eds.), *Restructuring for caring and effective education: Putting the puzzle together* (pp. 93–128). Baltimore, MD: Paul H. Brookes.

Kuhlthau, C. C., Maniotes, L. K., & Caspari, A. K. (2007). *Guided inquiry: Learning in the 21st century*. Westport, CT & London: Libraries Unlimited.

Leithwood, K., Harris, A., & Hopkins, D. (2008). Seven strong claims about successful school leadership. *School leadership and management, 28*(1), 27–42.

Leithwood, K., Harris, A., & Strauss, T. (2010). *Leading school turnaround: How successful leaders transform low-performing schools*. San Francisco, CA: Jossey-Bass.

Lieberman, A. (1992). School/university collaboration: A view from the inside. *Phi Delta Kappan*, 147–156.

Literacy and numeracy: Which country tops the league? (2013). *The Guardian*. Retrieved from https://www.theguardian.com/news/datablog/2013/oct/08/oecd-countries-numeracy-literacy-high-skills

Lovallo, D., & Sibony, O. (2006, February). Distortions and deceptions in strategic decisions. *McKinsey Quarterly, 1*, 19–29.

Mathieson, L., Murray-Close, D., Crick, N., Woods, K., Zimmer-Gembeck, M., Geiger, T., & Morales, J. (2007). Hostile intent attributions and relational aggression: The moderating roles of emotional sensitivity, gender, and victimization. Retrieved from http://www.uvm.edu/~socldevl/Publications/Mathieson%20et%20al%202011.pdf

Mind Tools. (2017). *The conscious competence ladder*. Retrieved from https://www.mindtools.com/pages/article/newISS_96.htm

Mourshed, M., Chijioke, C., & Barber, M. (2010, November). How the world's most improved school systems keep getting better. *McKinsey & Company*. Retrieved from http://mckinseyonsociety.com

National Center for Education Statistics. (2013). *PIAAC 2012/2014 results*. Retrieved from https://nces.ed.gov/surveys/piaac/results/summary.aspx

National Council of Teachers of English. (2001). Critical literacy: What is it, and what does it look like in elementary classrooms? *School Talk, 6*(3), 1–5.

New South Wales Department of Education. (2014). *Literacy continuum K–10*. Retrieved from https://education.nsw.gov.au/curriculum/literacy-and-numeracy/literacy/literacy-continuum

New South Wales Department of Education. (2017). *NSW numeracy continuum K–10*. Retrieved from https://education.nsw.gov.au/teaching-and-learning/curriculum/literacy-and-numeracy/literacy/literacy-continuum

Ontario Ministry of Education. (2006). *Ontario language arts curriculum*. Ottawa, ON: Queen's Printer.

Ontario Ministry of Education. (2007). *Teacher moderation: The collective assessment of student work*. Capacity Building Series, Literacy and Numeracy Secretariat #2. Retrieved from http://www.edu.gov.on.ca/eng/literacynumeracy/inspire/research/Teacher_Moderation.pdf

Ontario Ministry of Education. (2010a). *Collaborative teacher inquiry*. Capacity Building Series, Literacy and Numeracy Secretariat Special Edition #16. Retrieved from http://www.edu.gov.on.ca/eng/literacynumeracy/inspire/research/CBS_Collaborative_Teacher_Inquiry.pdf

Ontario Ministry of Education. (2010b). *Growing success: Assessment, evaluation and reporting in Ontario schools*. Retrieved from http://www.edu.gov.on.ca/eng/policyfunding/growSuccess.pdf

Ontario Ministry of Education. (2011a). *Getting started with student inquiry*. Capacity Building Series, Literacy and Numeracy Secretariat Special Edition #24. Retrieved from http://www.edu.gov.on.ca/eng/literacynumeracy/inspire/research/CBS_StudentInquiry.pdf

Ontario Ministry of Education. (2011b). *Professional learning cycle [DVD]*. Ottawa, ON: Queen's Printer.

Ontario Ministry of Education. (2012a). *Evaluation of the Ontario Ministry of Education's differentiated instruction professional learning strategy*. Request for Services No. 661, Final Report. Ottawa, ON: University of Ottawa.

Ontario Ministry of Education. (2012b). *The third teacher*. Capacity Building Series, Literacy and Numeracy Secretariat Special Edition #27. Retrieved from http://www.edu.gov.on.ca/eng/literacynumeracy/inspire/research/CBS_ThirdTeacher.pdf

Ontario Ministry of Education. (2013a). *Capacity building K–12*. Special Edition #32. Toronto, ON: Queen's Printer.

Ontario Ministry of Education. (2013b). *Inquiry-based learning*. Capacity Building Series, Literacy and Numeracy Secretariat Special Edition #32. Retrieved from http://www.education-leadership-ontario.ca/storage/6/1380680840/OLF_User_Guide_FINAL.pdf

Ontario Ministry of Education. (2013c). *Paying attention to literacy*. Toronto, ON: Queen's Printer.

Ontario Ministry of Education. (2014a). *Principals as co-learners: Supporting the promise of collaborative inquiry*. Capacity Building Series, Literacy and Numeracy Secretariat Special Edition #38. Retrieved from http://www.edu.gov.on.ca/eng/literacynumeracy/inspire/research/CBS_PrincipalsCoLearners.pdf

Ontario Ministry of Education. (2014b). *Collaborative inquiry in Ontario: What we have learned and where we are now*. Capacity Building Series, Literacy and Numeracy Secretariat Special Edition #39. Retrieved from http://www.edu.gov.on.ca/eng/literacynumeracy/inspire/research/CBS_CollaborativeInquiry.pdf

Ontario Ministry of Education. (2015a). *Inquiry-based learning: On transforming wonder into knowledge*. Capacity Building Series #32. Toronto, ON: Queen's Printer.

Ontario Ministry of Education. (2015b). *System leaders and collaborative inquiry*. Capacity Building K–12, Special Edition #42. Toronto, ON: Queen's Printer.

Ontario Ministry of Education. (2016a). *Growing success: The kindergarten addendum*. Retrieved from http://www.edu.gov.on.ca/eng/policyfunding/growingSuccessAddendum.html

Ontario Ministry of Education. (2016b). *2016 student achievement: Literacy planning resource grades 7–12*. Retrieved from http://edugains.ca/resourcesLiteracy/SystemLeader/Learning-oriented/2016_LiteracyPlanningResource.pdf

Ontario Ministry of Education. (2018). *Teacher learning and leadership program*. Retrieved from http://www.edu.gov.on.ca/eng/teacher/tllp.html

Organization for Economic Co-operation and Development. (2015). *Program for international student assessment (PISA)*. Retrieved from http://www.oecd.org/pisa/pisa-2015-results-in-focus.pdf

Organization for Economic Co-operation and Development. (2017). *Education at a glance 2017: OECD indicators*. Retrieved from http://dx.doi.org/10.1787/eag-2017-en

Patel, A. (2016). When it comes to high literacy, numeracy rates, Canada is low on the list: Report. *The Huffington Post Canada*. Retrieved from http://www.huffingtonpost.ca/2016/09/01/canada-literacy-rates_n_11817262.html

Peurach, D. J., & Glazer, J. L. (2016). Reading Recovery as an epistemic community: A case of occupational control in education. *Journal of Education for Students Placed at Risk, 21*(1), 1–9.

Planche B., Sharratt, L., & Belchetz, D. (2008, January). *Sustaining students' increased achievement through second order change: Do collaboration and leadership count?* Paper presented at International Congress of School Effectiveness and Improvement Conference (ICSEI), Auckland, New Zealand.

Robinson, M. A., Passantino, C., Acerra, M., Bae, L., Tiehen, K., Pido, E., . . . Langland, C. (2010, November). *School perspectives on collaborative inquiry: Lessons learned from New York City, 2009–2010*. Consortium for Policy Research in Education, Teachers College, Columbia University. Retrieved from www.cpre.org/school-perspectives-collaborative-inquiry-lessons-learned-new-york-city-2009-2010

Robinson, V. (2017). *Reduce change to increase improvement*. Retrieved from https://us.corwin.com/en-us/nam/reduce-change-to-increase-improvement/book249122

Robinson, V., Hohepa, M., & Lloyd, C. (2009). *School leadership and student outcomes: Identifying what works and why: Best evidence synthesis*. Wellington, New Zealand: Ministry of Education.

Robinson, V. M., Lloyd, C. A., & Rowe, K. J. (2008). The impact of leadership on student outcomes: An analysis of the differential effects of leadership types. *Educational Administration Quarterly, 44*(5), 564–588.

Rotman School of Management. (2018). *What is integrative thinking?* Retrieved from http://www.rotmanithink.ca/what-is-integrative-thinking

Ruurs, M., & Badr, N. A. (2016). *Stepping stones: A refugee family's journey* (Trans. F. Raheem). Victoria, BC: Orca.

Ryerson, R. (2017). Creating possibilities: Studying the student experience. *Educational Research, 59*(2). Retrieved from https://doi.org/10.1080/0013188 1.2017.1343091

Sahlberg, P. (2011). *Finnish lessons: What the world can learn from Finnish educa-tion*. New York, NY: Teachers College Press.

Scardamalia, M. (2002). Collective cognitive responsibility for the advancement of knowledge. In B. Smith (Ed.), *Liberal education in a knowledge society* (pp. 67–98). Chicago, IL: Open Court.

Scardamalia, M. (2016). *Knowledge building* [video transcript]. Toronto, ON: MediaFace.

Scardamalia, M., & Bereiter, C. (2003). Knowledge building. In *Encyclopedia of education* (pp. 1370–1373). New York, NY: Macmillan Reference.

Schwartz, S., & Bone, M. (1995). Retelling, relating, reflecting: Beyond the 3 Rs. Toronto, ON: Nelson Thomson Learning.

Shafritz, J. M., Ott, S. J., & Jang, Y. S. (2011). *Classics of organizational theory* (7th ed.). Belmont, CA: Wadsworth.

Sharratt, L. (1992). *The reflective practitioner*. Paper presented at the First Comenius Conference, Prague, Czechoslovakia.

Sharratt, L. (1996). *The influence of electronically available information on the stimu-lation of knowledge use and organizational learning in schools* (Unpublished doctoral dissertation). University of Toronto, Canada.

Sharratt, L. (2008–2018). *Learning walks and talks* [Training materials]. Australia, Canada, Chile.

Sharratt, L. (2013). Scaffolded literacy assessment and a model for teachers' pro-fessional development. In S. Elliott-Johns & D. Jarvis (Eds.), *Perspectives on transitions in schooling and instructional practice* (pp. 138–153). Toronto, ON: University of Toronto Press.

Sharratt, L. (2016). Setting the table for collaborative professionalism. *Principal Connections, 20*(1), 34–37. Retrieved from http://lynsharratt.com/wp-content/uploads/sites/4/2017/02/collective_professionalism.pdf

Sharratt, L., Coutts, J. D., & Harild, G. (2015). Good to great to innovate: What matters most? *Australian Educational Leadership Journal*.

Sharratt, L., Coutts, J., Hogarth, W., & Fullan, M. (2013). Reading recovery: A high return on investment for cost-conscious and student-achievement oriented education systems. *Journal of Reading Recovery, 13*(1), 53–60.

Sharratt, L., & Fullan, M. (2005). The school district that did the right things right. *Voices in Urban Education, 9*, 5–13.

Sharratt, L., & Fullan, M. (2006). Accomplishing district-wide reform. *Journal of School Leadership, 16*, 583–595.

Sharratt, L., & Fullan, M. (2009). *Realization: The change imperative for deepening district-wide reform*. Thousand Oaks, CA: Corwin.

Sharratt, L., & Fullan, M. (2012). *Putting FACES on the data: What great leaders do!* Thousand Oaks, CA: Corwin.

Sharratt, L., & Fullan, M. (2013). Capture the human side of learning. *Journal of Staff Development, 34*(1), 44–48.

Sharratt, L., & Harild, G. (2015). *Good to great to innovate: Recalculating the route to career readiness, K–12.* Thousand Oaks, CA: Corwin.

Sharratt, L., Hine, E., & Maika, D. (2015, February). Pedagogically focused leadership: Creating reciprocal and respectful relationships. *The Register, 17*(1), 35–39.

Sharratt, L., Ostinelli, G., & Cattaneo, A. (2010). *The role of the "knowledge-able other" in improving student achievement, school culture and teacher efficacy: Two case studies from Canadian and Swiss perspectives and experiences.* Paper presented at the International Congress for School Effectiveness and Improvement, Kuala Lumpur, Malaysia.

Sharratt, L., & Planche, B. (2016). *Leading collaborative learning: Empowering excellence.* Thousand Oaks, CA: Corwin.

Sharratt, M. (2004). *The impact of teacher leadership on students' literacy learning* (Unpublished master's thesis). University of Toronto, Canada.

Singer, T. W. (2015). *Opening doors to equity: A practical guide to observation-based professional learning.* Thousand Oaks, CA: Corwin.

Slavin, R. E. (2016). Getting to scale: Evidence, professionalism, and community. *Journal of Education for Students Placed at Risk, 21*(1), 60–63.

Smith, S. D. (1992). Professional partnerships and educational change: Effective collaboration over time. *Journal of Teacher Education, 43*(4), 243–256.

Stoll, L. (2015). Using evidence, learning and the role of professional learning communities. In C. Brown (Ed.), *Leading the use of research & evidence in schools.* London: IOE Press.

Thompson-Grove, G. (2000). *Atlas: Learning from student work.* Bloomington, IN: National School Reform Faculty. Retrieved from https://www.nsrfharmony.org/wp-content/uploads/2017/10/atlas_lfsw_0.pdf

TVO Teach Ontario. (2015). *Using authentic media texts to engage students and improve learning.* Retrieved from https://app-www.teachontario.ca/community/explore/teachontario-talks/blog/2015/09/28/using-authentic-media-texts-to-engage-students-and-improve-learning

The U.S. illiteracy rate hasn't changed in 10 years. (2017). *Huffpost.* Retrieved from https://www.huffingtonpost.com/2013/09/06/illiteracy-rate_n_3880355.html

Vygotsky, L. S. (1978). *Mind in society: The development of higher psychological processes* (4th ed.). Cambridge, MA: Harvard University Press.

Watterston, B., & Kimber, R. (2017). *System leadership: Informing the role of area supervisors.* Brisbane, AU: Brisbane Catholic Education.

What Works Clearinghouse. (2013). *Beginning reading intervention report: Reading Recovery.* Retrieved from http://ies.ed.gov/ncee/wwc/pdf/intervention_reports/wwc_readrecovery_071613.pdf

Willms, J. D., Friesen, S., & Milton, P. (2009). *What did you do in school today? Transforming classrooms through social, academic and intellectual development.* Toronto, ON: Canadian Education Association. Retrieved from: https://

www.edcan.ca/articles/2012-wdydist-research-series-report-one-the-relationship-between-student-engagement-and-academic-outcomes/

York Region District School Board. (2007). *Guidelines for literacy, 2007.* Retrieved from http://schools.yrdsb.ca/markville.ss/mm/literacy/GL-guidelines forliteracy.pdf

Zetlin, A. G., & Macleod, E. (1995). A school-university partnership working toward the restructure of an urban school and community. *Education and Urban Society, 27*(4), 411–420.

Zhang, J., Scardamalia, M., Reeve, R., & Messina, R. (2009). Designs for collective cognitive responsibility in knowledge building communities. *Journal of the Learning Sciences, 18*(1), 7–44.

Zhao, Y. (2018). *Reach for greatness: Personalizable education for all children.* Thousand Oaks, CA: Corwin.

Zimpher, N. L., & Howey, K. R. (Eds.). (2004). *University leadership in urban school renewal.* Westport, CT: Greenwood.

INDEX

Figures are indicated by f following the page number.

CORWIN LEADERSHIP

Anthony Kim & Alexis Gonzales-Black

Designed to foster flexibility and continuous innovation, this resource expands cutting-edge management and organizational techniques to empower schools with the agility and responsiveness vital to their new environment.

Jonathan Eckert

Explore the collective and reflective approach to progress, process, and programs that will build conditions that lead to strong leadership and teaching, which will improve student outcomes.

PJ Caposey

Offering a fresh perspective on teacher evaluation, this book guides administrators to transform their school culture and evaluation process to improve teacher practice and, ultimately, student achievement.

Dwight L. Carter & Mark White

Through understanding the past and envisioning the future, the authors use practical exercises and real-life examples to draw the blueprint for adapting schools to the age of hyper-change.

Raymond L. Smith & Julie R. Smith

This solid, sustainable, and laser-sharp focus on instructional leadership strategies for coaching might just be your most impactful investment toward student achievement.

Simon T. Bailey & Marceta F. Reilly

This engaging resource provides a simple, sustainable framework that will help you move your school from mediocrity to brilliance.

Debbie Silver & Dedra Stafford

Equip educators to develop resilient and mindful learners primed for academic growth and personal success.

Peter Gamwell & Jane Daly

Discover a new perspective on how to nurture creativity, innovation, leadership, and engagement.

Leadership That Makes an Impact

Steven Katz, Lisa Ain Dack, & John Malloy
Leverage the oppositional forces of top-down expectations and bottom-up experience to create an intelligent, responsive school.

Peter M. DeWitt
Centered on staff efficacy, these resources present discussion questions, vignettes, strategies, and action steps to improve school climate, leadership collaboration, and student growth.

Eric Sheninger
Harness digital resources to create a new school culture, increase communication and student engagement, facilitate real-time professional growth, and access new opportunities for your school.

Russell J. Quaglia, Kristine Fox, Deborah Young, Michael J. Corso, & Lisa L. Lande
Listen to your school's voice to see how you can increase engagement, involvement, and academic motivation.

Michael Fullan, Joanne Quinn, & Joanne McEachen
Learn the right drivers to mobilize complex, coherent, whole-system change and transform learning for all students.

CORWIN LEADERSHIP

A SAGE Publishing Company

CORWIN HAS ONE MISSION: to enhance education through intentional professional learning.

We build long-term relationships with our authors, educators, clients, and associations who partner with us to develop and continuously improve the best evidence-based practices that establish and support lifelong learning.

The Ontario Principals' Council (OPC) is a voluntary professional association representing 5,000 practising school leaders in elementary and secondary schools across Ontario. We believe that exemplary leadership results in outstanding schools and improved student achievement. We foster quality leadership through world-class professional services and supports, striving to continuously achieve "quality leadership—our principal product."

The Australian Council for Educational Leaders is a not-for-profit company that actively supports the development of educational leadership capabilities across Australia through conferences and workshops, leadership programs, in-house publications, online resources and bookshop. Access to these leadership focused opportunities is available for classroom teachers through to system leaders.